Cheryl Koenig OAM, is a motivational speaker and author. *With Just One Suitcase* is her fourth book. Her previous publications are *Paper Cranes* (2008), *The Courage to Care* (2007) and *There's always Hope: just alter the Dreams* (2006). Cheryl spends her spare time volunteering in the health care sector with a focus on government policy and services centred on people with disabilities and their carers. She currently sits on several committees in this capacity and was recognised for her contribution to the community in 2009 being named NSW Woman of the Year, and in 2014 receiving the Medal of the Order of Australia. Cheryl lives in Sydney with Rob, her husband of over thirty years and with whom she has two sons.

WITH JUST ONE SUITCASE

Cheryl Koenig

Published by Wild Dingo Press
Melbourne, Australia
books@wilddingopress.com.au
www.wilddingopress.com.au

First published by Wild Dingo Press 2015.

Text copyright© Cheryl Koenig

The moral right of the author has been asserted.

Except as permitted under the Australian Copyright Act 1968,
no part of this book may be reproduced, stored in a retrieval system,
or transmitted in any form or by any means, electronic, mechanical,
photocopying, recording, or otherwise without prior permission
of the copyright owner and the publisher of this book.

Cover design: Susan Miller, millervision@netspace.net.au
Layout: Midland Typesetters

Editors: Katia Ariel and Iris Breuer
Printed in Australia by Ligare

National Library in Australia
Cataloguing-in-Publications Data
Koenig, Cheryl, 1960–
With just one suitcase / Cheryl Koenig

 ISBN: 9780987178589 (paperback)

 World War, 1939-1945–Europe, Central.
 War victims–Europe, Central–Biography.
 Families–Europe, Central–Biography.
 Immigrants–Australia–Biography.
 Refugees–Australia–Biography.

 362.870994

The paper this book is printed on is in accordance
with the rules of the Forest Stewardship Council˚.
The FSC˚ promotes environmentally responsible,
socially beneficial and economically viable
management of the world's forests.

*Dedicated to my darling Rob.
May your hand continue to hold mine
and may we dance this dance together,
until the stars no longer shine.*

ACKNOWLEDGEMENTS

Warmest thanks to Wild Dingo Press, in particular Catherine Lewis, for her commitment to preserving tales which form part of the multi-dimensional fabric woven to combine the rich tapestry that is modern Australia. Although new in derivation and divergent in motivation, these tales continue today and the need for them to be told is significant. Working with you, Cathi, has been a wonderful experience. You are an amazing teacher—you have brought out the best in my writing, and thereby in me.

To Katia Ariel and Iris Breuer: your talented and insightful hands in the editing of this work proved invaluable. For that, as well as your sensitivity to the theme of familial love (both within and outside the pages of this book), I will always be grateful.

To Robert Hillman, author-extraordinaire: my sincere appreciation for your friendship and mentoring.

To my very special family: Robert, Jonathan, Chris, Danielle, Stephanie, my siblings—thank you for your love and patience with my, at times, fanatical pursuit of history.

Most importantly, however, my eternal gratitude to my patriarchs: Frici and Istvan. During the writing process—as I packed and unpacked my own small suitcase many times over in a personal battle for survival—your stories inspired me to stay strong, committed and hopeful. You each taught me that life may be tenuous and uncertain and sometimes crisis will follow crisis. And just like the *many* immigrants who have come to our shores with just one suitcase, you have demonstrated courage to rebuild from the ashes.

Indeed we understand ourselves, our identities, our roles in life, largely because of the stories we are told. And from the contents of my two fathers' suitcases, I have learnt that being surrounded by family—by a common humanity and a special interconnectedness—is the real measure of a successful and authentic life. I have that family. I have that life.

Finally, in closing Fred and Steven's suitcases, I consider the impact upon their *real* legacy: their grandchildren. I am pleased that I was blessed with the time to finish what I set out to do. Because their grandchildren, and indeed, the grandchildren of the many thousands whom they represent, only come to know their grandparents in the evening of their lives. And in that fading light, some might only see the weathered facade they present and perhaps consider this generation as old, unsteady, fragile or even withdrawn.

Some might never know the extraordinary early lives of their grandparents. I know mine did not. How could they when I only knew a fragment? Now my children will come to know how brave and adventurous their grandfathers truly were; and appreciate the poetry of genes from Katarina and Anna that have combined to make their own. And if for no other end result than this—knowing where it is you come from—it has been more than worthwhile. My hope is that it encourages other families to sit down and have the same conversations.

I used to think it was the big events that defined history, but I've learned it's not—it's the people. History is written by survivors.

Like a persistent archaeologist who digs and dusts until she finds the antiquities for which she searches, I have found more jewels than I had ever hoped for.

AUTHOR'S NOTE

How many of us, in our Australianness, forget that we are the product of people smugglers, of war or at the very least, of economic refugees? As the descendant of the central characters in this story who lived through World War Two and its aftermath, naturally it is my belief that to do justice to our label as a 'proud multicultural society' we need to continue the conversation about our immigration history, share in the revelation of stories from those whose courageous origins were lived out quietly with nobility and humility, embrace the kaleidoscope that is our identity.

The early lives of my father and father-in-law were narrated to me by them respectively (as was my grandmother's legend which she recounted many times over in the countless hours I spent with her before she passed away). It is based on the facts of their lives; however, creative licence was necessary in some parts of their stories in order to give depth to the narrative—especially in the days prior to their births and during their early childhoods. As I visited that era, it wasn't difficult to find the vision to give birth to the tale, from the lullabies their loved ones left behind, as the actual writing process spawned its own language, as facts emerged on the page. Language, however, does not give birth to a tale—rather the story must have the ability to bring forth the language. And always at the forefront of my mind during the creation of this story was that if I altered their history, I would alter, too, their achievements.

The strength of character portrayed by the many thousands of post-World War Two immigrants to grace our shores—their valour in the face of oppression, fearlessness in travelling halfway around the globe and their determination, with a work ethic to match—are just a few of the qualities that generations since will never truly possess. The naive may think that these settlers were disadvantaged—arriving in a new country young, alone and without financial assistance. But it is we, subsequent generations, who are the disadvantaged ones, as we will never know the feeling of triumph and sense of pride that comes from building a new life in a new country, *with just one suitcase.*

FAMILY TREE

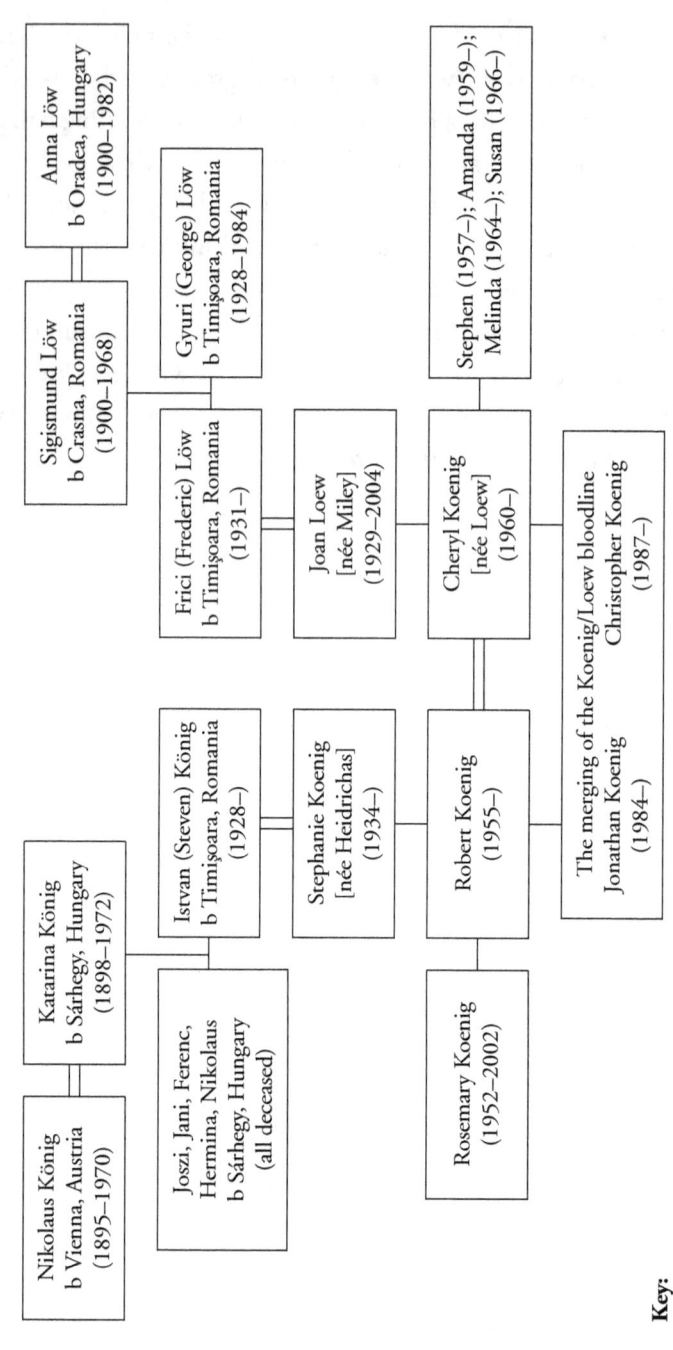

Key:
Double line connection = married to
Single line connection — related to

Central Characters
- Anna Löw (pronounced Lerv). Her children and grandchildren called her Anyu (pronounced Un-you), meaning 'mother' in Hungarian. When the family members came to Australia, they anglicised the spelling of their family name to Loew.
- Sigismund Löw. Also known as Apu (pronounced Ar-poo), meaning 'father' in Hungarian.
- Frici Löw (pronounced Fritzi Lerv). He anglicised his name to Frederic Loew when he came to Australia.
- Gyuri Löw (pronounced Jury Lerv). He anglicised his name to George Loew when he came to Australia.
- Istvan König (pronounced Ist-varn Ker-nig). He anglicised his name to Steven Koenig when he came to Australia.
- Istvan König's family: mother Katarina, father and one brother both called Nikolaus, sister Hermina, brothers Jani, Joszi (the letter 'J' is pronounced as a 'Y') and Ferenc (pronounced Ferenk).
- Stephanie's (Steven's wife) family name is Heidrichas (pronounced Hydrickas).

Central locations
- Timişoara (pronounced Timishara) is situated in south-west Romania, close to the Hungarian border.
- Chişoda (pronounced Kishoda) is a suburb of Timişoara.

'Sing in me, muse, and through me tell the story.'
Homer's *Odyssey*

1
Katarina

Timişoara, Romania
1938

The day has become ripe and the smoky aroma of fresh salami, salted pork and other cured meats wafts in the breeze to the hum of bartering voices and shuffling feet. The market is open for business this Saturday, just as it is every Saturday and Sunday. It is a carnival of stalls located in the suburb of Chişoda, south of the old baroque palace at the centre of Timişoara. You might sell all sorts of things here, but principally what can be eaten. That's the aroma that spices the air—what you might eat: not only cured meats of a dozen sorts, but also fresh meat, including the local favourite, *pacal*, known in the English-speaking world as 'tripe'.

This is not the English-speaking world, of course; this is western Romania, whose second largest city, Timişoara, sits squarely on the broad Oltenian plain that stretches farther west almost as far as Hungary and present-day Serbia. A long way to the east, across the Transylvanian Alps, lies the capital Bucharest and eventually the Black Sea. In the south, Romania shares a border with Bulgaria, and to the north beyond the Carpathians, with

Ukraine. For centuries, the country has been likely to argue with its neighbours, to be invaded by them, sometimes to exact revenge by marching an army in one direction or another with bloody intent. It's a fraught location for a country in a notoriously unruly region of Europe, large parts of which were once dominated by the acquisitive Ottomans. The culture of Romania at this time is a living festival of influences, including those of the Orient, Russia, western and eastern Europe, stretching all the way back to classical Greece.

On this day in 1938, Katarina König is busily selling the fare of her particular stall, which is to say living chickens, living geese and fresh vegetables from her kitchen garden. 'Busily' is perhaps going too far. Katarina is standing with her arms folded, the cuffs of her brown-grey smock rolled back from her wrists, silently urging customers to pay her some attention. Although eager for sales, she still nods and greets the gaze of those who pass by, through hazel eyes that hold the wisdom of a woman with four decades behind her. Short of stature, Katarina is a picture of heartiness, her weathered face punctuated with a round button nose under a high forehead, in keeping with her robust Slavic lineage. Dressed for function rather than form, she keeps her attire uncomplicated. Today being warm, she has donned a loose-fitting gypsy-style blouse over a buttoned-down ankle-length skirt which is purposely dark so as not to show the dirt that catches around her hem.

She is in the company of her youngest child, a boy of ten with unruly thick waves of brown hair and an alert expression. He is named Istvan. It is Istvan's task to get a good grip on the necks of the chickens and geese when a sale comes along, bind the legs and pass the birds over to the customer.

There is a lack of pretension in Katarina's manner as she picks up her broom and sweeps briskly at the feathers scattered by the lively protestations of her caged poultry. She pauses, tucking the broom under her substantial upper arm to regather strands of mousy brown hair that have worked their way loose from her rolled chignon and secure them out of toil's way. As she does this, she looks to her son who is watching inquisitively.

'Vanity is for people with no mission and too much time on their hands, my boy. I think this hair of mine would serve me better chopped short.'

'No, Mama. Don't. I like your hair the way it is. Papa does, too.'

Katarina's husband, Nikolaus, is a mechanical engineer of Austrian extraction who runs a flour mill in a rural outpost of Timişoara. Katarina's chickens supplement a household income that could, even without her contribution, keep her family in passable comfort, or in something like luxury compared with the vast majority of Romanians, for this is a country which, in broad regions, has yet to fully emerge from the feudalism of the Middle Ages.

Katarina's customers are drawn from every level of Timişoara's society: people of her own class, those a little less comfortable, the nervous middle class (Stalin and his collectivist political philosophy is just over there, beyond the Carpathians), the well-to-do, and even the occasional aristocrat—or at least the aristocrat's servants. And it will be one of Timişoara's well-to-do who will become her next customer this morning, for a brougham-landaulet[1] carriage drawn by a handsome Oldenburg horse[2] with

---

[1] Invented in the 19th century, this ornately designed closed carriage is pulled by a single horse. A driver sits behind the horse on an uncovered elevated bench.
[2] The tallest and heaviest of German horses originally used to pull coaches.

a groomed mane has just arrived and taken a place in the row of carriages outside the market. The fact that such carriages are still in use at a time when motor vehicles are crowding the streets of more sophisticated metropolises testifies to the tardy pace of development in Romania, but also captures its charm.

The woman who opens the door of the brougham and steps down reveals a charm of her own. She is dressed stylishly in a charcoal grey skirt and matching short-waisted jacket with black velvet lapels, white gloves, her jet-black hair attractively arranged beneath a cloche hat. She extends her gloved hand to help her son, aged around seven, down from the carriage. Dressed as impressively as his mother, he sports a spotless white shirt, royal-blue bow tie, navy braces, short grey trousers and highly polished black shoes. The boy doesn't appear quite as comfortable as his mother—a little as if he has been dressed for display. But the impression on anyone watching—Katarina, for example—is of quality.

Quality. Yes, that's the word. Katarina sighs, wondering how many chickens she would need to sell before she could afford a jacket and skirt from the same tailor as Mrs Löw. For, she knows the woman's name and has sold poultry to her in the past. She knows, too, that a charcoal suit with black velvet lapels made to order for her figure, would not give her the queenly appearance of Mrs Löw. Clothes might 'maketh the man', but it needs something more to 'make' the woman. Breeding, and the confidence that produces. And above all that, a certain gracefulness that no currency can procure; a knowledge that a hundred eyes are admiring you, without surrendering to conceit.

Katarina's supplementary wish is that her boys—her Istvan, especially—could go a full day as free of the blemishes of mud and soot as Mrs Löw's prince of a child. Oh, she is proud of her boys, loves them madly, but wouldn't it be wonderful to dress Istvan for once in a white shirt that remained white for longer than ten minutes; in shoes that looked shiny black for longer than thirty seconds?

As if to demonstrate that what we wish for might well be granted us with a few undesired entailments, Mrs Löw's son suddenly baulks at being led towards the squawking chickens at Katarina's stall.

'Frici, what is it?' says Mrs Löw. 'What's wrong with you?'

The boy has an expression of mingled horror and disgust on his small face.

'Anyu! Mama!' he wails, 'Not the chickens … No!'

'Frici, I must buy chickens. Be sensible now.'

Mrs Löw takes a firmer grip of her son's hand and urges him closer to the stall, and to the menacing chickens. She is embarrassed by her son's brief outburst and smiles at Katarina with an implicit appeal for sympathy that transcends class: *Boys! You have one, I have one. What can you say?*

Katarina's greeting conveys her ready acceptance of Anna Löw's entreaty.

'How are you today, Mrs Löw? Are you well?'

'I am very well, thank you. It's so nice of you to always remember my name.'

Her son, her Frici, is still resisting any closer approach to the chickens. Any onlooker would have thought the boy feared being eaten by the birds.

'It's not so difficult to remember,' Katarina replies. 'My family name is König, so we have something in common. You a lion, me a king.' Katarina laughs nervously and lowers her gaze, realising her careless chatter was perhaps too familiar with this high-class lady.

Was this going a little too far? Katarina comparing the king of the beasts and a human monarch? Or more to the point, placing a market-place chicken seller and an elegant woman of far higher social standing in the one frame? If she feels any unease, Anna Löw conceals it well.

'Good, from now on I will always remember *your* name, Mrs König, you may be sure of that,' she says, then immediately excuses herself to attend to the frankly ill-mannered behaviour of her son.

'Frici! Please stop pulling on my arm. Now see what you've done—my glove has fallen on the ground.'

Frici, unrepentant, wrenches free of his mother's grip and escapes into the crowd. The market is bustling by now; customers are crowding around the many stalls displaying the bounty of Timișoara and its rural hinterland—fruits and vegetables, cheeses in wheels and wedges, bright spring blooms ferried in from flower farms—daffodils, freesias and purple irises—and of course, the smallgoods that advertise themselves with their rich savouriness. Anna Löw, Katarina and even Istvan are able to observe Frici's rapid progress through the throng and all the way back to the Löw brougham. They watch while he opens the door and clambers inside.

Anna Löw, some of her poise forfeited in this confrontation, turns back to Katarina König with a hasty apology.

'Mrs König, I do apologise for my son. What must you think of him, and of me.'

'Not at all, Mrs Löw. The chickens alarm him. Who can explain these things? He's a fine boy.'

Anna Löw smiles in gratitude.

'I'd better hurry,' she says, 'before he takes off again. I will have one chicken and one large goose. There … that one,' she points, 'the fattest one, please. A nice fat liver for my liverwurst.'

'Istvan, take the money from the lady while I carry the poultry to her carriage.'

Istvan does as he is told. Mrs Löw thanks him and leads Katarina with the fat goose and the moderately plump chicken through the stalls and carts towards the carriage where her driver sits waiting, either patiently or in a daze of boredom.

'Would you mind placing them in the cage and my driver will secure it for me? Janos, can you do that? Make the birds secure in the cage?'

Frici, inside the carriage, is suffering a renewed outbreak of his chicken phobia.

'Frici, for heaven's sake, stop squirming like that. Mrs König, thank you so much. I will see you next time.'

When his mother returns, Istvan who is fearless not only where chickens are concerned, but in most things, blurts out, 'What a spoilt brat! If I carried on like that sissy, Papa would thrash me, I'm certain.'

His disgust is tempered with smugness, too, probably because he thinks that any father, given the choice, would prefer a son like him to one like this precious little Frici? If so, it's not what Istvan's mother is responding to when she admonishes him. No, she's thinking more of her son's insensitivity.

'Istvan, you should not say such a thing. Mrs Löw is one of my best customers. They are a lovely family and the other son is about your age.'

Istvan shrugs. It is not within his brief as a boy of ten to exercise charity in his mother's fashion.

'You can have him,' Istvan replies sullenly.

'Be kind,' persists Katarina König. 'Listen to me. Not long ago the boy was taken to the kosher butchery—you know, in town, where all my Jewish customers go—and he saw many birds, their necks cut, hanging upside down, still wriggling, just how they do when Papa kills them at home …' She pauses, noticing Istvan still smiling smugly.

'*Istvan*, are you listening? Living in town, not being brought up on a farm like you have, this was a shocking sight for him. I'm saying he saw *many*, not just the one. And he is younger than you. It scared him. The *shochet's* knife, the blood. Try to get into his shoes.'

The Löws are Jewish. The beasts they eat are slaughtered by the *shochet*, the ritual butcher, according to a process said to be formulated by Moses millennia past, and for reasons only Moses has ever fully understood. If the beast is killed by an accredited *shochet*, the meat is kosher. If not, it isn't.

Istvan repeats his verdict on the conduct of the Löws' irritating little princeling.

'He's a sissy.' He then punctuates his opinion with, 'and a Jew!'

Now, Katarina is an adoring mother and a patient one, but the way her son throws off that word—'a Jew!'—is something she won't countenance. She turns an infuriated face to her son and slaps her palm on the pile of old newspapers stacked on her table for the purpose of wrapping vegetables.

'I've taught you better than that. Are you that stupid?'

She means it. She sees in the smug anti-Semitism found everywhere in Romania not only cruelty but also a type of vulgarity. That it should surface in her son causes such a piercing disappointment that she is torn between weeping for him and slapping him. The hand she has brought down on the newspapers is a maternal deflection of the blow she might have landed on Istvan's cheek.

And Istvan is shocked. When does he ever see his mother react so strongly? His repentance is immediate and complete. He looks down, pretending to take a particularly close interest in counting the copper and silver *lei* from the morning's trade. He raises his head when he has mastered his emotions so that his mother can see the contrition on his face. But Katarina won't look at him. He touches her hand.

'Mama, I'm sorry. Truly.'

Katarina withholds the forgiveness her son craves for a few seconds longer. Then she looks down at his face, at his eyes.

'Good, Istvan. Good. Do you see how much I hate that sort of thing? Do you?'

'Yes, Mama.'

'Then, that's settled. Now go and see Mrs Nagy, and buy two sticks of hot *csabai*[3] so that I can make potato *krumpli*[4] tonight. Go on.'

Istvan, relieved and pleased to be back in his mother's good books, trots off a few steps to fulfil his errand. Then he stops.

'Not schnitzel?' he says.

Katarina shrugs. 'Will the veal be crumbed? Who knows if your sister listened to me.'

'Hermina said she's making a cake. *Beigli*[5].'

'*Beigli*?'

'Yes, that's what she said.'

---

3 Pronounced 'chah-buy': full-flavoured salami made from coarse minced pork, black peppercorns, paprika and red chilli.
4 Pronounced 'kroomply': potato bake layered with hard-boiled eggs, *csabai* and a generous amount of sour cream.
5 Pronounced 'baygly': yeast-dough cake filled with walnut stuffing and rolled into a log.

'Can a family survive on cake? What goes on in that girl's head?' Katarina shrugs and sighs.

Istvan heads off in search of Mrs Nagy's stall. Katarina, with four other sons and the not-entirely-reliable Hermina to occupy her thoughts, manages a moment of reverie alone at her stall: a short-waisted jacket with black velvet lapels hangs in her wardrobe, a servant brings her tea when she rings a small silver bell, her children line up in expensively tailored outfits to smile at her and accept, each of them, a kiss on a well-scrubbed cheek.

What Katarina doesn't know—how could she?—is that one day her bloodline will blend with that of the stunning woman whose wardrobe and elegance she covets. None of those composite children will live in Timişoara, nor even in Romania, but each of them will carry in their genetic make-up a certain amount of the poetry of Katarina and Anna, a certain amount of the poetry of Austria, of Hungary, and of this fertile land of mountains and plains in which geese grow fat.

2
Katarina

Born in the small mountain town of Sárhegy, in north-western Hungary not far from the Austrian border, Katarina is one of three children raised under the dome of Catholicism and under the roof of her grandparents' home. To Magyars[6], family is the centre of the social structure, with several generations of extended family very often living together.

It is here as a mere girl of sixteen at the beginning of World War One, that Katarina attends a military parade in which her two brothers are proudly marching off to battle with the Austro-Hungarian army. The day is bleak and she is shivering not only from the cold but from an intuition of some other impending darkness.

Katarina is a smiler; a lips-only, no-teeth smiler, with dimples in her round cheeks. So as her brothers pass by, she smiles stoically and gives a small wave. With tears glistening in her eyes, she is about to move away from the line of townspeople gathered along the side of the dirt road when the piercing grey eyes of a

---

6 Hungarians, also known as Magyars, are a nation and ethnic group who speak Hungarian and are primarily associated with Hungary.

dashing officer catch her gaze. She finds herself smiling at him, perhaps too broadly, and from beneath his military moustache, the corners of his mouth briefly lift in return.

This Great War, this 'war to end all wars', begins on 28 July 1914 with Austria-Hungary declaring war on Serbia. Those who understand, like her father, say it has been a long time coming, but the actual spark to the flame is the assassination of the heir to the Austro-Hungarian throne, Archduke Franz Ferdinand, in Sarajevo one month earlier. This war ends four years with the German armistice of 11 November 1918, but not before millions of innocent civilians are tragically wounded or killed, ranking it among one of the worst conflicts in human history. For the Austro-Hungarian army, it ends the lives of more than one million soldiers and wounds some three million. Of those who survive, many would later wish they did not.

As the months pass, Katarina writes many letters to her brothers who are stationed somewhere on the Serbian front, but not one is answered. The young men will be just two of many hundreds of thousands from the Austro-Hungarian army who go missing in action.

However, at his first opportunity for a lengthy leave of one month, the dashing young officer, who thinks often of the girl with the heartening smile, returns to the small mountain town to find this one who has occupied his thoughts. Their friendship quickly blossoms. And, with the imminent return to a landscape of warfare, they decide to marry. After the small family ceremony, Nikolaus returns to the Italian front where his regiment has been battling the Italians who joined Britain and France in May 1915. The bloody but indecisive fighting on the Italian front lasts for the next three and a half years.

Two months after her wedding, Katarina discovers she is pregnant. By the time a battle-weary Nikolaus returns permanently from war, his sporadic visits have borne him three boys under four years of age.

In the face of his war weariness (and no doubt his wife's), Nikolaus feels privileged, appreciative of his fortune. Oh, that's not to say fear doesn't catch him many times over—and change him, harden him—but he realises that he is fortunate not to have been swallowed by the carnage of his time. So, eager to move forward, he does his best to put the past behind. And despite unanswered questions about her brothers' fate, Katarina's joy to be reunited with Nikolaus is palpable.

For the next few years the grateful couple remain and make their home within her parents' crowded house in Sárhegy. Nikolaus is highly skilled in his engineering trade and a very hard worker, rapidly working his way up to the position of manager of the local timber mill during this time.

Time produces more children—several more—and two months before their sixth child is due, Nikolaus informs Katarina of his decision to take their young family across the border to Timişoara. 'In the hope of finding good business opportunities,' he explains to an incredulous Katarina, as she wonders how she will manage to pack and move in her condition.

'Men,' she mutters with a roll of her eyes before turning her back in that timeless female gesture of frustration. She would never question his judgement for Katarina is a woman of her times: a devoted and acquiescent wife, perhaps even a little intimidated by her spouse. But at times he frustrates her because he sees the world only in black and white—and more so, because he gets to decide what is black and what is white.

However, Katarina is not really surprised by the spontaneity of his decision because Nikolaus talks incessantly about his dream to own his own business. It has been this way since he returned from war. If only Nikolaus could see into a crystal ball, down the years some half a century later, he would see his grandson dream the same dream, speak the same words to *his* new wife, who in turn would mimic that timeless gesture.

Moving is a good decision and one Katarina doesn't regret for a moment. They have a fine life in Romania and this farmhouse feels large in comparison to the busy routine of three generations under the one roof. So here, on the outskirts of Timişoara, in the suburb of Chişoda, just beyond which lie constellations of quiet villages marked by a poverty that mirrors the very starkness of the landscape, Katarina is grateful, for she is well aware that the peasants of Romania are among the poorest in eastern Europe. She sees this for herself each week at her market stall when the poor beg for alms and forage for scraps. Nikolaus, in his worldly way, helps her appreciate that the situation is compounded not only by a high birth rate now that the war is over but even more by a lack of modern farming techniques and machinery. And with that, Katarina comprehends Nikolaus's enthusiasm to move here. She understands his eagerness to build machinery that he can use to harvest wheat crops for the farmers. Yes, she is content in the knowledge that her large family has settled into a comfortable, albeit modest, lifestyle.

'There but for the grace of God …' she says, blessing herself at the thought of those poor peasants.

In the small hours of 7 November 1928, Katarina awakes to the realisation that today will be no ordinary day. She doesn't rouse her husband yet, for she knows from experience that these things take time. And being the hardworking man he is, she knows too—as she listens to his gurgling snore reverberate within the timber panelling of their small bedroom—that he needs his sleep. Waves of pressure come and go within her rounded belly, but she lies still—thinking, planning, excited, even fearful, of what this day will bring.

As the morning gently tiptoes into the room, Nikolaus rubs his eyes and sits up on the side of the bed. He casts an intuitive look over his shoulder at his wife. She nods in affirmation to his unasked question, even managing a smile through the peak of a contraction. There is no need for conversation. He knows what to do—after all, this is the seventh time. Dressing, he walks to the bedroom door, but with hand on the doorknob he pauses, struck by the memory of Katarina's labour of two years ago. The calamity. He looks again to his wife in case there is something he need know for the midwife.

'Go,' she waves him off with another strained smile.

The spasm passes and Katarina relaxes her grip on the rolled towelling in her hands. At the foot of her bed, the midwife imbues an air of experience—perhaps even indifference?—as she busies herself folding piles of fresh sheets and towels, seldom glancing Katarina's way. Katarina quietly observes the efficient midwife and gauges her to be of equal vintage and as generously proportioned as herself, which meets her approval at least. Little babes cannot nestle against sharp ridges and bones, she considers.

Nikolaus enters the room carrying a bucket of steaming water in each hand. He places them on the floor where the midwife points. He turns and glances awkwardly at his wife, then quickly leaves. For this is not a man's place—not in 1928.

Another contraction washes over her. As if surrounded by wildfire, she is sweating and lost in a haze of pain. Closing her eyes, she succumbs to the contraction's intensity, softly moaning. It ends almost as quickly as it begins.

The hours pass slowly. The midwife is now standing over her mopping her brow a little too vigorously, as beads of sweat trickle down her face. She hears her husband's footfall against the timber floorboards as he paces outside the closed door. She knows he is anxious—she can hear it in the sharp tone he uses to admonish the children. This disruption to the household, to Nikolaus' work, she carries like an added mantle.

Outside, the rain falls softly. Nestled against her pain, Katarina's senses are so heightened that she can detect the earthy damp-grass smell of wet fields. The wind intensifies, rattling the windowpanes. Chill gusts find the cracks between the timbers of the house. She imagines the wind carrying away the last of the amber leaves that just yesterday were clinging futilely to the branches of the oak tree standing like a sentinel at the front gate. She loves that old tree, especially the way in which the wisteria vine encircles its trunk. But now, with the crispness of autumn, it has long since abandoned its lilac flowers and instead she thinks, could be likened to long thin arms, naked and tangled, reaching towards the sun, towards life. *Ooh ... this one is a determined little thing*, she notices in the shrinking interval between two contractions.

'Another big push, Mrs König. Don't stop now. You're doing very well. I just need one more big push.' The midwife's voice is composed as she urges Katarina on.

Oh yes, that's what they always say, Katarina thinks, though her politeness would never permit her to express her thoughts out loud—not even in the throes of labour. But Katarina knows it will take more than one push. It always does. And as the crucial time draws near, there is a sudden heaviness in her heart. She dreads the possibility that the outcome will be the same as her last labour. That one had been equally difficult, and in the end tragically unfulfilled, as the midwife handed her a silent infant. All day she has pushed these thoughts aside. Why must she now think of the image of her tiny blue babe, all but perfect in his stillness? What chance did one so tiny have with the cord coiled around his delicate throat? And how is it possible to sustain an unborn life for nine months, only to have it end in such cruel silence? These questions plague her mind with ungovernable guilt now, just as they have done for nearly two years.

Finally, the unmistakable wails of a newborn fill the room. A boy, she is told, another boy! *But is he all right? Please, dear God, let him be all right.* Her prayers are answered. He is wailing louder and she, too, is crying with relief. This one has survived.

'Istvan. His name will be Istvan,' she states, as the infant breathes a special life into her world that drapes bliss, awe and relief over her like a warm blanket.

On this more-than-common day in November 1928, as she gently cradles her strong little babe to her breast, she again feels competent and rewarded.

'All these sons—your father is a lucky man,' she says as she rocks him. 'But fortunately I have the blessing of one daughter to help me around the house. Your big sister, her name is Hermina. She is eight years old. How she will dote on you, little Istvan! But your brothers—they are a good many years older than you: Joszi is thirteen, Jani twelve, Ferenc ten. The gap is great between you and those boisterous boys, but hopefully not so great with your four-year-old brother, my fastidious little Nicky. I hope you will grow up to be close to him,' she says as she smiles fondly down upon the bundle of crinkled ruddy skin cooing softly in her arms.

For several years, regardless of distance, phase of motherhood or what weather the Lord sees fit for his followers—in fact, until Katarina commences working weekends at Chişoda markets—the König family don their Sunday best to walk to church. Prayers, of course, feature fervently in her daily routine, and being a God-fearing woman, Katarina is not afraid of death.

'It's simply nature's destiny,' she reiterates to her young at the passing of a domestic or farm creature.

At times Katarina worries about the recriminations of not keeping sacred the Lord's Day—will there come a day of reckoning? So she does her best to instil in her young family a moral fibre based upon the sound Christian ethos with which she was raised. To have a spiritual faith, she believes, is essential in one's journey. Secretly—because she knows most would think it sacrilege—Katarina envisages her dining table as symbolic of the altar her family rarely attends, for it is here that mother, father and six offspring come together as the sun sets, not solely to satisfy their hunger, but to thank the Lord for their blessings and partake with boisterous interest in each other's day. It is here, also, that father and offspring—as they pass brimming tureens of spicy soups or hearty goulash, or accompaniments such as *lescó*[7] or *lángos*[8], or platters of wafer-thin *palacsinta*[9]—silently give thanks for the sumptuous fare with which they are blessed. Oh yes, no doubt about it, Katarina is a good cook. Her kitchen is her place of solace, with the ritual of preparing

---

7 Pronounced 'letcho': side dish of stewed capsicum, tomato, onion, garlic, paprika and chilli.
8 Pronounced 'langosh': deep-fried flat bread made from flour, yeast, salt and water.
9 Pronounced 'palachinta': paper-thin pancake served savoury or sweet.

the large evening meal almost meditative—a calming period where she can turn back through the album of her mind to recapture watercolour memories of choice. Indeed now, as she peels potato after potato after potato (the staple of choice for the voracious König males) she looks out her kitchen window to where eleven-year-old Istvan is kicking his football and thanks the Lord for the wondrous day she was presented with her final gift from above.

As the seasons change colour many times over, a thin veneer of ivy claws its way up the front of the three-bedroom farmhouse and the old oak tree becomes further devoured by the heady sweetness of its weeping wisteria. Inside the modest home, Katarina's choice of decor exudes the vivacity of her Hungarian heritage, as she draws from a palette of warm orange tones. Her fondness for collecting bright hand-painted plates and decorative knick-knacks is proudly displayed along the timber sideboard and shelving that Nikolaus has carved.

As her children sprout and change like the foliage in her garden, Katarina discovers that each child takes differently from her. For the most part she watches on contentedly, even learning to keep her distance when the boys scuffle, for they are just as likely to bury the hatchet before she can unearth her wooden spoon. Naturally, the boys take her time, her space and, Lord knows, her patience—but they give it all back with a smile. Hermina, in comparison, is harder to mother. She takes things to heart and can behave sullenly for days. Only her father can restore her good mood. Perhaps she feels that his presence, his unassailable power—for he has a tightly controlled style and rigid approach—protects her from her brothers' taunts. Yes, Hermina appears happiest when her father is home, Katarina thinks, but wasn't she also this way with her own father, who when alive was the only man in the world who could do no wrong?

Each König child differs in aptitude and aspiration as the year, or the season, sanctions. As the elder sons embark on further study or trade, she knows Nikolaus is relieved to still have the hand of his youngest son and keenest worker, Istvan, to help him.

'Papa, can I drive the tractor?' the energetic boy calls out to his father as he eagerly follows him around, always underfoot. Hearing Nikolaus's reply, Katarina smiles to herself, all the while trying to maintain her balance as she turns this way then that, throwing feed to her many quacking geese, noisy rooster and his speckled-orange feathered friends that always seem to gather excitedly in the folds of her long skirt.

'No, my boy, you are still too young. But you worked hard today and I am happy with you. Maybe Mama has cooked your favourite dinner, chicken *paprikash* with *nokedli*[10]. Don't worry, I will make sure you get the largest helping—larger than your studious brothers—yes?'

---

10 Classic chicken-based creamy paprika stew served with small home-made egg dumplings.

3
Anna

Timişoara, Romania
1938

The driver of the carriage draws the reins tight in his leather-clad hands and brings the vehicle to a stop in front of a two-storey townhouse set amid a curved row of similar looking residences. Each facade is painted muted ochre and elegantly contrasted with black solid timber doors and wrought-iron window grilles. The second storey of each facade is adorned with motifs of birdlife intertwined with vines and foliage constructed in stucco of a similar design. The exclusive boulevard is situated close to the city centre of Timişoara, not far from the Politehnica University, one of the largest technical universities in all of central and eastern Europe. The city is made up of historic quarters, or neighbourhoods: Cetate, Elisabetin, Iosefin and Fabric. We are now in Elisabetin (or Erzsébetváros to the stylish Hungarian lady who is about to disembark), south and east of the Bega River which runs through the middle of the city and links all four neighbourhoods. In recent times a wave of construction has attracted many creative architects. They draw their inspiration from the Vienna Secession movement which was highly influential at the turn of the century in the Austro-Hungarian Empire to which the Banat region, where Timișoara is, once belonged. For this reason Timișoara is widely regarded as 'Little Vienna', a fact not lost upon Anna.

'Thank you, Janos,' Anna says to her driver as she carefully alights from the carriage and turns to help her son down the large step. 'Would you mind taking the poultry cage to the kosher kitchen before you return to the warehouse? And please inform the *shochet* I will have them picked up tomorrow.'

'Very well, Mrs Löw.' He turns his stocky frame towards her and tips his tweed cap in a gesture of respect, all the while keeping a firm hold of the reins in his other hand to ensure there is no movement on the cobblestone roadway until his charges are well clear of the carriage.

Anna bids him farewell and follows Frici inside the townhouse where they have lived for the past four years. Entering the foyer, she slips off her muddy ankle boots and begins to remove her gloves while greeting their live-in maid Ilinca, who is busy on hands and knees polishing the parquetry floor with an oiled rag.

'This one will need soaking after being on the ground,' she says with some frustration, examining both sides of the glove before placing it on the half-moon antique table. A gilt-framed mirror sits above the table. Anna surveys her appearance—turning first left, then right, removing her hat and running her fingers through her ebony bob.

'Goodness, how unkempt I look after that trip,' she remarks, not expecting a reply from the industrious Ilinca. Anna crosses the glossed floor, taking care not to slip in her stockinged feet. When she reaches the foot of the staircase she calls, 'Frici? Have you removed your shoes? I'm sure they're covered in horrible clay.'

Hearing no response from the boy, she calls out to their German nanny.

'*Frau Schröder? Können Sie bitte Frici's Schuhe ausziehen,*'[11] Anna wants her children to be multilingual like herself, so she insists the nanny speaks to her sons only in German. Other times at home the family speak Hungarian, but when out and about or at school, Anna has told the boys they must speak only Romanian. Being curious—as children are apt to be—they need to know why, and being the astute mother she is, Anna naturally tells them to ask their father.

'Well, boys, it's difficult to explain.' Sigismund is thinking of an uncomplicated explanation for what is indeed a complex situation about culture wars and long-held boundary issues. 'It's like this: Romanians—not me or any of our family, of course—are very ... how shall I put it ... territorial, protective over their land. It's been this way for hundreds of years. Why?' he asks rhetorically—forcing the boys to sit back down in their chairs, but not before they exchange knowing looks—'because other countries, like Hungary and Russia for instance, have actually invaded and fought many wars with us over our rich lands. So there is some ill feeling between our neighbours, you might say.'

Though not a 'hands-on' father, Sigismund enjoys these times of imparting wisdom to his sons. He is a man who believes in knowledge for the sake of knowledge, so he continues to explain that Romania has rich black soil because of its relatively low water table, which makes others covet its fertile agricultural region. He pauses, looks from one son's bored expression to the other, then adds, 'Anyway, boys, only no good comes from hate

---

11 'Frau Schröder? Can you remove Frici's shoes, please.'

or envy—especially over the country someone is born in, but even more so, over the religion one is born into.'

For this is 1938. Timișoara has a population of around ninety-two thousand, of which about ten per cent are Jewish. Not a reassuring statistic to belong to as the decade draws to a close.

Anna climbs the stairs to her bedroom, unbuttoning her waistcoat as she goes. She can't believe how Frici embarrassed her at the markets today. Yes, she knows he can be stubborn, even bad-tempered at times, but he's always been a well-*mannered* child—well, at least in public. As she enters her room, she removes her coat and sits down on the edge of the four-post mahogany bed. He has worn me out today, that *makacs kisfiú*, that wilful little boy. I must not tell Sigismund—he'll only lose his temper with him, and what good will that do anyone? Anyway … that's exactly where he gets *his* temperament from, she muses. After all, hasn't it always been so? That in the most intimate of ways, the experience of one generation will flow into the understanding of the next? She wishes Sigismund would display more affection with the boys, but it's simply not his way.

Anna slips off her gold-rope chain and coils its one-metre length into a ball. She places the heavy chain on her bedside table and leans back against the goose-down pillows. Their starched covers are intricately embroidered by her own hand—hers with the letter *A*, his with *S*. These were her gift to Sigismund on their first wedding anniversary. They lived then in an unassuming apartment in Chișoda. However, as Anna's life prior to wedlock was anything *but* unassuming, she was somewhat embarrassed by her small residence in the outer suburbs of the city. Nonetheless, she would soon find contentment, for it is here her two treasured sons would be born—Gyrui on 5 February 1928 and Frici on 10 April 1931.

Every narrative has a beginning. Anna and Sigismund's story unfurls in 1926, in Crasna, in the region of Sălaj, Romania. Born into the affluent Hönigsberg family of Nagyvarad, a neighbouring city to Crasna, Anna is an intelligent, stylish young lady of twenty-six. Typically, she enjoys a vibrant high-society lifestyle, was home-tutored, is fluent in four languages and displays an avid interest in cuisine. She has one elder sister—a celebrated actress—and two younger brothers who work in her father's burgeoning importing business. Sigismund on the other hand, is one of eleven children born into a working-class family which, despite strenuous efforts, struggles to prosper in its small corner store.

Crasna and Nagyvarad share a dynamic history of interchanging borders: Nagyvarad remains under Austro-Hungarian control until the end of the Great War when, like Crasna, it becomes part of Romania and is renamed Oradea. Despite this, Anna's family consider themselves Hungarian.

Anna's father is a self-made entrepreneur. Following the war, before many understand the ramifications of unstable and inadequate economic policies for agriculture, plus the vagaries of the Romanian climate, Mr Hönigsberg can see that there will be a market for imported foodstuffs. He begins in a small way in Oradea, but soon his business grows to incorporate warehouses throughout Romania and Hungary, and before long he is importing a wide range of uncommon fruits and speciality products. In his rapid expansion, he acquires farmland in the temperate regions of southern Italy and sends his two sons there to develop an orange orchard.

Growing up, Anna never tires of visiting her father in his business and weaving her way among the large baskets of citrus fruits, figs and other colourful and fragrant foodstuffs that fill his Oradea warehouse. She especially adores the pungent aroma of the Brazilian coffee beans and the crisp bite of a Tasmanian apple. As she grows into a sophisticated young woman, she embraces the latest trend of going to town to meet friends for coffee and pastries in the fashionable cafes that are springing up.

On this particular day in 1926, Anna, along with her mother and sister, is accompanying her father on a business trip to Crasna. The Hönigsberg women have spent the morning meandering through the town's pretty shops and the stores selling wines, apricot liqueur and pastries. At her mother's suggestion, they head off to visit and learn the history of Crasna's castle, which, as Anna discovers when she catches the heel of her shoe in a metal grate and is forced to listen to the tour guide's lecture, has not been inhabited since the seventeenth century.

'For centuries the town fell within the kingdom of Hungary', the tour guide's booming voice echoes through the castle with his tutorial, 'and remained within Hungarian borders until the Treaty of Trianon—a peace treaty drawn up at the end of the war by the Allies and Hungary—whereby Crasna was given to Romania.'

As she tries to no avail to pull her shoe free, a dark-haired stranger with soft voice and courteous manner steps up, seemingly out of nowhere. 'May I assist you?' Before any sound reaches her lips, he is bending down on one knee. He delicately removes her stockinged foot from her black court shoe and prises free the small heel held captive by squares of rusting iron.

'Crasna takes its name from the Slavic word meaning beautiful,' the guide continues.

But Anna only vaguely hears the guide as she slips her foot back into her shoe. Her cheeks blush with embarrassment but her keen eye observes the elegance of her rescuer's pin-stripe suit, crisp white shirt and a tie that matches the blue of his eyes. Catching herself, Anna quickly smiles and offers him her gloved hand, thanking him for his kindness. He asks her name, and she his in return. They make arrangements to meet for a coffee after the tour.

Less than a year later, they marry in what becomes Nagyvarad's social event of the calendar. With Anna's sister Elisabeta celebrated throughout Hungary and neighbouring parts, and her brother Miklós a well-known football player—representing Hungary in the 1924 Paris Olympics—the invitation list includes actors and directors, famous sportsmen, plus the political and well-heeled business associates of Mr Hönigsberg. That day, in front of a cast of hundreds, Sigismund tells his new bride that upon their first meeting, even within the shadowed light of the castle walls, he was captured by her beauty. How, as he handed back her trapped shoe, his desire to touch her hair as it fell in waves against the blush of her cheeks was maddening. But it was her guileless blue eyes that he fell for. Isn't it always the eyes? And as Sigismund avows his love, glasses clink to the happy couple and voices chorus their wishes for many years of uninterrupted bliss.

Even as her dark hair turns a soft, undulating silver and lines of weariness etch their way into her once perfect skin, Anna will retain the beauty Sigismund describes. However, her naivety, her innocence, will soon disappear.

Mr Hönigsberg, a gracious man, gifts his new son-in-law a branch of his importing business, located in Timișoara. Sigismund proves himself to be a keen businessman and the agency goes from strength to strength. A few years after Frici is born, Anna is delighted—in fact very much relieved—when they can afford a lavish townhouse close to the city centre. She is pleased, too, that her instincts, and her father's trust, have not been misplaced.

'Sigismund, do you have your pocket mirror inside your suit coat? You know I like your tie to sit perfectly straight.' She reaches up to kiss him goodbye as he sets off for work.

'Yes,' he replies, patting his breast pocket. 'And don't forget Mr Munteanu is coming this evening to trim my hair and attend to my manicure and pedicure.'

'My goodness, has it been a fortnight already? Where does the time go? Remind me to have a cushion ready to place in your barber's chair too, for the boys.'

They are not unalike in appearance, her sons. Their dark wiry hair and high-bridged noses are features inherited from their father. Gyuri is tall and slim, also like his father. Although three years younger and a good six centimetres shorter than his brother, Frici already has the more powerful, athletic build—one which will serve him well as before too long he will peek into the deserted alleyways where bigotry, and its companion, iniquity, lie lurking.

That evening, after Mr Munteanu has left, Anna ties her apron around her waist. Despite employing a cook, Anna oversees the preparation of each meal. She can't help but notice the anxious look on Frici's face.

'Don't fret, silly boy. I'm not cooking chicken with Mrs Dimitru tonight.'

'Good. Chicken, geese, ducks—all those birds you buy from the markets—I will never eat that stuff, not till I'm a hundred years old.'

'Well then Frici, you will be fine for another ninety-three years.'

As long as poultry is off the menu, Frici is usually close by her side in the kitchen. He loves to watch her instructing the Romanian cook on the secrets to creating traditional Hungarian fiery red goulashes. Or, even more, just as she is doing now without any assistance from Mrs Dimitru, preparing his favourite rolled *dobos*[12] cake which she fills with the rich dark chocolate cream that tantalises him with its heavenly aroma.

'Not yet, Frici.' She senses him sneaking up behind her ready to dip his finger into the lava of chocolate as it drips from the cake. He ignores her, ducks around her waist and traces his finger down the entire length of the rolled cake. 'Frici!' she shouts, stomping her foot. Her spatula is coated in chocolate cream but she tries to smack his hand away nonetheless, all the while conscious of not wanting to create further mess. The boy easily avoids her feeble attempt and dashes away, sucking his prized finger as he goes.

The Löw family espouse many traditions of Judaism, but they are observant in a way that is their own. It is customary for Anna to light the *Shabbat*[13] candles every Friday evening and they partake in traditional celebrations, such as Passover and

---

12 Pronounced 'dobosh': traditionally, this Hungarian torte has multiple layers of thin sponge filled with chocolate butter-cream, topped with a layer of caramel. Anna's version is rolled, omitting the caramel topping.
13 A Jewish ritual, these candles are lit by the eldest female of the household on Friday evenings to usher in the Jewish Sabbath, the seventh day of the week and day of rest.

Yom Kippur, attending Iosefin Synagogue on such important occasions. It is at Iosefin that the boys attend the Jewish primary school situated in the yard behind the synagogue. It is a thirty-minute walk each way—with their nanny in tow—every day except the Sabbath.

Both sets of grandparents dote on the young boys, but Sigismund's parents and family live closer so they visit more frequently. Anna ensures she keeps a special set of cutlery and dinnerware reserved as kosher—free from ever touching seafood such as lobster, crab, scallops and prawn; meat from pig, horse, camel or donkey; birds of prey, or even eggs containing blood-spots. Although she is well aware that she should not be cooking with or eating dairy food at the same time as meat, Anna occasionally breaks the rules of that doctrine and prays the loose lips of her children do not betray her to her in-laws.

With many aunties, uncles and cousins on both sides of the family, there is usually some sort of celebration to be had, about which there is never a complaint to be heard from the boys. But the one aunt they are most fond of visiting is Elisabeta whose stately home they enjoy playing in; their excited, fun-filled voices and slapping footsteps echoing throughout the great marble foyer. They are fixated, indeed obsessed, with repeatedly climbing the sweeping staircase, straddling the polished balustrade and sliding down the length of its enticing curve. Despite the many warnings to behave before they arrive at Aunt Elisabeta's, it is here they ignore the wrath of Sigismund. And when caught in the act, still their father's intimidating '*Nem, nem, nem!*'[14] cannot dissuade them.

---

14 'No' in Hungarian.

Certainly, to the Löws and Hönigsbergs, family is everything. As they gather with relatives for celebrations, the cornerstone of their tradition is an unswerving belief in *kavod* (respect and dignity), *chessed* (kindness) and *shalom bayit* (peace within the home). For with this way of life are obligations to certain morals and behaviour and, at the very least, a feeling of not wanting to disappoint or shame parents or grandparents. Later, when Frici discards his Jewishness as easily as a shirt, this model of family will, however, endure.

4
Katarina

Timişoara, Romania
1939

Approaching the age of 44, Katarina knows herself well enough to be assured of who she is. Generous with praise she observes her youngest grow into the masculine skin of his youth. She sees that this son, unlike his brothers, is even-tempered with a casual 'no-problem' disposition. Of course his interests are not found in school or in books—no real surprise there because eleven-year-old Istvan likes to roam carefree through nearby fields, forever chasing his well-worn football. But, most importantly, he likes nothing more than working with his hands alongside his father. And although a strict disciplinarian with his four older sons, Nikolaus has a gentler approach with his youngest, whose impish exuberance easily wins favour, much to the resentment of his siblings.

Istvan bears a strong resemblance in both manner and appearance to his father. Both have blunt features, outlined by strong, often stubbornly set, square jaws. As she observes them working hard together on this or on that, Katarina is amused by the same mannerism each has of flicking his sweaty brown fringe up and out of his eyes. However, it's the eyes that set them apart: Istvan's hazel eyes shine bright with enthusiasm and are haphazardly speckled with spots of brown, like a canvas at which an eccentric artist has randomly flayed his brush. Nikolaus too, has hazel eyes, but his are steely, she decides.

From a young age, Istvan displays a strongly competitive nature and Katarina has difficulty containing his energy and adventurous spirit, a spirit that is never daunted by the physicality of his older brothers or schoolboys who soon learn not to challenge him for his favourite possession—his football.

'Come on, Nicky, tackle me … see if you can get the ball.'

'You play too hard, Istvan. What's the point? You and I both know I can never beat you.'

Exhausted from a day's work in her rambling vegetable patch, Katarina stands up, removes her gardening gloves and, with the back of her sweaty hand, brushes away loose strands of hair that have escaped her bun.

'Mama, I'll carry your basket.' Istvan appears and takes her basket to the *nyári konyha*, the summer kitchen. This is a separate cottage at the rear of the main house which contains a cast-iron stove on small legs, a simple wooden table with bench seats and a small bed. It is here that Katarina spends the warmer months cooking for her hungry brood so as not to heat up the main house. Even though Romanian winters can dip below zero, the summer months of July and August can get as high as thirty degrees—and God forbid Nikolaus should stifle inside after a hard day's work.

'Thank you, darling,' she says as Istvan places the basket of vegetables on the long kitchen bench. 'Now go and find Hermina. I don't know what she's been doing all day, but tell her she needs to come and help me,' she adds as she lights the oven and prepares to roast a loin of pork from their own pigs.

Throughout the dampness of the frosty months of winter, Katarina uses the attic to dry her washing. The room is long and narrow with high tapered walls and is filled with the warm air that radiates from each of the open fires that keep the farmhouse comfortable. As Katarina unpegs her washing, she finds the heavy winter clothing has taken two days to dry. The sound of her son hurriedly dropping his school satchel inside the front door alerts Katarina that Istvan is home. 'Istvan, where are you going?' she quickly calls.

'I'm going to find Papa to see if he needs a hand.' He tears out the door before his mother can stop him.

That one never stops. Like his father in more ways than one, she thinks, tossing a pair of wooden pegs into a rusty old tin. As she folds the bedding, her thoughts drift to how quickly her robust boy has grown. She is proud of her strong-minded son— what mother wouldn't be?—but her intuition troubles her. There is something she just can't put her finger on.

'Nikolaus, what do you think Istvan should do when he leaves school?' she says as she pulls the goose eiderdown back and climbs onto the feather coverlet she has made to soften the horsehair mattress of their bed.

'I haven't given it much thought. We can discuss it when the time comes. He still has a few years to go.'

'Yes, I know, but he just seems so disinterested in study. I mean, Nicky knew he wanted to be a carpenter and already he loves his course. And Ferenc, too, knew early on that he wanted to be a chef. I know Jani and Joszi have not been as settled since they moved to Budapest, changing jobs, doing this, doing that—and of course I worry about them—but Istvan … I just can't picture what lies ahead for him.'

'Ah, woman, you drive me nuts with such talk. He's good with his hands. He learns fast and is good with numbers. Whatever he does, he'll be fine.'

5
Anna

Timişoara, Romania
1939

Despite earlier trepidation about going to synagogue—due to reports of gangs abusing or roughing up Jews who set out to pray—Anna is relieved to be enjoying the invigorating autumn air as she strolls hand-in-hand with her family along the wide boulevards through the cosmopolitan section of the city to Iosefin Synagogue. It is the eve of Yom Kippur,[15] so it is important that, as members of the Iosefin school community, they are seen to attend.

Anna looks towards the gardens that surround the city square, appreciative of the pretty borders of white daisies and vivid blue cornflowers, behind which are tiers of Romania's national flower, the *Rosa canina* (dog rose). She glances with admiration at the elegantly dressed crowds that are also out enjoying a walk, or more accurately, a personal parade. Her attention is interrupted, however, by the whims of her exploratory son as he tugs free from her grip and bends down to trace the intricate pattern of

---

15 Also known as Day of Atonement, it is the holiest day in the Jewish calendar; with central themes of atonement and repentance for sins of the previous year including a 24-hour period of fasting.

pavement cobblestones with his fingers. Each time she manages to regain her grip, a lamp post springs up in their way and Frici pulls free once more so he can swing himself around the pole like a chimpanzee.

'Look, Frici … see the peacocks, swans, owls and other birds drawn on the front of that building? See how colourful the peacock is—how he spreads his feathers so finely?'

'Yes, I see but I don't care.'

Anna recognises the whine in his voice and anticipates what will happen next.

'I don't want to go to *templom*[16]. The stupid singing of the prayers … it bores me! I'd rather go home and stay with Frau Schröder. Do I have to go?'

'Of course you must go with us. How many times must I tell you we are a family and as such will be seen as one. Now walk along nicely with all these people—we are being watched.' Her voice is tense as she looks around, suddenly noticing murmurs and glares. Worse still, she now is acutely aware of just how they are perceived by some non-Jews, as some hold their noses and others turn their backs when they pass by.

Gyuri notices her unease.

'Why didn't we drive in Apu's car, or take the carriage from the warehouse?'

'We will walk to *templom* just as we always have—like the rest of these good people,' she replies none too convincingly.

'Why?' Frici asks.

'Starting the car is like lighting a fire, and lighting a fire is not allowed on *Shabbat,* nor during holy times such as *Yom Kippur.*

'Why?'

---

16 Hungarian term used by Jews and Christians for place of worship.

'Always "why". If I tell you that the Torah says we cannot show we are stronger than nature on *Shabbat,* can you understand?'

'No.'

'Exactly. So don't always ask me why. Just be a good boy and do as I say.'

'Frici, leave your mother alone. Walk nicely along like your brother. I have told you both we will not show off in my car. It is for me to drive to work and special occasions—not for *templom*. You know that we are one of the few families to even own a car.'

'Now see how Apu is upset? Frici, listen to me. Stop touching the pavement, your good white clothes will get dirty. And stop with the questions, please!' She looks around, then adds, 'Oh, Sigismund, this was not such a good idea—especially after that terrible bombing in the theatre. I wish you hadn't worn your *Kittel*[17]—perhaps you should put your coat on …'

'Anna, they are just scowls and actions from unintelligent hypocrites. Do they think they can stop us from living our lives?' There is a sense of righteous outrage in his tone born of a social status and recognition that has to date guaranteed his and his family's security.

'I'm hungry, Anyu,' Frici whimpers.

'Oh Frici. Today of all days, when we are about to seek forgiveness for our wrongs, *please* behave yourself—especially in *templom*.'

When they arrive at the synagogue, Sigismund takes the hands of his sons and Anna proceeds alone up the narrow winding stairs to the mezzanine level to sit with the women. She gazes around the softly lit interior of this relatively new

---

17 White burial robe often worn by married men on Yom Kippur and other High Holidays symbolising the link to its use as a burial shroud and to the verse 'our sins shall be made as white as snow' (Isaiah 1:18).

synagogue, much preferring the Oriental architecture of the larger and older Citadel Synagogue on the Strada Mărășești, which she used to attend when she first moved to Timișoara. Her thoughts are broken when Rabbi Schick begins his prayers. As the haunting cadence of his chant fills the synagogue, Anna considers the young rabbi's appearance and silently approves. He is charismatic, she thinks, and tidy too, with his trimmed curly black hair and matching short beard, unlike his more traditional peers. Banal thoughts, but preferable to thinking about the walk back home.

When they arrive home, the nanny is waiting in the hallway with a small suitcase beside her.

'I am sorry, Mr and Mrs Löw,' she says, bowing her head so her platinum blonde fringe almost hides her blue eyes, 'but I must leave your employ immediately.'

'Why so suddenly, Helga?' Sigismund's facial expression retains its typical reserve as he goes through the routine of sliding off his coat, brushing it lightly with his gloved hand and hanging it carefully on the coat stand by the door. But there is an edge to his voice.

'I've had … there's a letter from my family. They are going back … returning to Berlin. They want me to go with them. I'm not permitted to say more. I'm sorry.'

'Well, if you must, of course … you must go then.'

Anna looks at her husband, surprised by his reserved tone.

'Thank you, Frau Schröder, you have been a wonderful help with the children,' she says as she opens the front door.

With small case in hand, Nanny Helga quickly brushes past. Anna closes the door and slides the bolt across, securing the family home.

6
Frici

September 1939

Frici is at war. He is at war with a worthy opponent: his brother. They are playing table tennis on the second-storey back terrace of their townhouse. The terrace is wide and under cover with a wrought-iron lattice grille and balustrade, just the right height and width to ensure wayward balls from young boys' bats don't escape. As they get older and more adept at the game—well, that's when the real arguments begin over who has to retrieve any wayward ball.

'Yes!' Frici pumps his fist, as he reaches the winning score of twenty-one.

'Best of three again?' Gyuri asks.

'No way—you lose.'

Frici has learnt to quit while he's ahead. He dashes inside to report his win to his parents. It's still and quiet upstairs, so he makes his way down the staircase. His mother is not in the kitchen, where he would expect to find her, and his father is not in the library, where he would normally find him reading his Sunday newspaper, so he begins searching room to room.

When he finds them in the sitting room, they look worryingly serious, and he watches from the doorway. Something stops him from disturbing them. They have moved the two formal lounge chairs out of place closer to the wall cabinet, which makes Frici curious, as he's never been allowed to move the furniture out of place. Then he observes his father reach out toward the small black dial of their new short-wave radio—a modern-looking piece of equipment with a round black speaker above dials that move a vertical red line through a series of tiny white numbers, all encased in burnished walnut wood with rounded edges, in keeping with the wall cabinet on which it proudly sits.

Yesterday, Sigismund had arrived home from work carrying a large cardboard box and Frici danced around his father like a curious puppy, begging him to reveal its contents. Even Gyuri showed some modest excitement. But Anna made them all wait until after dinner. Then, with the new-fangled device out of its package, the four of them knelt around it with much fascination and enthusiasm. Gyuri nearly ended the merriment when he snatched the instruction booklet from his brother and took over reading out the unusual words that Frici was stumbling over. But Frici soon got over his annoyance when the radio began to speak.

Now, however, Frici is cautious as he watches his parents from the doorway. They look distant, worried, as they listen to the different languages that momentarily break through the static while his father's fingers fiddle, turning knobs this way then that, delicately alternating between the many different channels of the tuner. Finally he settles on an English-speaking voice and leans back in his chair. Just as Frici decides it is safe to enter, they both suddenly sit forward again. His father's back becomes rigid and his mother's hand abruptly reaches out for his father's arm.

This morning the British ambassador in Berlin handed the German government a final note stating that, unless we heard from them by eleven o'clock that they were prepared at once to withdraw their troops from Poland, a state of war would exist between us. I have to tell you now that no such undertaking has been received, and that consequently this country is at war with Germany.

A five-second pause follows before the speaker continues:

You can imagine what a bitter blow it is to me that my long struggle to win peace has failed.[18]

'Sigismund! England at war with Germany! For God's sake, not another war!' The colour has drained from Anna's face. His father's hand comes down hard on the arm of the lounge chair, causing Frici to jump.

'I'm not surprised, not at all. Didn't I tell you this Hitler—he has been making furious speeches proclaiming Germany's right to other lands. And what with the invasion of Czechoslovakia six months ago, and now Poland, well … Chamberlain has no choice, now.'

'What does it mean for us, here?'

'Look, Anna, we're a long way away. We don't have to worry … yet, anyway.'

He stands up, paces a few steps, then comes back to his wife who has covered her eyes with her hands. He squats down and leans in to her, taking her hands in his. He says nothing, even as he reaches out and draws her close to his chest. Anna can't see her husband's face, but Frici can, and the portrait before him

---

18 Part of Britain's Prime Minister Neville Chamberlain's broadcast to the nation. For full transcript: http://www.bbc.co.uk/archive/ww2outbreak/7957.shtml?page=txt.

perplexes him: never before has he seen Sigismund's eyes dart from place to place, his hands jittery with tension.

How could Frici possibly comprehend the significance of today's date: what it will represent, how it will change his family. After all, he is not even nine years old. So the 'war to end all wars' didn't live up to its name. And today marks the beginning of what will become known as World War Two. Those belonging to Frici's parents' generation—who lived through a time where conscience was forsaken for shocking brutality—might appreciate to some extent what lies ahead. But even they will not fully grasp the impact this war will have on a global scale—how it will radically alter patterns of society and family existence, bring about an anguish, a rupture, that will destroy any capacity for logic. And even if they did, what could they possibly do about it?

Despite the date, some, like Sigismund, say the actual line in the sand was crossed months, if not years, earlier: 'almost as soon as the ink dried on the Treaty of Versailles'. Others argue it commenced in 1932 when Germany, under Chancellor Adolf Hitler, begins to secretly build up its army and weaponry and form strategic alliances with other countries.

But no one—from politician to businessman, from educator to student, from farmer to housewife—will envisage that, under this man named Hitler, a political and social bacterium will fester in the form of a virulent anti-Semitism. Jews will be scapegoated for all Germany's economic, social and political problems which Hitler will use to justify an industrialised genocide never before seen in human history. Anti-Semitism has, of course, existed for centuries. But Hitler's ideology adds a further dimension. It fixates on Jewishness not just as a religion or culture but as a race, casting the Jewish people as *Untermenschen* or subhumans and thereby removing their rights to be treated as part of human society.

A few months later, workers begin digging up their front lawn. 'What are they digging so deep for, Apu?

'It's a bunker, Frici. Most of your friends have cellars under their houses—we don't. I want an underground room, that's all.'

'Oh, I see,' he says. But he does not see at all.

'Later today you can help me with something,' his father says. 'We are going to cover the windows with paper.'

'But we have curtains.'

'Ah, but this is new.' His father's back is aching. With hands on hips, he stretches from side to side as he continues. 'The government needs everyone to tape black paper to the windows. They don't want any lights to be seen by pilots flying above at night. Pilots from other countries that do not like us.'

'Why would they not like us?'

'Not just us, Frici. You'll see. All your friends' houses will soon have their windows blackened too.'

7
Istvan

1940

Istvan is at home with just his mother and twenty-year-old sister Hermina. As yet unaffected by the ramifications of the continental conflict, they are happily preparing for Hermina's simple wedding to her beau, Hans, a young German and eager new recruit in the German army. The women are busy plucking chickens in the kitchen, while Istvan is sitting at the kitchen table sharpening his mother's long-bladed knife. His young hands are already hard with work.

'Istvan, be careful.'

'I know what I'm doing, Mama,' he says with the indignation of a twelve-year-old boy who knows everything. After all, his father has shown him many times how to hold the blade of the knife at a forty-five degree angle and slowly grind with whetstone from hilt to point—what father hasn't?

From the living room a composed Romanian voice can be heard crackling from the radio. Istvan stops sharpening the knife mid-stroke as the announcer's words catch his attention:

War has blazed a path of destruction across neighbouring countries of Romania ... As reported late last year, Britain and

France have tried to guarantee Romania's borders, but King Carol's refusal to allow the Red Army to cross its borders has kept Russia out of the pact and the guarantee has fallen apart. The hope of our government to remain neutral has all but disintegrated. Under counsel from the German government—whose leader, Adolf Hitler, sees value in our country as a key supplier of oil, grain and industrial products to the Nazi armies—King Carol has ceded hundreds of square kilometres of Romanian territory, with approximately four million of our population, to the Soviet Union and Hungary. Without a single gunshot fired, in a treaty between Germany and the USSR, Romania has ceded Basarabia and northern Bukovina to the USSR and north-western Transylvania to Hungary. King Carol is without internal or external political support. There are rallies throughout the country protesting against him as people consider him responsible for the loss of the aforementioned territories and for the violence in political life in this country. It is anticipated that King Carol will give up most of his decision-making powers in favour of General Ion Antonescu, allowing him to become Romania's head of state.

Not sure what to make of the grim daily news reports, and if truth be told, not really interested—despite his parents' new seriousness—Istvan continues on with his simple and, as yet, undisturbed days. His sister's wedding is a small affair celebrated with just a few close friends and family. In the days following, Hans, impatient to travel back to his homeland and join Hitler's war effort, leaves his new wife at home.

Soon after, Istvan farewells his older brothers Jani and Joszi, who had come home briefly from Budapest for Hermina's wedding. His other two brothers, Ferenc and Nick, now twenty-two and sixteen years of age respectively, leave with their older brothers to seek out better work opportunities in the capital in their trades as chef and carpenter.

'Goodbye, little Istvan,' Ferenc calls as they head down the long dirt drive and past the deep-rooted oak tree whose spreading canopy now covers half the front yard. The sunlight is dappled between the foliage on the thick branches, and the grass beneath is patchy, struggling to thrive. When they reach the road, with suitcases in hand, both boys turn for one last wave.

'We'll write as soon as we have news,' Nick calls.

'Goodbye,' Istvan waves, then just before they disappear from sight, yells, 'and don't call me little anymore!'

In their first letter home, which his father reads aloud as they gather around the glowing embers that light their small living room, Istvan can tell that all four brothers, like Hans, are caught up in a wave of patriotism. He lies on the hearth rug, the crackling flames warming through his whole body. Rolling over, he stares up at the exposed timber beams that support the attic and listens to the wood pop, until his mother and sister eventually retire.

'They say they have no choice but to join the Hungarian army. But knowing them, Papa, they are probably just saying that not to upset Mama.'

'You could be right. Perhaps they foolishly want to follow in my footsteps, thinking it will all be over very soon. But that's what we all thought about the last war. Damn propaganda does nothing to help. They tell the young ones they will have adventures, be heroes …'

'Do they get paid to be in the army?'

'Yes, but what good is money at the risk of your life? Anyway, be careful around your mother—she's on tenterhooks now.'

Tired, Istvan soon makes his way to bed. His bedroom is not large, but with his brothers gone it certainly feels that way. He changes into his flannel pyjamas, slides into bed and pulls the eiderdown up to his chin.

Suddenly he hears his mother cry out from her bedroom.

'*Why*, Nikolaus? *Why* must our sons be made to fight in a war which we know nothing about? Why can't these generals leave us in peace? We should never have let them go into Hungary.'

'There is nothing we can do, Katarina,' he hears his father reply. 'All men over the age of eighteen will soon be conscripted—mark my words.'

'But it's *their* war, not ours. Not Jani's or Joszi's.'

'Did you hear the news? King Carol abdicated today,' Istvan says to his mother as he dumps his school satchel inside the front door and removes his coat. 'Everyone at school is talking about it.'

'Yes, it's on the radio, over and over. And what can this new one—a nineteen-year-old for goodness sake—do as king? Particularly at a time like this. Bah!' Her grievance with all things political is still evident and Istvan thinks he should not have broached the subject, especially when she continues, 'and what are your clever teachers and friends saying about Prime Minister Antonescu and his "Iron Guard"?'

'I don't know, Mama. Nothing, I suppose.'

'Of course, they must say something.' She is standing in the kitchen doorway with the meat cleaver in her hand. Istvan thinks that right about now would be a good time to see if his father needs help in the yard.

'No good will come of it, that much I know,' her voice trails after him as Istvan makes his escape.

He finds his father in the piggery, a large shed that Nikolaus has converted into two levels. As well as holding pigs on each level, the shed houses a large grinder which processes weeds and roots into feed. The engineer inside Nikolaus has the whole procedure of feeding several hundred pigs down to a fine art. He has built a dozen long metal barrows—which sit on wheels—that he conveys from the grinder along each line of pigs whose hungry snouts protrude from his precisely constructed metal barricades. As they work side by side, Nikolaus tells his son the ins and outs of feeding pigs.

'Pigs will eat all the food you give them and still whine for more. Overweight pigs are a real problem, Istvan. A pig that is overweight can get sick, even die. Never trust a pig to tell you if it's hungry,' he laughs.

Of course Istvan has heard this many times, and is busy thinking about another topic altogether. Somewhat unexpectedly, Istvan asks his father what the Iron Guard is. Nikolaus explains the grim facts to his son briskly, and with little pleasure in the details.

'Ah, the Iron Guard ... Quite a sinister assemblage, really. An ultra-nationalistic fascist group. Some call them "Legionnaires". They're particularly active against Jews, communists and other minority groups, such as the *cigàny* [gypsies]. You see, Istvan, throughout parts of the country—but now here, too—there's increasing violence on the streets, not only against these groups but also against those who stand up to oppose the Iron Guard's thuggery. So you must be very careful when you're out and about. These people are also said to be behind a lot of political assassinations. They have the support and are funded by their friends, the German Nazis. Very soon, I fear, the Iron Guard will become the largest fascist movement in the Balkans. How things will affect us, I have no idea. But I tell you this much: it's a worry.

'Glad we're not Jewish then, eh, Papa?'

'For sure. But be very careful about what I've just told you, Istvan. In fact, it's better you say nothing at all. Not to anyone. Especially not to your mother.'

Late autumn. Istvan rests his elbows on the windowsill and stares through the misty pane, taking in the sight of his small world as a new day begins to breathe. An unseasonable early dusting of snow covers the ground and he wishes he could stay home from school and work with his father. There will be much work to be done today, he thinks. The spring vegetable seeds will need to be planted now before the mould seeps into the dirt, and the barns will need to be prepared for keeping the animals warm through winter.

'Istvan? Are you ready? You'll be late if you don't come now and eat your eggs and *szalonna*[19].'

'I'm coming, Mama,' he replies as he reluctantly begins to dress.

He gulps down his eggs, followed by a warm milk coffee in which he dips his mother's freshly baked bread. In the background the now familiar sound of the early morning radio can be heard. The voice, though well-known, now carries a disquieting tone:

> *… therefore, it is now official that as of 23 November, Romania has formally joined the Axis Powers.*[20]

---

19 Hungarian pronunciation 'sah-lon-na': a smoked pork product, or back bacon with rind.
20 The Axis Powers was the title Germany, Italy and Japan gave themselves after they signed a tripartite pact on 27 September 1940. These three countries believed that they would be connected by an 'axis'—such as depicts latitude and longitude on a map—and the world would revolve around that connection. Romania joined the Axis coalition in November 1941.

'Istvan?'

He knows what his mother is about to ask, and quickly replies, 'The main leader of the Axis Powers is Hitler.'

'Of course,' his mother interrupts.

'Let me finish, Mama. The others who have joined with Germany are Italy, Japan, and of course now there is us and Hungary. I think that's all—maybe some other small countries—I can't remember everything they told us at school.'

8
Frici

1941

Frici deftly tiptoes into his mother's bedroom, away from the pursuing footsteps of his brother, and hides inside her tall mahogany wardrobe. After several stifling minutes between her long velvet robes and woollen dresses, he smiles like a fiend in the dark for he knows he has outwitted Gyuri in their game of hide and seek. He climbs out of the wardrobe, moves to his mother's dressing table and strokes her soft hairbrush—enjoying the way the bristles caress his fingertips. The corner of an envelope is protruding from underneath her crystal dresser set. Playing detective, he carefully slides it out, reads his mother's name and address scrawled across the front, then turns it over and concludes it has already been opened. Checking over his shoulder—as any good detective would—he listens for approaching footsteps. With no one in close proximity, he quickly pulls out the folded cream paper from within. His eyes travel over the fluid script:

My dearest sister,
I must write quickly now, as I fear that time will not do us any favours. Things are not good here in Iasi. There have been

mass deportations of Jewish families to labour camps. Police and soldiers, willingly supported by mobs—people who we once considered friends!—are rounding up hundreds, or perhaps even thousands, by the day. Up until now most have gone by train—to where?—only God knows the truth! But now there are not enough trains to take them away. With my own eyes I have seen hundreds of these pitiable men, women and even children forced to march through the thickest of snow storms. The children, Anna, how sad it is to hear them cry from the cold. Even sadder to see the old ones fall down, only to be beaten. Only yesterday, as a group of people marked with a yellow Star of David on their chests trekked past the building where we have been hiding with four other families (it is safer for all if I do not say where), I saw an elderly man stumble and fall. He tried to get up but couldn't. Next minute a Nazi soldier approached and took out his pistol and shot him. Then I heard the soldier shout to the others: 'Don't look so shocked—thousands of your people are dead—what is one more?'

Can it be true? I pray not, but I fear the worst.

We have survived thus far only for the graciousness and kind heart of a dentist and his family, who let us, along with the other families, live in his attic. We are cramped and must share everything—beds, chamber pot, meagre amounts of food. How the girls hate to be so unclean—as you would my sweet, meticulous sister—but we are alive! Though as each day passes I am filled with a heavy feeling that it is only a matter of time before we are discovered—then what will become of us, dearest Anna?

I pray that you, Sigismund and the children are safe and well. I have heard that parts of south-western Romania are protected from this terror. I hope that this is correct. It is so difficult to know what is true and what is not. I cannot write again—it is too dangerous for our compassionate guardians.

Dear, dear Anna, my memories of our happy times together will be what I carry inside my heart wherever my journey takes me. Please pray that these most terrible days come to an end and we will all be together again soon.

All my love,
Elisabeta

Frici carefully folds the letter and replaces it exactly. For months now he has quietly observed his parents listening to their short-wave radio for hours on end, their expressions so focused they often don't notice his presence. And he also sees how quickly they discard the newspapers, before he or Gyuri can read them, when only a short time ago Apu had insisted that they both read the paper each night. 'Smart men have a knowledge of current affairs,' he used to say.

Frici does not quite understand this war, but he senses an atmosphere of trepidation in the people around him. And now, having read his auntie's letter, his suspicions of disquiet are confirmed.

Some weeks later, Frici enters the library and selects his favourite novel, *Journey to the Centre of the Earth*, to read for a second time. He lies down on the chesterfield lounge, where the musty smell of old books and fine leather exhale a comforting scent, immersing himself in the adventures of Professor Von Hardwigg, his nephew Harry and guide Hans, as the trio plunge through an old volcano in Iceland. All of a sudden he is distracted by a distant sound, like the clap of thunder approaching. Gradually the roar becomes louder and louder, making the windowpanes rattle and the crystal chandelier above him shiver. He jumps up off the settee, skittles through the hallway and out through the front door onto the front steps of the house. The ground trembles with fear beneath his feet.

'Frici! Frici! Come back inside at once!' his mother shrieks as she follows swiftly behind. But instead he stands mesmerised by the sight of tanks, trucks, motorbikes and marching troops as they pass down his street and onto the main street of Timişoara.

'What's happening?'

'I don't know, Frici, but it is not good, not good at all ...'

'Apu will know—won't he, Anyu?'

'Yes, yes, we'll ask Apu. Now, *please* come inside.'

Later that afternoon, Frici sits at the kitchen table with his schoolbooks spread out over its red-and-white chequered cloth. Instead of working, he has his elbows resting on the table, two hands cupping his chin, engrossed in the ritual of Mrs Dimitru—the dour-faced and rather obdurate family cook—stuffing large green capsicums with cooked onions, rice and minced meat.

'Can I help you stand them in the pot, Mrs Dimitru?'

'No, Frici. Your mother said you were to finish your schoolwork.' Her tone is firm as she wedges the stuffed vegetables upright inside the largest of her cast-iron pots, pausing every so often to look over her spectacles in Frici's direction. He quickly turns to his books each time and pretends to write.

Next, she roughly dices several tomatoes and onions and places them over and around the capsicums. As the tomatoes simmer down into a thick red sauce Anna enters the kitchen with a list in hand and the two women disappear into the larder to discuss the coming week's menu. Every few minutes, Frici sneaks up to the pot, lifts the lid, and furtively dunks torn pieces of bread into its bubbling liquid, making sure not to trickle even a drop onto his clothes or his mother will surely fuss—nor drip any on the floor or Mrs Dimitru will give him one of her long, hard scowls. So occupied is he with repeating this stealthy antic, he doesn't hear his father enter the kitchen.

'Aha, Frici, caught you!' At least his father is smiling. 'Dinner smells good tonight, Mrs Dimitru,' he says as the women reappear from the larder. 'I hope Frici has left enough sauce for us all,' he adds, kissing his wife on the cheek.

'Apu, did you see all the tanks and soldiers parading down the street today?'

'Yes, I did.'

'What are they doing here in Timişoara?'

'They're travelling through on their way to Yugoslavia. Listen, Frici, we are still safe here, so I don't want you to worry, all right? Now leave us a moment, will you. I need to speak to your mother alone.' He guides Anna out of the kitchen, across the foyer and into the library.

Frici leaves his parents and walks towards the staircase. When he hears his father begin to speak in a hushed tone, he tiptoes back to eavesdrop from just outside the open door.

'Anna, don't be alarmed, but I've heard that German and Romanian soldiers have begun to round up men over the age of eighteen to join the army.'

He hears his mother's sharp intake of breath.

'Jews too ... you are sure?'

'No.' His father's voice is tight. 'People are talking. People who should be well-informed—business associates—but even more so, people I trust, like Janos, who has links to the dissident movement. And the talk is they won't take Jews in the army. But there are worsening reports of harassment.'

'God help us, Sigismund! Are we safe?'

'For now, yes. Try not to alarm the boys, Anna. Listen to me now. I've made provisions, used my contacts ...'

His father pauses for a moment and when his voice comes again it is hoarse with anger.

'If I didn't work with food, there is simply no way we could eat this well. Even basics like flour and butter are hard to get. I'm sorry to say we're going to have to let Mrs Dimitru go.'

'Oh dear, Sigismund. I don't mind doing the cooking, but poor Mrs Dimitru …'

'Look, I don't do this lightly, Anna, and although I can't explain fully now, I fear it will be safer not only for us, but for her as well. Don't look so distressed, I'll ensure she's well paid.'

Frici can hear his father's footsteps pacing over the floorboards. He's not concerned about losing Mrs Dimitru—he prefers his mother's cooking on Sundays anyhow—but he knows his father's remarks about the harassment of Jews are true because only yesterday his older friend and neighbour, Viktor Bossel, told him that these attacks are worsening. The previous night their mutual friend Alex Gerrard, who lives around the corner alone with his mother Olga, was frightened half to death by a rock that came smashing through their front window. Viktor then showed him a copy of *Curierul Israelit* (the Israelite Courier). Frici scanned the headlines:

PRIME MINISTER ANTONESCU INTENT ON CLEANSING THE LAND OF JEWS

JEWISH ENTERPRISES BURDENED BY HEAVY TAXES WITH THE AIM OF RUINING THEM

AN ORDER HAS BEEN ISSUED FOR TIMIȘOARIAN JEWS TO REMAIN AT THEIR HOME ADDRESS

Lately their dinners are without laughter, often without conversation. The silence tonight is only broken by a clinking of silverware. Until a sudden rap on the front door disrupts the meal.

'I'll get it,' Sigismund says, as he pushes back his chair.

Serious voices can be heard in the hallway. Frici is getting up to see who they belong to, when Sigismund re-enters the dining room and curtly instructs the boys to go to their rooms. From the tone of his father's voice, Frici knows not to say a word and instead looks inquisitively towards his brother, who acknowledges his unspoken question with a shrug as he gets up and moves past his father. Frici immediately follows his brother into the hallway and up the staircase, but not before taking a surreptitious look at the two solemn men in dark suits.

'Gentlemen,' his father says, 'please come this way—into the library.'

'Hurry up boys,' his mother says, her voice strained as she follows them up the stairs.

Unbeknown to his mother, Frici keeps his door ajar and waits until he hears the click of her bedroom door closing. Quietly, he creeps back down the stairs and leans against the thickness of the highly glossed library doors. Despite being barely discernible, the stern voices that penetrate the wood make Frici afraid for his father. As the voices grow louder and footsteps approach the door, Frici makes a silent dash back up the stairs and hops into bed. He lies awake trembling for some time, wondering about the men in dark suits.

As the days wear on, an aura of urgency begins to surround everyone, especially Anna. At the sound of an air-raid alarm, a loud *clang* echoes through the house as Anna drops whatever she is holding and dashes around in a panicked state, calling her sons' names. Together they race into the front yard, lift the handle of the hinged door to the bunker that lies hidden under their manicured lawn and descend the four-metre ladder, taking care not to slip on its steel rungs. Once inside, Gyuri lights the kerosene lamps hanging from two large wooden rafters that support the reinforced concrete ceiling. When illuminated the small room lends a strange light to their faces as they sit and stare at each other. Narrow shelves, which are built down one side, are stocked with tins of food. 'In case you get hungry,' his mother had replied to Frici's look of uncertainty on their first tour of the bunker. But so far they are never in there long enough to get hungry. After twenty minutes or so, the sirens usually stop. Only then does Anna—in an attempt at composure—stand up, brush her clothes down, and declare, 'False alarm. Thank goodness. Back into the house, boys.'

The next evening, as Frici sits in the kitchen doing his schoolwork, he looks up from his books into his mother's face as she prepares dinner. She is alternating between stirring the goulash and dropping matzo-ball dumplings into his favourite soup. The grandfather clock strikes six o'clock. With the first few chimes, there is a slight tightening of her jaw. After the sixth and final chime, fear clouds her eyes, for this is the time Sigismund should be home from work. She dries her hands on the kitchen towel and goes into the foyer. Frici knows what she's doing—he has seen her habit of staring at the hallway clock, waiting nervously for the metallic sound of his father's key turning the lock of the front door. How he hates this war. And this man called Hitler—he would like to punch him hard on the nose.

9
Istvan

1941

The months pass quietly with an eerie calm for Istvan and his family, in a landscape now in transition, destined to change for the worse. Letters from Jani, Joszi, Ferenc and Nicky are few. Their words are shaped carefully, so the family must rely on disquieting rumours and confusing propaganda, which hang heavy like the smell of thunder before a storm.

School, for thirteen-year-old Istvan, is a small two-room timber building located a few kilometres from home. Much to the delight of all but a few studious types, schooldays have been cut in half, due to the war causing a shortage of teachers, as well as books and writing implements. Sitting at his wooden desk, Istvan's stomach begins to groan. He's pleased for it means he'll soon be able to go home for lunch—now the largest meal of the day. He hopes his mother has made cabbage rolls, or something equally substantial, so that he can work non-stop with his father until sundown. The sound of the small bell interrupts his thoughts of food. The students pack up their simple belongings and file out of the room. Istvan is joined by his friend Andor, and together they begin the half-hour trek home.

Istvan is only partly listening to Andor's tedious talk about war affairs—as if he doesn't get his fill of that in school—but he nods his head and tries to say 'mmm' in all the right places, all the while kicking loose stones to the side of the dusty road as he goes. Andor's commentary drones on. And on. Soon he is extolling his father's logic behind the shortage of good food and other essentials. Andor's father is an opinionated Romanian who believes that the blame lies squarely at the feet of the refugees flooding into their city from neighbouring Transylvania. Istvan, too young to be involved in the rhetoric, responds humorously.

'Really, Andor? So far we are both doing all right. Anyway, you could stand to lose a few kilos.' With his free hand he softly punches Andor in his rotund belly.

Still trying to impress the imperturbable Istvan, Andor continues, 'Well, what about this, then: my father says there have been more Romanian troops sent to fight Russia than all of Germany's other allies combined. Did you know that, smarty?'

'So, what of it?'

At last, sensing a modicum of curiosity from his indifferent friend, Andor—who, like his father, enjoys regaling others with informed opinion—explains that Romania is in competition with Hungary to win Hitler's favour, and that the government believes by providing extra troops as well as equipment and oil to Nazi Germany, it will regain northern Transylvania—land which Romania is bitter about losing to Hungary after the last war.

'I see. Now I understand what happened at our farm a few weeks ago—it's all to do with stupid land.'

Andor almost chokes on the apple he is munching, stunned by his friend's interest.

'What do you mean?'

'You know that my mother is Hungarian, right?'

'Yes.'

'Well, one night this lot of scruffy Romanian men came to our house, yelling and screaming, and even throwing rocks through our windows. Papa made us all go up into the attic. I tore a slit in the black paper covering the window and peered out. Couldn't see much—it was so dark—but I saw that Papa had his gun and I could tell he was furious. I heard him threatening to blow their heads off if they didn't get lost.'

'Did they go?'

Istvan smirks.

'They left running with their tails between their legs.'

'Did they ever come back?'

'No way, they'd be too frightened. I've never seen my dad so angry.'

The following Sunday, the two friends decide to pay a visit to Istvan's Uncle Dieter who owns a hotel in Timișoara near the Opera House. They board a tram that departs from Chișoda—the last stop on the line—which will take them into the city centre. Uncle Dieter is pleased to see Istvan and takes the boys through the stylish foyer into the restaurant where he orders a slice of poppyseed cake and a small cup of hot chocolate for each boy. Uncle Dieter apologises that the cake is a few days old, and perhaps a bit dry, but flour and eggs are not so easy to obtain, even for merchants.

Having had their fill, the boys say goodbye to Uncle Dieter. It's mid-afternoon and there are a lot of people meandering along the main square, Piata Victorier, which stretches down to Piata Operei, where the elegant baroque Opera House sits framed by tailored parks and rose gardens. Pigeons flutter at their feet as they amble past the museums, shops and cafeterias on their way to the tram stop.

As their tram trudges through the streets, it clangs and creaks against the rails and soon comes to a stop outside a large school with high black metal gates. Several neatly uniformed boys board. Istvan notices that each child has a number sewn onto his uniform, and asks Andor if he knows the reason.

'Oh, that's to let us know they're Jewish kids.'

'I don't get it.'

'It's their identification numbers, you know, so we can complain to the authorities about them if we want to.'

Istvan remains quiet. He knows the school is a Jewish one, but he has never noticed the numbers before. They must be a new thing. He continues to gaze out the window and spots a gang of rowdy adolescents hanging around outside the gates. They're all wearing identical brown shirts. His brow draws together, as he observes them taunt the smaller Jewish boys trying to pass by quickly.

'What are you looking at, Istvan?'

'Over there, by the gates, see? Those boys are picking on the Jewish kids as they leave.'

'Oh, that—so what? Who cares about the *Jews*?' Andor's eyes narrow. 'My father says they are getting what they deserve. Says that Antonescu is doing a good thing restricting them, says that the Jews have had it too good for too long.'

'Ah, you talk such rubbish, Andor. I like you best when you keep your stupid mouth shut.' Annoyance breeds silence for the next eight kilometres, until the tram comes to Andor's stop with a sudden jolt. He stands up, steps over his friend's legs, hesitantly says goodbye. But Istvan doesn't reply. Instead turns his head and mutters one word: 'Idiot.'

10
Frici

1943

For the first few years of war, Sigismund invests heavily in protecting his family, as well as procuring covert warranties with corrupt officials to ensure his business is able to operate in some capacity. Without one, he cannot afford the other. As such, the face of anti-Semitism hovers around the periphery of Frici's life. Oh, he hasn't escaped the casual slurs and venomous taunts, of course. And just because he is too young to retaliate, doesn't mean he hasn't been keeping score. As the world turns and the seasons grow dim, a cosseted boy grows into a fiery adolescent.

Frici, now almost thirteen, attends his first day of high school at Israelite Lyceum. Professor Neumann, a young rabbi who has just completed his rabbinical studies in Budapest, lectures the class about the growing fanaticism of Hitler's youth. Frici sits riveted through the professor's tutorial.

'Unfortunately, there will be days when, as you leave the school grounds, you will notice gangs of young men clad in brown shirts and khaki shorts. This group of small-minded fanatics has infiltrated our city and is growing in numbers. They model themselves on a Nazi organisation known as the SA or "Stormtroopers" which functions as a paramilitary faction of the National Socialist German Worker's Party, or Nazi Party.

'Boys, we now live in times of great hardship. Jews have been forced into labour detachments; the threat of the deportation to Transnistria is ever-present. In parts of Romania, Jewish students and teachers have been expelled from schools and deprived of any rights. Regardless, I will continue my endeavour to inspire children and adults with the power of hope for the dawn of a decent life. We must preserve the Jewish spiritual life. The practice of compassion—'love the other'—is prescribed in the Torah thirty-six times. This is just one guiding example that gives me the strength to keep the flame of Judaism alive and proud within the community of Timișoara. Please do not engage in retaliation as you leave the school grounds.'

A few days later, as Frici walks the short distance home from school, he finds himself accosted by an older youth wearing a brown shirt.

'Come on, Jew-boy, let's see what you're made of!' he yells, as he crosses over the tramlines that run down the middle of the leafy avenue and dashes towards Frici.

Frici has never seen him before, but has definitely noticed the type of brown shirt he is wearing. Rabbi Neumann's words run hazily through his mind, along with Gyuri's warning that he should steer clear of anyone wearing this particular uniform: 'They're bad guys, Frici. They hate us. Run home if you see any.'

Ignoring his warnings, Frici yells back, 'I'll show you what I'm made of!' He drops his schoolbag and charges at the older boy, knocking him to the ground. Rolling around on the pavement, they exchange blows. One minute Frici is on top, the next the other boy. Suddenly Frici feels a strong arm pull him by the scruff of his neck off the felled boy. As he lands on his feet and turns around, his first thoughts are that this brawny youth standing before him must be another Brownshirt member. Just as Frici is about to swing a punch in his direction, the intermediary pushes him out of the way and quickly steps between him and the brown-shirted youth.

'Get lost! Leave him alone,' Istvan shouts, centimetres away from the face of the thug.

'Who are you, some sort of Jew-lover?'

'Get lost *now*, while you still can,' Istvan retorts. 'There are two of us now. Do you want to fight us both?'

The brown-shirted youth raises his fists and opens his mouth to speak, but then takes a furtive glance around and notices he is alone, without reinforcements. Slowly, he backs away, but not before hurling another insult towards Frici.

'You'll get what's coming to you Jew-boy—not today, but just beware.'

Frici turns to look at the solidly built teenager with the mop of brown hair that almost covers his hazel eyes.

'I didn't need your help.'

'Maybe you did—maybe you didn't. Hard to tell from where I was standing. It seems as if you should be thanking me, though.'

'Oh right, thanks for *nothing*.' The acrid taste of blood trickles from his nose into his mouth. He turns around looking for the youth in the brown shirt, ready to follow him. Incensed, he paces back and forth looking up and down the street.

Suddenly, Gyuri appears beside him and grabs him by the arm.

'You idiot! I told you to run if you saw any Brownshirts after you.'

'*You* can run if you like. But *I'll* never run.'

'You're just lucky that other big boy showed up when he did. Your nose is bloodied. What will Anyu say? Don't you care that she'll be upset?'

'Of course I care. But still, I will *never* run from a fight.'

With the after-school physical and psychological taunts getting worse, and despite Frici's protestations, Sigismund decides to take action.

'From tomorrow, boys, I will send Janos to meet you after school and bring you home.'

'Why, Apu? You need him at work. Let me take care of these thugs. I'm not scared of them!'

'Frici, you will do as you're told. I won't hear further talk like this.'

A reluctant Frici does as his father bids. However, once home he sneaks back out of the house and makes his way past the closed doors and drawn curtains of the frightened neighbourhood towards the nearby sporting field, where he loves to kick around his football. With his natural muscularity, he excels in most sports. Already, during his first year of high school, he has been selected for rowing, table tennis and cross-country running. But of far greater significance to Frici is his being asked to play in the elite Kadima football club's team for sixteen-year-olds despite being three years younger. Fast and agile he surely is, but it is here that his superior ball dexterity, which he has honed through hours of practice, comes to the fore. He proudly holds the record at school for the length of time he can juggle the ball between foot and knee and his head, and wonders why Gyuri is not impressed by such agility. Every player in the Kadima squad has been given a strip embossed with a single capital letter taken from the team name. Each time Frici pulls his jersey over his head and stands back to take in his reflection in a mirror, he feels a surge of pride as he admires the large 'D' on his chest.

This afternoon, as Frici sets up two large rocks to mark as goalposts in the empty field, the same strapping boy who intervened in his fight approaches, carrying a well-worn football under his arm.

'Want a game?' he asks, flicking his untamed brown hair from his eyes.

Frici appraises him through a guarded squint. He can tell the boy is a few years older, perhaps his brother's age, and even though he likes the thought of opposing a stronger player, he still harbours some resentment towards him. Seconds pass before Frici shrugs and casually replies, 'Sure'.

They mark another pair of goalposts with rocks and begin to play. Frici is surprised by the skill of his opponent, the way he uses his broad shoulders to fend him off the ball. But he refuses to be outplayed and jostles him just as hard. They continue to play vigorously, taking equal turns with possession, each producing every trick they can muster. Almost an hour ticks by, yet such is their determination that neither concedes a goal.

'Let's blow the final whistle,' says the older one as he comes to a sweaty halt.

With hands on his knees, Frici tries to catch his breath, 'Sure. Thanks for the game. Anyway, what's your name?'

'Istvan. Yours?'

'Frici.'

'How about we meet up again one day?'

'Sure, why not? I come here nearly every day.'

Suddenly realising he will be in serious trouble if he is not home before his father, he turns towards home, calling over his shoulder as he takes off, 'See you later then, Istvan.'

Over the following weeks, whenever he can sneak away unnoticed, Frici returns to the park, hopeful his new friend might turn up to play, but each time he practises alone.

A letter has arrived from Sigismund's newly married nephew, Imre Lengyel. All of Sigismund's immediate family still live in the Romanian town of Crasna in the county of Sălaj in the north-west region of Transylvania, two hundred kilometres from Timişoara. The letter informs Sigismund that most of the Jews from the county have been rounded up and placed in a ghetto. Unless part of a select few who manage to flee, some 8,500 Jews from the towns of Crasna, Cehu Silvaniei, Jibou, Şimleu Silvaniei, Supuru de Jos, Tăşnad, and Zalău are concentrated in the Klein Brickyard of Cehei, a small village in the Sălaj county, that lies on the floodplains of the Crasna River. The ghetto is run by Commander Krasznai, a particularly cruel man, with a special unit of gendarmes from Budapest acting as guards. It is a marshy and muddy location and the brick-drying sheds are limited, so many of the inmates are compelled to live under the open sky.

Sigismund is stoic in front of his family, doing his best not to unravel. But inside the hurt is raw, gnawing at him like an ulcer. There is little he can do but pray for some word that his parents and siblings are somehow surviving this nightmare.

Weeks turn into months, but no word arrives.

11
Frici

1944

Perhaps Anna's family will be safe in Oradea? Not likely. Oradea is situated only ten kilometres from the north-west border of Romania and Hungary, 170 kilometres from Timişoara. The Mezey Timber Yard in the town has been appropriated to create one of the largest and most overcrowded ghettos in all of Romania and Hungary. The Jews of Oradea, who constitute about one-third of the town's population, are crammed into quarters where more than a dozen must share a small room. Like every other ghetto, this one suffers from a severe shortage of food, but the inmates also suffer the punishing measures of a merciless local administration. The city government regularly cuts off the electricity and water.

What Anna doesn't know at the beginning of 1944 is that save for two members of her large family, the rest will be deported with the 'evacuation' of Jews concentrated in the Mezey Timber Yard on 23 May. For many, including Anna's relatives, the final destination is that most notorious of death camps: Auschwitz in Poland.

A loud banging on the front door disturbs the evening household just as Anna is saying goodnight to Frici from the hallway. Frici sits up and listens to the familiar calm step of his father on the timber floorboards of the hall below.

'Take your hands off me! Where are you going to take me? My papers … Let me get my papers!'

'Sigismund! Where are you taking my husband?' Anna yells from the landing.

Quickly throwing back his satin-quilted eiderdown, Frici jumps out of bed and tears down the stairs two at a time, arriving in the hallway only to see the retreating back of his father as he is being dragged away by uniformed men. Gyuri joins his brother and in an unusual display of brotherly affection, places his arm around Frici's shoulders. Frici opens his mouth to say something in return, but there is a wad of emotion plugging his throat. Then, hearing their mother's sobs from the landing, they both quickly climb back up the stairs. Covering her face with her hands, Anna sinks to her knees.

'Anyu, Anyu …' Frici finds his voice, but his heart feels as if it is suspended in mid-air.

Anna wraps her arms about Frici's waist so tightly, he thinks he might actually break in half. Gyuri stands behind her stroking her hair. Minutes elapse, then finally, using both boys for support, she stands and lets them guide her towards her bedroom.

'Oh God, my God, what shall we do … What shall we do?' she says, as she lies down on her bed. 'My chest—so tight. The air—the air has seeped out of the room.'

'I'll open the window, Anyu. Try and stay calm. And breathe. We can't do anything until morning,' Gyuri attempts to replicate his father's tone, but none-too-convincingly. After Anna finally settles, Gyuri walks towards the door and signals for his brother to join him.

'No, Frici. Stay with me. Please!'

'All right, Anyu.'

He moves to his mother's side and lies down next to her. She takes his hand in hers.

The night trudges heavily uphill. Every now and then Frici reaches across with his handkerchief to dry his mother's tears as rivulets course down her cheeks. Somewhere in the long stretch of darkness, he dozes off and as the dawn blushes through the open curtains he awakes to the metallic sound of the front door unlocking. Frici leaps out of bed and races down the stairs to find his tired, shaken father standing hunched over in the foyer. Frici runs straight to him, almost knocking him off his unsteady legs with his embrace.

'What has become of this world? What madness now exists?' Sigismund reaches for a chair. He looks up, hearing a noise from the landing above.

'Anna? Anna, my love, don't cry. I'm home.'

She runs to him and buries her face in his chest, sobbing. 'I was so scared … so very scared.'

With one arm around Anna's waist and with haunted eyes downcast, Sigismund does not hold back—describing a terrifying night, and one that is happening in every town in Europe where the Nazis have overrun civil society and the law.

'They took hundreds of us to Electrica Football Stadium. Everyone was confused and frightened—many yelling in a panic.' He pauses before continuing. 'They have taken lots of people away. Who knows what will become of them? Me? Thank God, I had this.' Reaching into his coat pocket, he produces a folded piece of paper. 'If I did not have this paper saying I'm a qualified train driver … God forbid!'

'I don't understand—how would that help you?'

'The conscripted soldiers, and others sent to labour camps, are being sent by trains—many, many trains travelling all over Romania—so there's a shortage of train drivers.'

'But I never knew you were a train driver,' Frici replies, puzzled.

'I'm not. It's late, Frici, and I am very, very tired.'

'No, Apu, it's early morning, but let me help you up the stairs.'

'And Frici?'

'Yes?'

'If anyone asks you what my profession is—you must say train driver. Tell your brother, will you?'

'Yes, of course.'

Sigismund tries to operate his business in a reduced capacity, but with each passing month it becomes more difficult. With virtually all Jewish businesses forcibly closed or taken over, and daily news of further disappearances reaching them, Frici begins to understand that his father's security is guaranteed by the greediness of certain people. He comes to appreciate that their survival is influenced by money, status and the corruptibility of government officials.

One chilly morning, delivering yet another bag full of scarce fruit to the police station, he realises that his father's oranges have taken on greater value than people.

Crippled by extreme anxiety, Anna scarcely lets her sons leave the house. Like all of his friends, Frici's schooling has ended, and he grows more bored as each colourless day passes into the next. Often, when he is supposed to be studying English in his room, he ventures outside with his football and kicks it against the brick wall of a closed haberdashery shop at the end of his street.

One afternoon, he is suddenly set on by a pack of young men all clad in the familiar brown shirts he now detests. As one encircles his arms and torso from behind, another begins throwing punches into his chest and stomach. Frici tightens his stomach muscles in an attempt to lessen the sharpness of the blows.

'Wait!' comes the abrupt call from one who Frici thinks must be their leader. 'Let me take him on by myself. Listen here, Jew,' he stabs his finger hard in Frici's chest. 'Your reputation precedes you. You like to fight, yes?'

'Not really. I—'

'Shut up, liar! This is how it will work: one-on-one, me versus you. If I win, you come with us. If you win—which you won't, disgusting pig—you get to live another day. Is that fair?'

'Hardly call it fair—you're much older and taller than me.'

'How old are you, anyway?'

In an effort to mentally prepare, Frici vies for time.

'I'm only thirteen.'

'Thirteen, eh? You're a liar like all your kind. You're big enough to fight.'

As a circle of Brownshirts surround their solitary opponent, Frici raises his fists near his face and begins mockingly throwing punches at his taller adversary. The older boy laughs assuredly as he circles Frici, who keeps up his feigned attempt to box. 'Ha-ha! So we have a little Jew-boxer, do we?'

Frici waits, biding his time carefully, watching his flaxen adversary's confidence grow in front of his encouraging gang. Then, timing his movement with speed and precision, he swiftly closes the distance between them and begins swinging genuine punches. He lands a hard right fist into the unsuspecting soft underbelly of his foe, doubling him over.

'*Now* we are of equal height!' Frici yells, and using all his strength he sends a sharp left hook square on the boy's jaw, knocking him to the ground. Frici then pounces. He quickly straddles the felled boy and grabbing a fistful of hair in each hand, turns the boy's face toward the road and drags his cheek hard across the cobblestones.

'Ahh! Stop, stop!'

A hush falls over the band of onlookers who, until that moment, have been chanting their leader on. Climbing unsteadily to his feet, the Brownshirt wipes the blood from his face with the back of his hand.

'You surprise me, Jew. Small yet tough. Let him go,' he orders, with a rub of his jaw.

With that Frici turns and heads home as fast as he can. He is smiling as he runs, carrying his newly acquired lesson like a jewel: *always* catch them off guard.

12
Istvan

1944

The sweat trickles down Istvan's back. He spits on his palms, then grips the wooden handle of the axe and swings it high over his head and forcefully down into large chunks of timber, splintering each into smaller pieces so that he can stock the wood-fired stove in preparation for the evening meal. Warm for June, he thinks, as he gathers the chopped wood in his arms and carefully carries it into the *nyári konyha*.

All of a sudden he is startled by an unfamiliar and tremendous roar. He looks out of the small kitchen window and into a sky that he has never seen before: shadows created by hundreds of black planes swarming overhead, their wingspans blocking the sun's rays, as ominous as a swarm of locusts gathering to a stream before a fire.

He runs outside, bewildered by the sight. Air-raid sirens ring out around him. A deafening noise attacks his eardrums, so loud the sky seems to split. He brings his hands up to his ears. *Bombs. They are bombing Timişoara.*

He runs back into the summer kitchen where his mother stands frozen with panic, gripping the back of the wooden bench seating. He immediately senses why she is afraid—not because they are in danger at home, but because Papa is at work in his storeroom in the city. (Ever the entrepreneur, Nikolaus has recently ventured into a new business, where he buys and sells farm machinery.) From the terrified look in his mother's eyes, Istvan realises she, too, thinks him to be in harm's way.

'I'm going to find him.' He feigns a calmness he doesn't feel, as he heads for the door.

'No, Istvan! Come back. It's too dangerous!'

'Don't worry about me, Mama. I'll be all right. I have to go.'

He sets off running towards the city, taking a shortcut along the bank of the Bega River. Jumping over small bushes and up and over smooth boulders, he follows the river's natural curve, winding for several kilometres, before he makes his way onto the cobblestone streets that will lead him to his father's storeroom. Despite his legs becoming heavy and the dull ache of a stitch in his side, he never stops running. Never slows his pace. The closer he gets to the city centre, the more rubble he has to climb over. Many of the buildings that remain standing have large fractures and shattered windows.

Fear mounts in his chest when he sees cars and trams upturned and hears the sounds of people crying and moaning. Nothing in his fifteen years of life has prepared him for the sight of bodies strewn across the road. He tries not to look at the sight of bloodied torsos with limbs torn off. Head down, he almost bumps straight into a leg dangling from a lamp post. Quickly sidestepping its mangled flesh, he looks away. But no matter where he looks he sees the stain of blood and smells what he will come to recognise as its unmistakable stench. He wants to stop and help, but is desperate to get to his father to make sure he is unharmed. So he keeps up his frantic pace, trying his best to block out the catastrophe unfurling before his eyes.

When Istvan finally arrives at the storeroom, he finds his stunned father standing outside with his workers—everyone covered in white dust. He throws himself into his father's embrace.

'Son, I am all right, I think. Shocked. But no, not hurt. Dug myself free. I … I was buried under all these layers of rubble.' There is disbelief in his voice as he lifts some sheets of plywood and drops them back down, sending a cloud of dust skyward.

'Look behind you, Papa, the whole building is flattened,' Istvan says, wiping his face on his sleeve while his father turns to look, quickly heading back towards the ruins.

'Quick, help me lift some of this rubble. There may be others not so lucky. Hey, you guys, come and help,' Nikolaus calls to his workers, who are brushing themselves off agitatedly. Within minutes Istvan can hear trapped people calling for help. He and his father toil side by side, digging and heaving through the wreckage without a break, long into the night.

Exhausted, they return home to a distraught Katarina. 'Istvan … Nikolaus … My God, I was so worried. I wish you would have sent word that you were all right. You can't imagine what has been running through my mind.'

'The city, near the station, has been razed to the ground. There must be hundreds trapped and God knows how many dead. We haven't stopped working. And we couldn't spare anyone, especially Istvan here,' Nikolaus rubs his son's sandy head. 'He did the work of two men.'

Finally in bed after comforting his nervous and hungry stomach with bean soup and crusty bread, Istvan tosses and turns. His eyes are closed but he can still see mountains of rubble—see blood-drenched body parts protruding—see himself digging and digging, sometimes able to set someone free, but many times finding the wide eyes of the motionless. In the stillness of the night, he can again hear the soft wails of the trapped, calling for help.

'Who can do such things to other human beings?' he asks of the darkness.

The next morning a thunderous knock on the timber door of the farmhouse beckons Istvan from his bedroom. Upon opening it, he is startled by four tall soldiers standing squarely with guns in hand. As he takes in the grim appearance of their khaki uniforms and distinctive metal helmets with the low-shielding lip almost covering their eyes, his insides contract. The light from the rising sun catches their brass buttons and reflects in his eyes, so Istvan stares down at their black knee-high boots. His throat is dry and no words will come.

Suddenly the soldier in front barks, 'Nikolaus König? We have orders for Nikolaus König to come with us.' Without waiting for a reply, they push past Istvan and into the small sitting room.

Nikolaus calmly comes forward.

'No need to come into my house and terrify my family. I will come with you.'

They ignore him as if he hasn't spoken at all and begin entering the other rooms of the house. Istvan follows them, though he knows well enough to keep a safe distance. He stands in the doorways of each bedroom door and watches as they open wardrobes, move bookcases and look under beds. When one of the soldiers grabs him by the shoulder, he feels the strong fingers penetrate through his clothing, searing his skin with malevolent intent.

'Attic? Do you have an attic?'

Istvan looks from the scowl before him into the resigned face of his father, who slowly nods his head.

'Yes,' he replies, 'I'll show you.'

Two of the soldiers follow him to the rear of the house and up the small, steep staircase that leads to the attic, while the other two leave to search the *nyári konyha*, barns and sheds. Finding no one else at home other than Katarina and Hermina, who stand petrified and huddled against the kitchen sink, the soldier in charge barks at Nikolaus, 'You have other sons, yes? Where are they? We will find out, you know.' Looking at Istvan he adds, 'How old is this one? He looks eighteen.'

Istvan stands silent and solemn. He fights hard to control this new sensation that trembles within. Suddenly his mother rushes in from the kitchen and stands in front of him with her arms spread wide.

'He is only fifteen!' she screams. 'Get away from him. Away! How *dare* you come into my house like this. Your mighty army already has my four other sons—'

'Katarina! Stop now!'

For the first time in her life, she ignores Nikolaus's command and continues louder than Istvan has ever heard.

'And now you will take my husband. He has fought for you once already—is that not enough?' Her screams turn to sobs. 'What price must a mother pay for your stupid war? Why give birth to sons only to sacrifice them ... *for what ... for what?*'

Ignoring her cries, the soldiers take Nikolaus by the arms and lead him out of the house. Istvan stands in the doorway grasping its timber frame and stares in disbelief as his father is taken away like a criminal. As they place Nikolaus in the rear of a small army truck, his father gives one last half-wave, before the doors are clanged shut. For a moment, Istvan stands transfixed, unaware that his hands have closed into white-knuckled fists. Then, as the engine starts and the army truck begins to drive away, he tears out of the house and follows it down the long drive. When he gets to the old oak tree at the edge of their property, he stops and watches the truck bump down the dirt road until it can no longer be seen. He wraps his arms about the wide trunk, tears of despair streaming down his face, kicking his old boots hard into the rough bark and stubbing his toe. After a few moments he walks back to the house, drying his cheeks on his shirt sleeve so that his mother can't trace their tracks.

'What will they do to him, Mama?'

Wiping her tears, Katarina replies; 'Oh, Istvan, I don't know. All we can do now is pray … pray to God that Papa and your brothers do not get sent to the front. That's all we can do …'

They hug each other, trying to draw strength and give comfort at the same time.

'Don't cry, Mama. I'm sure when the army sees how clever Papa is, they will use him to build their machinery.' He silently hopes he is right. 'I might be too young for this conscription, but I promise to look after you and Hermina. You will see. And soon everyone will be home again.'

Katarina can barely function. Distraught, she goes softer and sadder through her days, not recognising the strange woman in her mirror. Since the age of sixteen she has not only loved, but been guided, by Nikolaus. Of course he infuriates her at times with his fastidiousness and rigidity, and Lord knows he has the sensitivity of a blunt knife, but without him she feels as small as a snowflake in a blizzard. How will she survive?

Within weeks, needing money, Katarina must take her dwindling supply of poultry to market.

'Ah, I wouldn't fret too much, Katarina,' Mr Nagy from the cured-meat stall says within earshot of Istvan. Mr Nagy, who fought in the Great War, wears a battered old cap and walks with a stick. 'They wouldn't have sent him to war. Engineers like Nikolaus are needed—necessary during times of war—to repair bombed railroads and bridges or fortify artillery. He's probably been sent to a work camp. My guess? Somewhere not too far from here.'

Katarina smiles, briefly relieved, until the old man continues, 'But don't get your hopes up too high. Many men die in these work camps from malnutrition and excessive physical work.'

After two months of anguish, a brief letter arrives from Nikolaus. Mr Nagy has guessed correctly. Standing in the hallway, Katarina says nothing, only stares vacantly at the floor as her fingers loosen their grip on the letter, letting it flutter to the ground.

13
Frici

1944

'Frici, are you ready? Janos is here with the carriage to take you to *Templom*.'

Stomping down the stairs, Frici exclaims sulkily, 'Anyu, you never let me out, but for this you will? Surely it's not important now.'

'Just as your brother celebrated his coming of age three years ago, you shall be no different. It *is* important—that's all you should know.'

'The only good thing that will come of this, is that Apu will let Mr Munteanu shave me each morning when he comes to shave him and Gyuri.'

Not even a war can get Frici out of this ritual: the Bar Mitzvah. However, the ceremony will be no elaborate celebration. Frici will read a portion of the Torah to a small congregation and be blessed by the rabbi, taking on the mantle of Jewish 'manhood'. It will, in fact, be undertaken in secret, as at this time in Europe, such rituals are rarely undertaken at all.

After the service Rabbi Schick takes Frici aside from the other boys.

'Frici, I am told you were seen to enter a non-kosher delicatessen—that you purchased some salami and ham. This cannot be allowed if you want to be permitted to publicly read from the Torah.'

'No, Rabbi. This is not true. That person must have mistaken me for someone else.'

He casts his eyes downwards over the length of the rabbi's long dark coat, mortified not by his sin but rather by being exposed. He continues fumbling his way through an alibi, but can feel the colour stain his cheeks from perpetuating a lie to one so hallowed. *If this should get back to my mother, she will surely faint from humiliation.*

As the months pass, a procession of men in dark suits continue to knock on their door. Each time Frici is disappointed to be sent to his room, although he doesn't need to hear what is being said to feel the animosity slowly rising like a sea disturbed by conflicting currents.

One evening after dinner an arrhythmic thumping on the front door beckons his father once more. Frici silently follows him into the hallway and watches as he ushers in a sinister-looking man wearing a trench coat that looks too long on his short body. Frici gapes at the man with his single strand of black hair combed over his egg-shaped head. As if reading his mind, the man glares back at him. His beady eyes are as cold and pale as frosted glass, his limp moustache doing nothing to conceal his synthetic smile. This man has never been to the house before.

'Yes, Apu, I'm going to my room,' Frici pre-empts his father's stern look. Just as he reaches the top of the staircase, the yelling starts.

'Haven't I paid you handsomely? Why can't we continue as we have been doing? We have an *agreement!*'

'Calm down, Mr Löw. All I'm trying to say is that it is not possible to provide you with adequate protection any longer.'

'Tell me why things must stop now? Are you afraid our transactions will be discovered?'

'What can I say? Even a stupid dog knows what happens when he steals the sausage once too often. Sooner or later he will get caught. I am not so stupid, Mr Löw.'

'And if I increase the payment, can you help my family get away—to the countryside—somewhere safe? Surely that is not unreasonable?'

'All right, but it will need to be a considerable sum. I will have to pay the police to escort you. And of course there are the farmers who you will live with. They will need to be looked after. Do you have that sort of money?'

'It can be arranged.'

'Good. We will have to act swiftly. Be ready tomorrow night.'

The next evening, as Frici squashes his football boots and training gear into his small suitcase, he looks up as his father's frame fills his bedroom door.

'We can take only the bare necessities, Frici.'

'I understand,' he replies, 'but I *have* to take my football gear. I need to practise for the Ripensia team trials. You know how long I've dreamed of playing professionally. Anyway, how long will we be gone?'

'I have no idea. I know the trials are coming up—hopefully we will be back in time. Be ready as quickly as you can.'

As all four gather in the hallway, Sigismund assesses the baggage. 'Anna, do you have your good jewellery?'

'Yes *drágám*[21], it's among our clothes in the blue suitcase.'

'Good. The police car has come. We'd better go.' Sigismund picks up the blue suitcase with one hand while holding his briefcase in the other. Frici can guess at its contents.

Crammed into the rear seat of the small black Fiat alongside his mother, who sits between him and his brother, Frici can feel her apprehension. No words are exchanged between his father and the driver, whose face Frici cannot see from behind. As they head east through the city boulevards that are all but deserted except for a scattering of dark vehicles and a few scurrying pedestrians, it begins to drizzle. Frici knows not to speak. He looks out the window as they head down the stately esplanade of the Victory Square. He knows the names of all the monumental buildings that occupy the square: the Lloyd Palace, the Lofler Palace, the Dauerbac Palace and the Merbi Palace. Usually they look so regal and impressive, but tonight they look cold and insubstantial. Through the mist that closes in like a sheer grey curtain around the square, his eyes strain to locate his favourite statue which he knows to be in the middle—the Wolf Statue. At school he has learnt that it was a gift from Rome in 1926, a symbol of the Latin roots of the Romanian people. He loves the way the mother wolf is sculpted: she is watchful and alert, ready to pounce. Her eyes defy anyone to come too close. At this moment, he understands exactly how she feels.

As they continue eastward out of the city through the outer suburbs and into the unlit countryside, Frici lays his head against the window of the car. He awakens with a start as the car hobbles up a long dirt drive towards an isolated farmhouse.

'You're here. Go inside. You're expected.' These are the only words uttered by the faceless driver.

---

21 Meaning 'darling' in Hungarian.

14
Istvan

1944

'You must go to school today, Istvan. You have already missed too much.'

'No, I want to stay home and help you. Papa would want me to.'

'All right. Today I am too tired to argue with you. Hermina, we must change the bed sheets today. Prepare the larger boiler so we can launder them.'

Reluctantly Hermina shuffles to the kitchen. She has grown heavy with melancholy, not having heard from her husband for over two years.

'And Istvan?'

'Yes, Mama?'

'You can chop the firewood for the stove, then feed the animals. Take care not to give them too many scraps. And the yard is a mess—do what you can. After you have done these things you can dig up a few potatoes and onions and fetch two eggs from the henhouse. I don't want to use another chicken for dinner tonight—we need them for their eggs—so I will make *nokedli* with fried onion and potato.'

Istvan races about the farm diligently performing his tasks, and returns to the house laden with the firewood and food. Following a lunch of homemade bread and cheese, he sits at the kitchen table and watches his mother push, pull and pummel the dough into compliance. The day is not overly warm, yet Katarina's face glistens with sweat, and flour clings to the dampness of her forearms, narrowly avoiding the sleeves which she has turned up to her elbow.

'Fetch me some water, can you, darling?' she says, blowing away from her face wisps of hair that have worked their way loose from her bun. 'I must sit down. I feel very tired. Can you ask Hermina to come and help me with the dinner?'

'Hermina! Mama needs you,' he calls as he walks towards her bedroom. Suddenly a loud bang resounds from the kitchen. Istvan turns on his heel and runs straight back, to find his mother slumped on the floor.

'Mama, what's wrong? Hermina, come quickly. Help me get her up and into bed.'

'I'm all right. I don't know what happened. Everything just went black.' She leans into her son's strong grip as he guides her towards her bedroom.

'Mama, *please* don't get sick. I promised I would take care of you. Nothing must happen to you.'

'You worry for nothing. I am just tired, that's all. Nothing a good night's rest can't fix.'

The next day Katarina is too weak to get out of bed and struggles to eat breakfast. Istvan forages through the vegetable garden, encouraged when he finds enough to make an enticing soup. He has watched his mother cook so often that he knows he can manage, even without his sister's help. Hermina is busy making herself beautiful for the moment that Hans strolls in the front door.

'Here, Mama, I've made you some soup. You must eat.'
'What would I do without you, my darling son?'
But when he returns to her bedroom the bowl is still full.
'I'm going to town to fetch the doctor.'
'No, Istvan. How can we pay for him? We have no money. We will have to give him one of our last chickens. We can't afford to. I'll be all right! Just give me some more time.'

Time does Katarina no favours. After several days, she remains listless. Finally, Istvan ignores his mother's pleas and heads off to town in search of a doctor.

'You won't find a doctor in there. The place is empty.'

At the sound of a gruff female voice, Istvan turns to see a plainly dressed woman with dark braids twisted around her head. Her two young children, dressed in frayed and dirty clothing, stare at him as they pass the two-storey townhouse on whose door he is knocking.

'All the young ones have been taken away to the war. At the far end of this street lives an elderly doctor—he is the only one left. Try him,' she calls as she trundles off after her children.

Istvan calls back his thanks and makes his way down the long curving street. Apart from the woman who gave the directions, the street is empty. No sign of life anywhere, not even stray cats or dogs. It's not yet winter, but the day feels bleak.

The snowy-haired doctor with tufts of bushy white brows is a kind man, but also a very busy one. He promises to visit in a day or two.

'She's very weak and tired. This war has taken its toll on many like her. I have left a tonic so make certain she takes it each day. It will give her back her appetite. She must eat to regain her strength.'

'Thank you, Doctor. But ... I'm sorry, but we don't have any money,' Hermina mumbles. 'If you wait a moment, Istvan is fetching you a chicken.'

'No, no, no. I won't take the last of your chickens—your mother will need proper nutrition,' the doctor replies as Istvan appears carrying a wriggling orange-feathered hen. 'Just give me a few eggs. That will do.'

15
Frici

1944

Frici is at first uncertain of his new surroundings and especially of the dishevelled-looking farmer with his hawk-like face. His wife, although also untidy, seems much more pleasant. She is round and diminutive and has to take two steps for each one of her husband's.

The Löws are shown to two small bedrooms, each containing two single beds. The room he and Gyuri are given is spartan yet clean. Against one wall stands a painted wardrobe—empty, Frici discovers—and on the opposite wall a bookcase with a few books neatly stacked amid small boxes of pine cones and assorted rocks.

'This is clearly a boy's room,' Frici says to his brother as he peers at the wall-hanging of brightly coloured butterflies, their wings pinned neatly behind glass.

'Yes. Perhaps their sons have been sent to fight. These people don't look much older than Anyu and Apu.'

Their father's face, tempered now like steel, appears in the doorway. He tells them to keep their voices down, then pulls out his pocket watch which dangles from his vest on a gold chain.

'It's late,' he says. 'Go to bed.'

The next morning, Frici rises before his brother and slips on his flannel robe. He follows his nose to the kitchen where his father is already seated and talking with the farmer.

'Good morning, sir,' Frici says to the farmer, sliding up next to his father on the bench of the built-in nook.

'Good morning, young son,' the farmer replies.

Sigismund explains that he and the farmer have decided none of them should reveal their true names but instead use pseudonyms to avoid betraying each other should the authorities question them at some point in the future.

After a filling breakfast of fried eggs and homemade sausage, Frici politely thanks the farmer's wife and asks the farmer what duties he can lend a hand with. The farmer smiles, raises his brow and nods his approval towards Sigismund, indicating he is impressed with his son's offer of assistance. The gesture is lost on Sigismund, who has far more pressing things on his mind than whether or not his son can milk a cow.

Which is precisely where the farmer takes Frici: to the barn to teach him how to milk the cows. When it's Frici's turn to wrap his hands around the teats of the swollen udder, they feel as slippery as wet soap to him. When he does manage to express a tiny amount, it barely wets his hand, let alone go anywhere near the empty bucket. The farmer tells him he is yanking on the teats, when he needs to squeeze his fingers sequentially: 'From middle to pinkie. Be gentle yet firm'.

Not one to give in easily, Frici persists, and persists—much to the discontent of the cows—until finally he develops the correct technique. Afterwards, the farmer shows him how he puts his Murakoz draught horse[22] to work in the paddock, all the

---

22 Developed from the Mura region of Hungary, Poland and Yugoslavia, in 1920 approximately twenty per cent of the horses in Hungary and Romania were Murakoz. World War Two brought many losses and along with mechanisation of farming practices, the breed has never regained its pre-war numbers.

while patiently answering Frici's many questions about horses and ploughing the land. This way of life is as foreign to him as another planet.

'And you asked about this type of horse. Generally speaking, they have a tall, muscular build, with an upright shoulder, just like Star here,' he says, patting his horse affectionately. 'Makes them well-suited for pulling. Look here—see their powerful hindquarters?'

Frici enjoys working with the large animals, especially brushing down the draught horse's long white mane and rubbing his soft velvet nose. But when the farmer asks him to feed the chickens and gather some eggs, he shakes his head and takes off like a bolt of lightning, leaving the farmer scratching his head in puzzlement.

When Frici is finished with his morning chores, he finds relief from the vacant hours by practising football in the wide open fields. He trains hard, often with only the company of dozing dogs and the lugubrious mooing of the cows dotted around the naked landscape. As much as he is beginning to enjoy the solitude and fresh country air, he hopes they will soon return to the city for the impending Ripensia trials so that all his training is not for naught.

Anna keeps busy helping the farmer's wife with the cooking whilst Gyuri is usually found lying on his bed reading or studying English. Sigismund, too, rarely ventures outside. His manner and complexion grow more lethargic with each passing day. Today he is sitting sombrely at the kitchen table reading *Vestul*, a political newspaper that the farmer brings home from his regular visits to town. As usual, he has the radio on and every now and then he stands up and relocates it, trying to find better reception—a familiar scene that usually ends in him throwing his hands in the air and cursing under his breath.

This evening, though, as Frici sits bored by the sight of his father fiddling with the round black dials of the radio, he is suddenly startled to see him leap to his feet: 'Quick, come quickly everyone. Listen … a broadcast from King Michael.'

> *And so, my fellow Romanians, on this the evening of 23 August 1944, I have issued a cease-fire, and proclaimed Romania's loyalty to the Allies. An armistice, offered by Great Britain, the United States and the USSR will be signed on 12 September 1944. We are now at war with Germany.*

'I don't understand, Apu, how can that be?'

Gyuri shoulders him. 'If you spent more time reading and taking an interest in current affairs instead of kicking that stupid ball around, you might.'

'Gyuri, that's enough. Listen Frici, it's complicated. I'll explain later.'

Sigismund is suddenly wary, unsure of how much to reveal in front of his hosts. Trust is a precious commodity these days—for a fee, or under pressure, people will reveal each other's secrets. Friend about friend, neighbour about neighbour, employee about employer. One careless remark could see you inside a blackened cell, or worse.

What Sigismund will explain to his son once alone is, as he says, complicated. But he will choose his words thoughtfully. He will explain that the Romanian economy has been ruined by the heavy cost of war and the recent destructive bombing by the Allies, particularly in Bucharest, has made things even worse. Inflation has skyrocketed, generating acrimony and sedition among the people—even those who supported the Germans and the war. King Michael, who has been nothing more than a figurehead for the last few years, has led a successful coup and deposed the wretched Antonescu dictatorship.

Within a few days, Sigismund informs them of his decision to return home.

'Pack your things, boys, it should now be safe to go home. And Frici, it looks as though you will make your trials after all!'

16
Istvan

1945

As the shortened sunlight hours fade into early evening, sixteen-year-old Istvan is tired because now he has all the responsibilities around the farm. With no correspondence for almost a year from the four eldest sons, the anguish only adds to Katarina's fatigue, who, although slowly regaining her health, is a shadow of her once robust self. And with each passing month without word from Hans, Hermina also grows more forlorn.

Joszi, Jani and Ferenc have been part of the Magyar Honvédség, the Hungarian defence force, since they left for Budapest in 1940. At first, aged only sixteen, Nick was too young, but the war effort produces an abundance of work for builders and carpenters. Two years later, however, he is conscripted. Somehow the brothers escape injury in Hungary's quest for territorial gain on the Yugoslav front and, even more miraculously, escape the huge loss of life the Hungarian troops sustain in their recent support of Hitler's troops on the Russian front.

One evening as Istvan and his mother and sister settle around the kitchen table for an early dinner of spicy goulash that he has prepared—with potatoes replacing their once abundant meat supply—the door to the farmhouse almost rips off its hinges as Jani bursts through.

'My God!' Katarina screams, knocking over her bowl of soup as she stumbles to her feet.

Jani's face is almost unrecognisable from the angry lattice of multiple cuts and abrasions. Small ruby pools are forming on the timber floor, streams from the deep lacerations to his neck and forearms.

'Clean me up, Mama. Hurry. I'm not sure if I was followed or not. But either way I have to leave here as fast as possible. The army will only find me if I stay too long.'

'Jani, what happened to you?' Istvan jumps in.

'What *happened* to me? I don't even know where to begin. Wash and bandage me, please, Mama, while I tell you.'

Katarina hurries to the sink and fills a basin with warm water, sending Hermina to fetch some long clean rags. She returns quickly to Jani's side and begins to gently soak his bloodied wounds, taking care not to further rip his torn skin that is mangled with glass and blackened with tar.

'Don't worry about hurting me, Mama, just hurry,' his voice is hoarse and urgent. 'Now, I'll try to explain. I was sent to fight—'

'Where?'

'Don't interrupt, Istvan, it's not important where. These places have no names. They all look and smell the same. If they do have a name, it would be *hell*.'

For the next few minutes, like a leaf caught in a vortex, Jani revisits that place of hell.

'… packed in like sardines, we are. Knee deep in cold, muddy, rat-infested trenches below a graveyard of khaki limbs lying in puddles of bloody dirt. I can't even find the words to describe the smell of blood and rotting flesh. Bullets whistle past my head. Bombs explode. All around the earth shakes. I can't sleep for fear of not waking up. We're so close to the Soviet trenches, between the bombs and grenades, I swear I can hear them talking … even praying. I can't explain how frightening it is … not knowing when your turn will come to rise and attack. To run to a certain death, lambs to the slaughter.'

He shakes his head and is suddenly back in the kitchen with his family.

'Couldn't believe how lucky I was when reinforcements arrived and our battalion was relieved and sent back to Hungary. But I just couldn't take the thought of having to return to that hell hole, so two nights ago I deserted.'

'Jani!'

'Yes, Mama, I deserted the army. Papa may be embarrassed to hear that, but I'm not sorry—only sorry that I got caught. When I found myself on a train to Bucharest to be imprisoned and court-martialled, I knew I had to escape. So I told the guard that I had to use the toilet and then hurled myself through the small toilet window of the moving train. Be careful Mama, I think there is still glass in those deep cuts on my neck … ah!'

Later that night, dressed in clean, warm clothing and with a basket of bread, cheese and soup, Jani leaves. The following day the military police come. They search the farm from top to bottom but find no trace of him ever being there.

Some weeks later, as spring declares its presence and the majestic barren oak tree begins to tooth new leaves from its heavy furrowed bark, Katarina is busy sowing cabbage seeds in her vegetable patch. She looks up to see what she first thinks to be a stranger approaching. A straight, spare figure in ragged clothing walks unsteadily up the drive. She straightens up and takes a few apprehensive steps towards him. Then she stops in her tracks.

'Nikolaus? Is it you?'

He nods, too weak to call back. She breaks into a run, not stopping until she has reached him and pulled his wasted frame into her comforting embrace. Once inside the farmhouse, Nikolaus drops into the softness of the worn sofa. He folds his stick-like arms, as if to hold himself together.

'Where is everybody?' his voice huskier and quieter than she recalls.

'Hermina is in town. She will be back shortly. But Istvan? Oh, Nikolaus, you missed him by just a few short days …'

Katarina tells her husband of a letter that arrived barely a week earlier. She goes to her bedroom to fetch it so that he can read it for himself. He takes the letter from her hand, turns it over and reads aloud.

'An official decree from the People's Republic of Romania …' He skims silently over the first few lines, then continues, *'All families of Hungarian or German descent are considered opponents of the new regime and as such must surrender one person from each family to be interned in the labour camps of Russia for a period of up to five years. Such persons may be either a male aged seventeen to forty-five or female aged eighteen to thirty-five.'*

Katarina explains that with only she and Hermina at home, sixteen-year-old Istvan, as expected, volunteered. She sits beside her husband and takes his hand in hers. Not wanting to meet his eyes with her own, she stares into the middle distance almost trance-like, as she relives the grim finality of their son's departure, recalling the scene, with a shiver.

'It was raining heavily, without letting up. There were so many families like us seeing off our loved ones. Everyone was just huddled together, holding hands, touching faces, clinging to clothing—all of us praying for a miracle. And when the voice called over the loudspeaker telling the men to board the train, soldiers moved down the platform, roughly separating those who wouldn't let go.

'My heart felt like a heavy stone in my chest, and as grey as the platform I was standing on, Nikolaus. I just couldn't find any words of comfort for my boy. If he was frightened, he didn't show me—of course he wouldn't. Not my Istvan. But I was terrified for him!

'My darling boy climbed up on the old cattle train and looked down at me and Hermina. As he reached down to take the basket of food from me, we were all crying. Everyone was. But not Istvan, no, no. I noticed he swallowed hard, though.

'Then the train began to pull away …' Katarina pauses and gathers the loose folds of her skirt in bunches in her lap. After several seconds, she regathers herself and continues.

'He was leaning out of the open doorway. The yelling and crying around us got louder. But when Istvan spoke it felt as if everyone else fell silent, because it was his words alone that I could hear … like chains of lead, tying me to my grief: "Goodbye, Mama. Keep strong. I'll be back very soon".'

As she finishes her story Katarina turns to her husband, eyes brimming, but full of pride.

'Our son, Nikolaus. You have taught him well to be a man. But I wish with all my heart he was still my little boy.'

With that, she reaches up and wipes the single tear that has escaped down his cheek. Smiling through tears at the stranger before her, she rests her head on his bony shoulder. Hearing only the thumping inside her chest, she closes her eyes and gives thanks to the Lord that her Nikolaus has returned, and promises Him she will serve Him forever more if he keeps safe Joszi, Jani, Ferenc and Nicky, and especially young Istvan. *Don't let him suffer, Lord.*

Before year's end, Katarina's prayers will be answered for her four eldest sons. They have all been spared serious physical injury during the final bloody conflict of a combined Hungarian and German attempt to hold off the crushing invasion of Budapest by Soviet troops. Even with Germany's help, Hungary is unable to hold the capital against the Red Army and their newest ally, Romania. The city falls on 13 February 1945.

17
Frici

1945

'Everyone thinks things will be all right. The *good* people have won the war.'

Frici's father doesn't look up from his plate as the family sit eating their evening meal from their now limited supply of provisions. His sober tone continues to the clatter of cutlery against plates.

'I hear that there are great celebrations in England and America. Even in some parts of Europe—in Paris and Rome—they dance in the streets. But what have we got to celebrate? Naive. That's what we were … are … here in these parts. "Let the Russians have eastern Europe." That's what the West said. "So what? The war is over." Does anyone even care about the utter turmoil we are forced to endure?'

'Yes, you're right, Siga[23], Anna responds.

'Even now, the naive don't understand that although the war is over, another one has begun,' Sigismund continues.

'What do you mean, Apu?'

---

[23] Anna's term of endearment she often used with Sigismund—an abbreviation of his name.

'A war against poverty, unemployment. It is not a time for celebrating, Frici. It's not as simple as that.'

'It never is,' his mother adds with resignation.

Frici casts a cautious glance towards the new guests seated opposite him. His cousin Imre Lengyel and his wife Sari don't look up from their plates, they don't respond. Frici isn't surprised. His father's nephew arrived on their doorstep only days earlier, barely recognisable, barely conversant. From a once well-built man of ninety-five kilograms, he is now sixty kilograms at most, and his thick dark hair has turned grey, like his skin. His wife, although slimmer than Frici recalls from their festive pre-war wedding, still retains a curvaceous figure. Short dark curls frame a heart-shaped face with high cheekbones and perfectly arched brows. However, white crescents now appear in her lips, as if she has bitten long and hard into the lower one. And the dark almond eyes that Frici recalls now hold a large expectant look, as if she has drunk too much coffee.

Imre and Sari tell of being separated from the rest of Sigismund's family in the ghetto of Crasna—told by authorities that they are being deported to 'work camps'. They recall seeing thousands sent on such journeys each week. Naively, they believed that this was a better fate than milling around the squalid ghetto day and night. Anywhere else must surely be better. Imre remembers that even when they arrived at this camp that stretched for kilometres, with tall barbed-wire fencing, and walked beneath a metal sign reading: *Arbeit Macht Frei* [Work Sets You Free], they think nothing else—after all, that's what the sign says. Then everything goes at speed. Separations begin: left, right, left, right, young man, young woman. Children under sixteen ripped from their mothers' arms. Elderly pushed and prodded, herded like cattle.

Screams.

Silence.

Auschwitz.

Imre anticipates his fate with the taut nerves of a caged animal awaiting its slaughter. But as each day passes, and he is still breathing, he is amazed. *Why me*, he thinks, *I am no different from all the others*. Nevertheless he asks no questions, follows orders, keeps his eyes down. He rarely sees Sari and is kept busy burying the dead in mass graves. Only after they are liberated by the Russian troops does he discover the truth behind their survival—his wife's 'betrayal', which eats like a poisonous worm into his very core.

As soon as they are able to find transport, the pair make their way back to Crasna. They discover nobody and nothing remains from their past, as if they, their entire families, have never existed. Their homes and neighbourhoods are inhabited by strangers now: civilian and soldiers alike.

Oh, yes, Frici can tell terrible things must have occurred in this place called Auschwitz. Not that they actually say much in front of him, but he has been listening to snippets of conversation. In fact, for the first time in his life, he discovers that there is much to be learnt from the unspoken. The way Imre looks at Sari with disgust. The way Sari returns Imre's contempt with incredulous eyes and stiffened posture. Then there is his mother's body language. Anna, whose wartime emotional pendulum hovered tentatively between panic and melancholy, now sways at regular intervals between pity and guilt—guilt for surviving, no less. And her continual worrying about Imre and Sari not eating enough knows no limits. Imre she would gladly force-feed if he could keep down more than the tiny quantities he toys with.

The drums of time keep beating as the tension between his cousins reaches a crescendo. One night Frici is awoken from his slumber by Imre shouting.

'Whore! That's what you are. I can't even stand to look at you.'

'Don't you think I *know* that? Don't look at me then. It would be a thousand times better than what your eyes are calling me day in, day out.'

'You, Sari, you *disgust* me. I don't understand *why?* How *could* you? Yes, yes, they were monsters—I, all of us, will live with the nightmares for the rest of our days. I will never be able to rid myself of that, that … stench of burning human flesh. It sickens me to even utter, give life to the words. Yes, we all know that if Satan exists, he wears the Nazi uniform. But now … don't you see? *You* are no better. *You* are one of them.'

'Good God, Imre. I have told you before and before and before. But I see now you will *never* understand. You think that you, me, either one of us would be standing here today—here in this most *beautiful, pristine* home of your uncle's—if I had refused to do what they asked of me?'

'Who knows? Maybe. There were others who survived without resorting to the filthy things you did.'

'What others, Imre? Show me the *others!*' The sound of her voice echoes through the wall, fast and high like a piano trill. The argument continues well into the night. Frici places his pillow over his head until the commotion eventually ceases.

The next morning, as a leisurely sun rises and pulls with it shadows across Frici's bed, he awakes to an unusually quiet household. He gets up, pulls his robe around himself, scratches his head and wonders at the contrast of calm to the previous night, indeed the previous few months. He saunters downstairs to the kitchen and finds his mother crying into the breakfast of semolina she is stirring on the stove.

'What's wrong, Anyu?'

'They are gone—Imre and Sari. No word, no note, nothing. Beds made and gone. Frici, how do we live with this? You know what Sari said to me yesterday?'

She continues without waiting for his reply.

'She said, "Aunt Anna, why has life has been so kind to you? Don't judge me as Imre has, please. Being afraid makes one alone, even if surrounded by many just as scared".'

Anna pauses, reflecting for a moment, then adds, 'Of course, I told her I do not judge. What she did, she must have deemed necessary. An evil commandant, she told me—he was the one who made her do these ... these *unspeakable* things, Frici.'

'I see.'

'Yes. But what you don't see is that I feel so terrible, so *guilty*.'

'Anyu—'

'Oh, yes, I know what you will say: why should I feel such shame? Well, I just cannot come to terms with how this ... this random pointer of fate decides such things—who lives, who dies, who must do unspeakable things just to survive. How do any of us know what we would do to survive in such impossible circumstances?'

'I don't know, Anyu. Really I have no clue.'

He pulls a chair out from the kitchen table and slumps his lanky fifteen-year-old self into it, thinking about how much things have changed between him, Gyuri and Imre. Imre is a few years older than Gyrui, and even though months would often pass without them seeing each other, as cousins they shared a special bond. But now, that bond feels so tenuous, lost in an idyllic time of innocent childhood. And perhaps it will never recover. For Imre and Sari, dreams were stolen from them, the sanctity of their marriage destroyed. Having survived the nightmare of Auschwitz, can they awaken from its legacy of shame, guilt, betrayal and despair? But for Frici and his family—whom Sari describes as lucky—dreams still harbour hope and their reality breathes of a future.

Tragically, it seems unlikely that Imre and Sari ever recover—they are never heard from again.

When Frici first hears rumours of mysterious disappearances, rapes and random shootings, he naively believes they are exaggerated tales. Impossible, he thinks—no one can get away with that. But they have and they are. Throughout Romania, thousands are being imprisoned daily for political, economic or no apparent reason. Stalin assures the other Allied leaders that the USSR will allow the eastern European countries it occupies after the war to re-establish their independence as democratic republics, although he will never allow that to take place.

Using intimidation, including overt methods of demoralisation and ideological subversion against citizens and rigged elections, the occupying Soviet military engineer the emergence of communist governments across the region. Before long, Romania's scarce post-war resources are further drained by taxes that feed straight back to Stalin and allow the Soviet Union to control Romania's major sources of income. Anyone trying to flee from this brutal regime of terror, if caught, can expect death or, if they're lucky, torture and the gulag. And not only for those who try to flee but also for those who speak out against the regime. Romanians will be trapped for the next forty years 'behind the Iron Curtain'.

An agitated Sigismund has much to say about the state of affairs, but always within the sanctuary of his own walls. He throws his morning paper aside and begins to eat the boiled eggs that Anna has set down before him.

'At least the new communist government is not discriminatory—not like the fascists who persecuted us and other minority groups,' then adds facetiously, 'that is, of course, unless you happen to be wealthy, or considered a capitalist. Only then will you find discrimination of the most unpalatable kind. As for your business—that will be forcibly taken. And your nice house … overrun by Russian soldiers.'

He is preparing her for what he knows is inevitable. He has seen it happening to his friends. He knows that before long his connections will no longer be able to offer protection from the new communist regime. Within days of Sigismund's prediction, the family is forced to surrender several rooms of their home to the comfort of two brash Russian soldiers who take up residence within.

'What are we going to do, Sigismund?' Frici hears his mother sobbing from her bedroom. 'I just can't bear the thought of these filthy soldiers in our house.'

Sigismund wrestles his tie off, flings it onto the floor, then roughly undoes his shirt buttons—ripping one off in the process—before thrashing his arms free and tossing the shirt across the bedroom. Anna, suddenly silenced by this uncharacteristic wild behaviour, stares at him for some seconds before quietly picking up his strewn clothes.

'What can we do, you ask? At the moment, there is not a damn thing we *can* do. We must appear to *tolerate* them. Just as we have, for years, been *tolerated* under this cloud, this virus, of anti-Semitism!' he spits out. 'Hopefully this new regime … this blasted tyranny, will learn how it feels to be in the position of being *tolerated*.'

Not surprisingly—least of all to him—Frici is successful in his football try-outs for the elite Ripensia Club. Next, he has his sights set on the impending trials for the National Youth League. But his brief euphoria is shattered by a devastating episode that occurs only days after the trials.

One evening, still clad in the yellow-and-red football uniform of the club, Frici arrives home from training beside himself with shock. Not wanting to face his mother's questions, he sneaks up the staircase, bumping into Gyuri on the landing. Gyuri questions him about his ashen appearance and he is almost incoherent as he stumbles for words.

'Outside, just now … on our street. A Russian soldier stops a man. Demands he hand over his watch. Viktor told me they are fascinated with watches. But the man … he refused to hand it over. So the soldier took out his gun and shoots: *Bang, bang!* Blasts him dead, Gyuri. I saw it with my own eyes.'

As his brother opens his mouth, Frici holds up his hand, signalling him not to speak. What could Gyuri possibly say to comfort him, he thinks. He turns on his heel and trudges into his room. Removing his sweaty clothes he knows full well that the scene he has just witnessed will appear before him many times over before dawn.

18

Istvan

1945

Crammed onto hard wooden benches, the terrified passengers begin their journey from Romania to Russia. Istvan is trying his utmost not to let the darkness—his own, that of the carriage, the sky through the slats and that of his fellow passengers—consume him. Opposite him is a sour-faced man who sits with his arms wrapped around himself as if he is afraid the other passengers will contaminate him.

Soon, a voice breaks the silence.

'You're Istvan, Nikolaus's son, aren't you?' A scruffy young man stands with feet apart trying to maintain his balance on the rocking train as he lurches rhythmically towards Istvan.

'Yes,' Istvan replies, staring up into a familiar face from his neighbourhood. 'Sorry, but I can't recall you're name.'

'Tibor, I live with my mother a few kilometres down the road from your farmhouse.'

'Yes, of course. Tibor. I've been to your farm once, with my father,' Istvan says, sliding farther along the wooden bench and receiving dark scowls from the row of passengers already jammed in thigh to thigh, elbow to elbow. 'Here, have a seat. Do you have any food to eat?'

'No. My stomach is aching from hunger.'

'Have my bread and my last egg. I've eaten enough today.'

'You're too kind, Istvan, and I'm afraid I'm too hungry to say no.'

Gulping down the hard-boiled egg, he continues, 'I've left my mother all alone. I don't know how she'll cope without me.'

'Me too. Although my sister is home, but she's not much help, unfortunately.'

'You heard about my brother and father?'

'Yes. I am very sorry.' Istvan knows they both died fighting in the Hungarian army.

They talk for some time, Tibor explaining that he wasn't especially close to his father. Naturally he was sad to lose him, but his father often drank too much whisky and rough-handled his mother. Whenever Tibor tried to stand up to him, his father would beat him too.

'So, there was a distance between us. But my brother …' The corners of his mouth twitch. 'We were very close. Just one year separating us. Him I miss more than anything.'

Istvan can't bring himself to mention his own father and brothers. Since Jani's fleeting visit, they have heard nothing. He has no idea if any of them are safe or well. And it is a subject which he just doesn't want to think about. Not here, not now on this wretched cavalcade.

After several days on the train, Istvan begins to feel a heaviness in his arms and legs as he tries to move about. As the train trudges on, sweat begins to pour from his brow yet at the same time he shivers uncontrollably from the cold. Istvan continues to tremble as the knots in his stomach make him double over in spasm. Finally, after much stopping and starting, the train comes to its final grinding halt, hissing clouds of steam at a deserted railway station that bears a sign in Cyrillic lettering that Istvan cannot read. But he knows it means he is in the Soviet Union. Famished and weary, passengers are instructed to disembark and form a long line. They exchange uncertain looks, but no one speaks.

Stepping down off the train, he pulls his jacket tighter about him with his one free hand and notices many do the same as they fall in behind each other. His legs feel weak and unsteady, probably from sitting too long, he thinks. Orders are given to keep walking.

Hours pass and the dishevelled procession shuffles against the wind. Each new gust cuts into Istvan like a knife. Finely stencilled deciduous trees stand along the roadway but offer little protection as they bow to nature. Underfoot, the road is gelatinous sludge that makes his steps progressively more difficult. Finally the line comes to a halt. Looking up at high brick fences, Istvan wonders whether they are destined to be labourers or prisoners, as a crosswind blows him sideways. He regains his balance, rubs his eyes, but suddenly the fences begin to blur and his legs begin to buckle.

19
Katarina

1945

'Nikolaus? Nikolaus? Where are you?' Katarina shouts as she rushes into the farmhouse, almost tripping over the front doormat in her haste.

'Here. I am right here,' he replies from the bedroom where he is lying down, still weak, despite being home for many months.

'Agnes has had a letter from Tibor—*oh, dear God, Nikolaus!*'

'What is it, Katarina? Please, tell me.'

'Tibor says that he met Istvan on the train to Russia, and that Istvan became ill on the train. The last time he saw him was when he was carried by stretcher into the camp hospital. He hasn't seen him since! *It can't be so! Please tell me it can't be so …*' She begins sinking to her knees.

'Listen to me now.'

He grips her firmly by the shoulders, perhaps a little too firmly, but he wants her to see sense. He tells her there are thousands in these work camps. To this, he can personally attest. Those interned are usually sent to do various jobs, so it is possible that Tibor is doing something completely different from Istvan. And the eating, if you can call it that, is staggered so that not everyone eats at the same time.

'Believe me, woman, Istvan is all right. He is smart and resilient. And he's strong. Dry your eyes. This is no time for tears.'

Frici's mother, Anna, aged 30, Timişoara – 1930.

Istvan's mother, Katarina, aged 30, Timişoara – 1928.

Istvan's sister and parents. *L to R:* Hermina, Katarina and her husband Nikolaus, Timişoara – 1940.

Istvan (on right), aged 21, and his brother Nick, in Naples prior to boarding *SS General Muir* bound for Sydney – 1950.

Bathurst Migrant Camp – 1950.

Fred (formerly Frici), aged 19, walking down Bondi Road, Bondi, not long after arriving in Sydney – 1949.
The smart suit was bought in Salzburg, Austria, before he left Europe for a new life in Australia.

Fred (far right), aged 20, wearing his favourite 'D' shirt from Kadima Football Club (in Timişoara) playing in a table tennis tournament in Sydney – 1950.

Steven's wedding in 1951.
L to R: Steven (formerly Istvan), Stephanie (Steffie) and her parents William and Stefania (Mutti) Heidrichas, with others.

Fred and Joan (later to become the author's parents) on an early date in Kogarah Hotel, Sydney – 1955.

Steven's children: Robert, aged 2, on the left, and Rosemary, aged 5 – 1957.

Sigismund (Apu) holding Cheryl (Cherie-ke) at her christening – 1960.

Steven's family at the St George Budapest Soccer Club Dining Room.
L to R: Robert, aged 14; Steven; Rosemary, aged 17; Steven's wife, Stephanie – 1969.

Steven returns to visit family in Chişoda where he was born, on the outskirts of Timişoara. Here with his niece, Evelyn (holding the ball) and some neighbourhood children (and their pet goat!) – 1974.

Cheryl (author) and Robert's wedding in 1979. The couple are photographed here with Cheryl's grandmother Anyu, aged 79.

Joan, being sworn in as Mayor of Hurstville – 1984.

Christopher Koenig's wedding in 2013.
L to R: Cheryl (author); her father Fred (Frici), aged 82; Steven (Istvan) aged 85; Danielle; Christopher (author's son); Stephanie and Robert (author's husband).

Cheryl receives her OAM from Governor Bashir.
L to R: Robert, Jonathan (author's eldest son), Cheryl, Governor Bashir, Fred – 2014.

20
Frici

1946

Now that Frici is nearly sixteen, his father has agreed to let him buy a motorbike from the army surplus machinery warehouse. The local Russian soldiers are keen to sell unwanted vehicles and they are going cheap. When Frici hands over the cash, the soldier pockets it without recording any transaction.

The next day, Frici heads off on his newly acquired motorbike to deliver flour to the local baker, who opens his shop just for family and close friends as long as they supply him with the much-needed and highly prized flour. As he nears the corner where the bakery stands, Frici pulls over on the empty street with its abandoned shops. A man in a long black overcoat and matching wide-brimmed hat appears from nowhere and grabs him by the arm.

'Get off your bike,' he orders. 'You're coming with me.'

Frici notices the small pistol in the man's free hand and his mind races with thoughts of stories he has heard about people vanishing. Suddenly caught up in the most sinister situation of his young life, he tries to act normally, to hold back the panic that threatens to engulf him. Remembering his street fights, he recalls the importance of catching his opponent off guard and realises he must stay vigilant yet calm, while formulating his getaway. He turns the engine off and alights as instructed, but keeps hold of both handles—one hand firmly holding the clutch in, the other ensuring the bike stays in gear.

'No problem, sir. I'll come with you, but please let me bring my bike.'

The darkly clad man nods his assent and they begin walking down the deserted street away from the baker's shop, his grip on Frici's arm tightening as they go. As they walk in silence, Frici gradually quickens his pace. *Easy ... easy ... keep your wits.* Step by step, he steadily increases his tempo. Soon they are moving at a canter.

'Slow down!' comes the order. But Frici does the opposite. He quickens his pace until he is running as fast as he can. Then, in one swift movement, he straddles the bike and drops the clutch, forcing the engine to sputter and start. As he speeds off, the bag of flour falls from the bike and bursts open on the hard cobbles, leaving his would-be abductor choking and blinded by a thick white cloud.

He maintains a frantic speed till he approaches his street and, as the bike slows down, so too does his heartbeat.

'There'll be no bread in our house tonight,' he puffs, never before so elated at an absence of food.

As the austere winter of 1946 deepens, some of Frici's friends are forced to live in the dank cellars of their own homes as Russian soldiers commandeer their houses. Frici thinks it won't be long before his family, too, is required to surrender even more of their home to the Russian military. Despite having just qualified for the National Youth Football Squad of Romania, he knows he must urge his parents to find a way to leave. At first Sigismund and Anna are reluctant as they have heard too many stories of people being shot while trying desperately to escape across borders. Their fear solidifies when his father's closest friend is also caught, robbed and shot dead.

However, when Sigismund is compelled to close down what little remains of the family business, he finally relents and agrees it is time to start making plans for their eventual escape.

One evening Sigismund takes his sons into his bedroom and locks the door.

'We have to act discreetly,' he whispers. 'You are not to repeat anything we tell you—not even to your friends. All plans must remain our family's secret. You are never to talk about this anywhere near the ears of the unwelcome inhabitants of our house. If they suspect anything at all—*anything*—they will expose us. Do you understand the gravity of what I am saying?'

'Yes, Apu,' the brothers say in unison.

'Good. Now listen carefully—we'll have few opportunities to talk like this without raising suspicion.' He lowers his voice even further and proceeds to tell them that prior to, and even during, the early years of the war, he was secretly sending large sums of money to his family's Swiss bank account, held jointly by his father, brothers and some cousins. Naturally, he has also kept some hidden at home. Through dependable sources, he has found what he hopes are reliable people-smugglers who are willing to take them across the border into Hungary.

'Then what, Apu? Won't we still be in a communist country?'

'Yes. I am working on the next stages, Gyuri. Anyway, so we don't raise suspicion, first you two will both leave, after which another family will be smuggled. Then, two weeks later your mother and I will follow and meet up with you in Budapest.'

A few more unobserved family meetings transpire where arrangements are discussed and preparations made. Then early one evening, as the two Russian soldiers swill Sigismund's fine brandy, laughing raucously as they play cards in what was once his library, Frici and Gyuri quietly prepare to leave.

Under instructions to pack only the bare necessities into just one suitcase between them, Anna is, of course, supervising the packing. She ensures her boys each have three pressed shirts, two pairs of trousers with a jacket, vest and tie to match both, another woollen cardigan, additional footwear, plus, of course, warm singlets, pyjamas and plenty of underwear. Frici sneaks in his prized stamp collection, then closes the bulging lid with a final push. The suitcase heaves its sigh of goodbye and Anna exhales her grief, as her heart crushes into countless pieces.

'Please, *please* be careful,' she barely whispers, before turning to bury her face in Sigismund's chest. *'I can't do this … I just can't …'* Every single part of her feels hollow, from the backs of her knees to the ridges of her collarbones.

'Shh, Anna,' Sigismund comforts, 'this is the only way. We have discussed it many times.'

He turns and hugs his sons with a fierceness Frici has never felt before. And when he speaks, his voice catches.

'Stick to the instructions and … and stay safe, my sons.'

They creep silently down the stairs and out of the house. Their escape has been purposely scheduled for a moonless night when not even a shadow is discernible. Through the darkness, they furtively weave their way through the city streets to a pre-arranged meeting place in a laneway on the edge of town.

Shortly, a middle-aged couple joins them—Lutwak, a business associate of their father's, and his wife Betty. They acknowledge each other through nods. Almost immediately, two men dressed in dark clothing and quiet walking shoes—attired as they have instructed the escapees to dress—emerge from under a shop canopy and approach them.

Wordlessly, they set off, making their way out of the city on quickened foot, all the while looking backwards over their shoulders and hurriedly ducking into unlit alleys and doorways at the sound of echoed footsteps or unexpected voices that intermittently resonate against the silence of the otherwise quiet city. Soon they are traversing farmland. They continue walking throughout the night, only stopping for brief rests every couple of hours.

Swapping the suitcase to his right hand, Frici looks at his watch. In the darkness, he can barely see the hands, but he estimates that it's close to four in the morning. The bearded guide, whose eyes are only just visible below his black cap, stops and gathers everyone close around him.

'Right, listen carefully,' he whispers, and goes on to explain that although scarce in numbers in the quiet of the countryside, groups of Russian soldiers are still menacingly present, patrolling the border on foot. Frici looks around, and then asks where the actual border is, as he can't see any fences.

'We are heading towards it now.'

The guide points in the direction of a distant farmhouse and informs them it is situated right on the Hungarian/Romanian border. The farmers, he explains, are part of the 'Organisation'. They purposely plough their land in different directions so that the actual border is barely determinable—appearing only as intermittent deep trenches in the unfenced cultivated land—making it the ideal place to cross.

'From now on,' the man continues in his gruff whisper, 'follow instructions without answering. Only use sign language. And when we stop briefly at the farmhouse for refreshments, do not talk to the man and woman. Do not give them your names, or ask theirs.'

When they reach the farmhouse door, the guide taps gently on the timber using an unusual rhythm. The solid door squeaks open and a heavily built elderly man in mud-spattered clothing ushers them into a sparse but warm cottage. Showing them to the kitchen, he gestures for them to sit at the table, which is already set with enamel cups and plates. A small round woman with wisps of silver hair escaping from her loose bun dries her hands down her apron as she turns and greets them with a small smile. Frici smiles back uneasily. In a soft voice, she asks her tense visitors if they would prefer tea or coffee to drink with their bread and salami.

'Coffee please.' They each reply. After only fifteen minutes' respite, they are told they must set off again while there are still dark hours left and civilisation sleeps.

'Before you go, boys, eat some cake and have a glass of milk,' the farmer's wife says. Cupping Frici's face in her hands she asks, 'What age are you, darling?'

'Sixteen.'

'Sixteen, yes? My God, you are so young! I pray that He blesses you and keeps you safe.'

Nodding their gratitude to these kind and courageous farming folk, the fugitives and their guides make their way out into the bracing night and continue across the fields where the shadows of the surrounding hills fill the undulations of carefully cultivated land. In the uninterrupted blackness, it is difficult to see what lies ahead. Suddenly Lutwak's wife Betty trips and falls head first into the soft dirt of a deep trench that marks the edge of the border.

'Ah!' she cries out loudly.

They all freeze mid-step as her cry echoes against the silent hills. In the distance, Frici can hear a crescendo of Russian voices approaching.

'Into the ditch—quickly!' one of the guides whispers urgently. Startled, they all turn and quickly jump into the trench.

Lutwak places a hand over his wife's mouth.

'Shut up, Betty,' he whispers against her ear as she begins to cry quietly.

Frici is sure the thundering of his rapid heartbeat will lead the soldiers directly to them, and the sickening possibility that they are within metres of the border and now hiding in what could prove to be their collective grave, is not lost upon him. As the minutes drag on, the Russian voices grow fainter until gradually they can no longer be heard. Cautiously, six pairs of eyes peer out over the edge of the dirt mound to confirm that the soldiers have retreated.

When they are finally safely across the border, they are confronted with a wide expanse of water. The tranquil, soft ripples of a lake, illuminated by the faint glow of the sickle-shaped moon, which has decided to make an appearance from behind its veil of clouds, suggest a calm that neither Frici nor Gyuri feel. Frici looks at his brother with eyes that silently question whether they can trust their aides. Gyuri's eyes reply with unease. In the pale glow from the low moon, Frici surreptitiously peers at the unshaven and shabbily dressed men, suddenly wary. As if they have somehow heard his thoughts, he quickly averts his glance as both men glare back shrewdly. Having made this crossing numerous times, the people-smugglers have an old wooden rowing boat hidden in the dense shrubbery that meets the lake's edge. As swiftly and quietly as possible, the party of six drag it into the shallow waters, clamber in and begin to row in earnest.

Frici's unspoken doubts continue.

They must know we all carry large sums of money … They could toss us out of the boat when we reach the middle of this deep lake with its black waters and no one would ever know …

'Stop rowing!' the bearded man whispers as a broad torch light flickers across the ripples of water in the direction of their vessel.

21
Istvan

1946

Twenty-one, twenty-two, twenty-three ... Are you watching, Nicky? I can juggle my football to one hundred. Twenty-nine, thirty, thirty-one ... Istvan awakens with a start. He is cold and uncomfortable. Where is he? And what is he lying on that is so hard—a table? He turns his head and sees a blurry figure in a white coat standing over him.

'Who are you?'

'You're finally awake now, eh!'

'Where am I?' Istvan asks, rubbing his eyes.

'You're in the camp hospital. You have a fever, but I think you'll be fine in a day or two. You need some food and water. There's no point in you remaining here, though. You're young and fit. Ready to work.'

'Yes, I feel fine,' he lies, rising unsteadily to his feet. 'Just tell me where I have to go.'

The light is thin and even the air of the camp seems bleak, as Istvan is taken under guard to long wooden barracks. Inside, he sees at least a hundred shivering bodies. Some stand, huddled like lost sheep, while others sit on lean straw beds covered by threadbare blankets. He's handed a pyjama-like set of clothing to change into.

'Are they joking?' Istvan whispers to the man next him. 'Is this a mock attempt to protect us against the cold?'

'The cold will be the least of our worries,' the man whispers back. 'My name's Radu. You?'

'Istvan.'

Looking about him to make certain he can't be overheard, Radu whispers, 'Like all of us here you would have been told we were going to work camps, yes?'

Istvan nods.

'Well, they're called labour camps, but really we'll be treated like prisoners of war—no different.'

Within days, Istvan will know Radu to be correct.

Unable to sleep that night because his body is trembling with cold, he continues to speak softly to his new friend who, although ten years older than him, so in his mid-twenties, doesn't seem as robust as Istvan.

'Radu? Are you awake?'

'Yes. What's the matter?'

'How long can we each survive on cabbage soup and one piece of stale bread for breakfast, lunch and dinner?'

'You're just a kid, so let me help you understand.' Even through the wooden bunk, his voice carries a harshness. 'Of the one thousand incarcerated here, no single person has any way of knowing if he will be in the many hundreds of detainees not to last, if he will be one of those who die from excessive physical work, or lack of nourishment or severe cold. If you believe in God, Istvan, pray for the strength to survive. Pray you will not be one of the hundreds to die.'

Istvan soon discovers that each day is a ghastly re-enactment of the one before. After breakfast, along with a hundred or so other prisoners, he is taken by truck to a nearby railway line where he shovels coal for the steam trains till sundown. Upon returning to camp in the early evening, the prisoners gather in the large canteen and are given the same scant meal of cabbage soup and stale bread for dinner. Immediately after they finish eating, they return to their barracks and attempt to survive the bone-piercing cold of the Russian night.

Towards the middle of the year, as the days begin to lengthen and the sun contains the promise of warmth, Istvan decides that he cannot endure much more of this unrelenting toil and unbearable living conditions. If he is to survive, he needs to make his escape from this hell-hole, and fast. Within days an opportunity arises while his team of prisoners are on a work detail outside the camp and close to the railway line. The guards have wandered back to their hut and are preoccupied with chatting and playing cards. He drops his shovel and takes off as fast as he can down the train tracks, ignoring the furious Russian voices calling after him.

'Stop!'

Incredibly, he manages to avoid being captured and eventually, tired and parched, comes to a deserted railway station, where he drops exhausted onto a rickety old bench. Not long after, however, he recoils in shock as two German shepherd dogs, snarling at the leash, loom before him. He looks up from the vicious teeth that are drooling centimetres from his body and into the eyes of his captors.

'Stupid boy,' one says, in Russian, though Istvan can gather his intent. 'How far did you think you could get?'

Grabbing him roughly by the arms, they drag him into a waiting truck. His punishment is same-day transfer to a work camp with tighter security. The living conditions are virtually identical but the work is backbreaking. Long days are spent loading trucks with heavy crates—whose contents are never disclosed to the prisoners—under the vigilant glare of armed soldiers.

Several months pass and once again Istvan decides he can take no more. He waits until night falls then silently creeps towards the dormitory door.

'Istvan? Where are you going?' a male voice asks as the door creaks open.

'Shh, Láslo. It's better you don't know.'

He creeps across the barren yard and leans flat against an icy wall near the camp's exit. Time hangs heavily but he stays near the gate watching and waiting for the guards to swap duty. Aside from freezing to death or getting shot, what could possibly go wrong? As soon as he notices the disruption in surveillance he's been waiting for, he sneaks out of camp and quietly crunches his way down the limestone road towards the promise of nothingness. For twenty minutes or so he walks with just the moonlight to guide him, before he hears a truck's engine resonate against the black tree trunks that form a wall along the roadway. He starts to run, but realising it is hopeless, stops and turns around, squinting blindly into the bright lights of the advancing vehicle.

22
Frici

1946

The rowing boat drifts on the slow-moving current. Its occupants are paralysed, frightened to breathe. To Frici, even the gentle sound of water lapping against the side of the vessel resembles giant waves crashing against cliffs. The flickering torchlight arcs back and forward within centimetres of the dinghy, mesmerising Frici. *We are so close ... Don't let them see us now.* When he steals a glance at the others sitting opposite him, only the whites of their eyes are visible against the black ink of night. As the ominous beam finally circles back towards the shoreline, Betty sighs in relief. But no one speaks. The people-smugglers silently slip the oars through the dark water.

They take turns rowing, two at a time, but when it is Lutwak and Betty's turn, Frici takes the oar from Betty's hands.

'Let me,' he whispers.

An hour or so later, when Frici's arms are aching so badly he doesn't think he can row another stroke, they are ordered by the men to get out of the boat.

'This is as far as we can take you. Wade ashore and follow

the road north to the train station. Fifteen minutes—that's all it should take. Keep your heads down. Talk to no one.'

When Frici steps out of the boat, he is dismayed to discover his legs sink knee-deep into mud. The chill of water is biting their legs, but with their one suitcase held high between them, the brothers, along with their companions, reach the shoreline without falling. In their mud-clad shoes, all six proceed to squelch along the road in what they believe is the right direction. In the very early hours of the morning, it is still dark and a low mist hangs over the road by the lake. They continue walking for nearly thirty minutes before Gyuri realises they must be heading in the wrong direction as they still haven't reached the train station.

'Damn it, Frici, we've come the wrong way. Now we must turn around and retrace our stupid muddy footsteps.'

Betty plonks herself down on a boulder by the side of the road.

'I'm sorry but I simply can't go on. I'm absolutely exhausted and my ankle is extremely sore from my fall.'

'You must get up and move, Betty,' Lutwak urges, with anxiety creeping into his voice. 'We must reach the station by sunrise or we'll miss the early train.'

Frici turns back and helps her to her feet, taking her large black leather handbag.

'What on earth do you have in here? It weighs a tonne!'

'Oh, I thought I'd bake some *pogácsa*[24] in case we got hungry,' she replies, nervously looking towards Lutwak, who rolls his eyes in reply.

The group marches on, quickening their pace as a crisp dawn rises to meet them. Finally, as they round a curve, to Frici's

---

24 Cheese biscuits.

enormous relief, a train station appears. With hope in sight, he is able to encourage the group to move even faster.

They approach the ticket counter. The uniformed official looks up, her gaze more accusatory than enquiring, as she peers over the top of black square-framed spectacles which sit low on the bridge of her nose under a fringe of henna hair. Despite inward trepidation, Frici feigns composure as he asks, 'May I purchase four tickets to Budapest, please?'

The clerk leans forward on the counter with her elbows and slowly peruses the two young men and the middle-aged couple. Observing the muddy condition of their clothes, she purses her lips and casts them a shrewd look. Oh yes, there is no doubting from that look—she knows they're fugitives. When she disappears behind her counter, Frici strains to hear voices whispering in haste. For the third time since leaving the safety of their parent's home, his chest tightens with dread. He listens anxiously to the staccato tones of a Hungarian male and female, voices rising and falling in the pitch of disagreement, catching the lengthened vowels of their dialect, knowing that his own accent betrays him. He looks at Gyuri and they both glance at Lutwak and Betty. From the frozen expressions on their companions' faces, the brothers realise that they are about to panic and perhaps give the game away.

Losing his nerve, Lutwak whispers, 'Frici, she knows where we've come from. We have to make a run for it before it's too late.'

'Wait, Lutwak.' Frici grabs hold of his arm firmly by the elbow. 'There are soldiers and secret police everywhere. If we run for it, we won't get far before we get caught and most likely shot. We have to keep our nerve—it's the safer bet. If she refuses to sell us—' he stops mid-sentence as suddenly the ticket lady reappears. Ever so casually, and without so much as a word, she sells them their train tickets.

'Fortune is our friend this brisk and misty morning,' Gyuri says into his brother's ear as they turn and head towards the platform.

'Pompous idiot,' Frici whispers back.

Arriving in Budapest, they head straight to the main synagogue, where arrangements have been made for the group to meet up with their safe-house hosts. They sit together inside the synagogue, too exhausted to talk after their harrowing journey and apprehensive about what awaits them in the next weeks. At the sound of the heavy door opening behind them, Frici turns to see a balding man with a pock-scarred face and nose bent to one side. He sits down behind them. Shortly after, a miniature elderly woman, with a headscarf tied under the chin of a weathered face, joins him. They make brisk introductions. From now on, the boys are separated from Lutwak and Betty, who both stand ready to leave with the man. Looks are exchanged but no words. They don't know if they will survive this next stage, if they will reach their journey's end, or even where that end might be. Frici and Gyuri leave with the woman to a different safe house, to await Anna and Sigismund's arrival.

Their room is unadorned and sparsely furnished, containing just two single beds, a table and two chairs. The locked window fails to foil a chill draught from seeping into the oppressive space. They have been instructed not to leave the premises, nor mingle with anyone inside. An elderly lady with a sullen expression and smelling of mothballs brings up their meals, giving them little excuse to leave their room.

With little to do to alleviate their boredom, the brothers play endless games of five-card-draw poker. Or, while Gyuri immerses himself in discarded newspapers, Frici hones the masterful skill of building tall houses from the deck of cards.

'It's been over two weeks, Gyuri, and they're not here yet. What do you think is going on?' Frici exhales, then holds his breath and painstakingly angles two cards in place to complete the roof of his five-storey tower.

'I don't know. We just have to sit tight. It's no good jumping to conclusions.' Gyuri casually tosses his paper aside, the slight breeze enough to demolish the precarious multi-storey mansion.

The days drag on without any word from their parents, and the brothers begin to despair. Then one morning when the old woman arrives with their breakfast tray, a letter has been placed against the pot of coffee. It is from their father.

'This letter has already been opened,' Frici remarks as he passes the envelope to his brother.

Taking the letter, Gyuri notices that it is written with the pre-arranged names and codes the family discussed before the boys' escape. As he watches his brother read, Frici notices his eyes growing wider with every line he scans.

'Tell me. What does it say?'

'Apu says that on the very next run after ours, the people-smugglers and their escapees were all caught and shot. Not only this but, Frici, the elderly farmer and his kind wife have also been shot. For "aiding absconders," he says.'

They sit in shocked silence for some minutes, scarcely believing the lethal brutality to which the regime has stooped to keep its citizens from leaving their country. Hasn't Europe seen enough unspeakable death and destruction for the last six years with the march of fascism across the continent, and its eventual defeat? Haven't the communists promised a workers' paradise where citizens will thrive with the redistribution of wealth and finally enjoy rights and a voice never before seen in Romania? So many questions …

The news means indefinite cancellation of escape plans for his parents who, Frici suddenly realises, will be put under immense pressure from their Russian boarders to reveal their sons' whereabouts.

'I only hope, Gyuri, that they have well-rehearsed the tale of us visiting Anyu's relatives in Oradea—especially when I don't show up for my first competition game in the youth squad.'

'As long as Anyu holds her nerve, they should be all right.' With that, Gyuri rolls his eyes and collapses on the bed, and Frici, too, realises that *that* will be easier said than done. After careful thought, Gyuri announces, 'We have no choice but to carry on to the next stage without them.'

The next stage involves instructions to meet up with a man known only as 'the Major', whom Sigismund has indirectly paid a large sum of money to in order to aid in their escape.

A few days later at a designated office, they meet the Major. He speaks only briefly to the brothers, but enough to tell them he has arranged for them to be safely escorted by car across the Hungarian border into Austria, after which they will be placed on a train to Vienna.

'Vienna has been divided into zones by the Allies and when you disembark from the train you will still be in the Soviet zone of the city,' he informs them in a brusque manner, before adding, 'Here are the instructions on how to find the safe offices of the US's Central Intelligence Agency. Don't lose them.'

Arriving in Vienna two days later, they follow their instructions and make their way through the maze of paved streets and laneways. Frici looks up at the once proud and elegant buildings he remembers from family holidays in this cultural centre of Europe. He is shocked by the number of buildings that are now unsightly piles of rubble and others that are barely standing, their facades mutilated and crumbling. What were once architectural marvels, famous throughout the world, are now crying out in distress from disfigurement.

Carefully, they follow the route on their map, safely reaching the building appropriated by the occupying US Military. When shown up to the CIA office, Frici looks swiftly to his brother, who mirrors his incredulity. Somehow, having arrived there before them, the Major is sitting at a desk in deep discussions with a CIA officer. He turns, acknowledges them with a cursory nod and continues talking.

A few minutes later, he stands to leave and as he passes them speaks in fluent Hungarian.

'Unfortunately—despite my cover as the head of Soviet Secret Police in Budapest—my *transactions* have been discovered and now I, too, must disappear.'

The brothers exchange another look, bewildered by what has transpired. They have only moments to absorb the extraordinariness of the situation, before they are beckoned by the same CIA officer. Shrugging, Frici quickly adjusts his thoughts to the present as he settles into the Major's now vacant seat.

The official gives Frici and Gyuri their final set of instructions on how to get to the Allied-occupied Austrian city of Salzburg. They are given train tickets and told which train to board and from where. He instructs them to purchase a German newspaper each and to sit apart, in different carriages. They are also given the name of a small nondescript station well before Salzburg, at which to disembark. Upon alighting, they are informed, they will notice six other escapees who will be under the same instructions. They are not to mingle with them, but instead immediately leave the station via the southern gates where they will find a large black limousine waiting for them.

Frici and Gyuri follow their instructions to the letter. At the station exit, Frici takes the lead in the small group of escapees milling about the limousine. When he opens the passenger door of the waiting car, he is startled to hear a gruff, distinctly American voice bark in English, 'Get in. Get in quickly.'

They drive for some hours and then quite abruptly the driver stops the car.

'Up ahead a road border-control is set up. Get out here, go through those thick bushes you see on the right, then climb the steep hill that lies behind. When you come down the other side, I'll be waiting for you. Now go, quickly!'

It all goes according to plan with Frici lugging their suitcase through the dense grove and then up and down the steep rise in the countryside. After coasting down the slope, taking care not to fall, they reach the loose gravel by the side of the road where the black limo is waiting as promised. After only a short drive this time, the driver stops the car and utters what is for his eight apprehensive passengers a most surreal statement.

'You can get out here. You won't have any more problems. Congratulations! Now you are free people.'

23
Istvan
1947

A Russian winter smothers the land, forcing plants and other life to weep a lament. One night Istvan's dormitory door swings open suddenly and two soldiers march in, bringing with them a foreboding chill. The arctic wind blows tiny stars of snow around their bulky frames—covered in long, sheepskin coats—before coming to rest on the seal fur of their Cossack hats. One of the soldiers begins calling out names from a list. Eleven names are called out before the metallic voice announces, 'Istvan König'.

Istvan rises from his bunk and joins the other unsuspecting detainees. They are ordered to 'move', and are taken to a waiting truck. On a narrow serpentine road filled with jarring potholes, the journey rolls on and Istvan is unable to sleep. As the darkness inside the truck gradually lightens in degrees of khaki, he stares out apprehensively at the tops of the pine trees that rise gracefully towards the sun as it ignites the first sign of day. Through the splintered light, he sees a battered road sign ahead and as it nears he can just make out the black lettering.

'Kiev,' he says to the others who sit with folded arms, silent and brooding. 'We're in Kiev.'

As the truck begins to slow, Istvan notices seemingly endless brick walls topped with rolls of barbed wire. The truck drives through high wooden gates, which open only long enough to allow the vehicle to pass through before clanging shut, coming to a stop inside a much larger work camp than their last one. The rear doors to the truck squeal open and the passengers are ordered to get out.

Sleet starts to fall, finding the skin on Istvan's neck and in between his tattered pyjamas, stinging like tiny electric shocks. As the latest arrivals stand hunched over in the snow, they are given a brief rundown on their new camp. There are eight barracks, each holding over three hundred detainees. There is a hospital, a dining hall, some small outhouses, a headquarters building and a separate punishment block with small holding cells.

'That's for prisoners who disobey the camp rules,' the official voice emphasises.

The dozen new detainees are sent to their long prison-like dormitory buildings. Once inside, Istvan's eyes are drawn to the rusty steel bars fitted to each tiny window under which wooden bunk beds are stacked in threes. The bunks are filled with men whose skin has all but melted from their bodies and whose ashen faces and hollow eyes rattle Istvan's grasp of humanity.

One of the silent men from the truck journey speaks for the first time.

'We are all failed escapees, am I not correct? Well, let me tell you now there will be no escaping from this menagerie. This is a "strafe camp". It is a punishment camp—the strictest kind of camp. We are all being punished for trying to escape.'

The sight and smell of so many rotting and cramped bodies assails Istvan's senses.

'This is worse than the holding pens my father built back home for the pigs,' he whispers to the man who now has a voice.

At first it is hard for Istvan to believe that conditions could be worse than before, but reality doesn't take long to set in as he and the other new arrivals surrender to their routine. Each day begins with a wake-up call at five o'clock followed by breakfast half an hour later. At six, a roll call takes place in the yard, after which all the healthy prisoners march under escort for one hour, through whatever weather conditions prevail, to a steel foundry where, with two armed soldiers watching over every dozen or so men, they are put to work melding die castings for tools and locomotive parts. They labour until sunset. After marching back to camp, they are given an evening meal—a thicker version of the morning's soup, served in tin cups. After dinner, all prisoners need to fulfil their camp duties: chop firewood, shovel snow or repair buildings. Finally at eleven o'clock they are allowed to sleep.

One morning, after consuming a watery grey potato soup, Istvan looks at the long line of prisoners still waiting for their paltry ration and decides he will rejoin the queue for a second helping. As he places his battered old cup out for a refill, the butt of a long rifle jabs him between the shoulder blades.

'Do you think we are stupid or blind or both?' The soldier snarls through thin, angry lips. 'Your insolence shall be punished. Come with me. Now!'

Istvan is locked up in an isolation cell less than one metre by one metre with no information about how long he is to remain there. *They think they can break me*, he thinks at first, *but it will take more than this to break my will.* However, with each passing hour the sucking hunger pain in his stomach worsens, gradually weakening his resolve until he vows he will do whatever it takes to never again be placed in confinement. He is released after eight hours.

But only two weeks later, he is provoked to act again. He and a group of fellow prisoners are marching to work when, without warning, an older man marching next to him suddenly collapses to the ground. His flaccid body hits the dirt with a thud. Before the feeble prisoner has time to climb back onto his feet, a young soldier stands over him and begins hitting him repeatedly with the butt of his gun. Istvan reacts instinctively, pulling the soldier off the prostrate, bleeding man. Seconds later he feels an agonising sharpness radiate down his spine as the butt from another soldier's gun slams into the back of his neck. He collapses to his knees. Stunned and in excruciating pain, he slowly climbs back to his feet and is immediately dragged out of the line and taken to one of the superior officers.

'You're a troublemaker, aren't you? Silence!' the officer shouts, as Istvan opens his mouth to answer. 'Your punishment for the crime of retaliation will be another stint in solitary.'

The door swings shut. The unforgiving sound of two metal bolts being drawn and locked sends chills down his spine as he comprehends that he is imprisoned once more in the tiniest of darkened spaces. *I've done this once. I can do it again.* For the first stretch (an hour? ten minutes?), he tries to distract himself by staying connected to the outside. He listens for voices. They are muffled. He hears the engine of a truck starting, though he can't hear the sound of the tyres because the ground is covered in slush and snow. It grows quiet. With the quietness, he can hear the song of a bird. *The bird is free ...* He feels his rage mounting. With not enough room to swing his arms, he stomps his feet in an effort to keep the cold from freezing his veins. He marches intermittently as time dips and morphs. If he stands still the cold will envelop him, anaesthetising him into a sleep from which he will never wake. Soon his rage turns to anxiety. *Who am I? What is the world really like? What is my reason for being here—to live a helpless existence in a bottomless pit of foul, stale odour which I will never become accustomed to?*

He knows he has to control his straying thoughts. From beneath the cell door, he focuses on a sliver of light from the outside world. He imagines the light being warm and wrapping itself around him. Then he thinks about his home: how warm he felt lying in the fields on a summer evening and watching the fading sunlight splay over the crests of the clouds between the hills in the distance. His thoughts turn to his love for his mother and father. He pictures their faces in turn, then together with those of his siblings, in a collage of shelter and affection, wrapping them round him like a thick blanket, reminding him of where he has come from and who he is.

When the doors finally open some twenty-four hours later, he topples out frozen stiff, with his arms pinned to his side like a wooden toy soldier. It takes several hours for his cramped muscles to thaw.

'Here Istvan, take my blanket tonight,' offers Emil from the bunk below.

'No. Keep it. I will be all right,' he says through clenched teeth as he rubs his aching body.

Istvan comes to the conclusion that in order to survive and maintain what is left of his once strong physique, he must use his resourcefulness to gain favour and perhaps prevent further shedding of weight. He knows that the amount of food prisoners receive depends on how much work they complete. But even a full ration is barely enough food for survival, and the weak who do not fulfil their strict work quotas slowly starve to death. With this realisation, he changes his mindset and begins to work as hard as he can. He also decides to learn Russian and German which, when combined with his Hungarian and Romanian, will give him four groups of people he can communicate with.

Istvan's plan works. In a matter of weeks, he is made an interpreter in the camp. He is given a red armband to wear, which allows him to move freely around the camp as necessary for his new role. As he gains the acquaintance of more and more officials, he is able to acquire more food and provisions. Having even a meagre amount more than what is given to the ordinary detainees helps him to fortify his health.

A year passes, and the enterprising young Istvan proves himself to be an asset to the camp with his diligent work ethic. For this reason, combined with his interpreting role, he is given even more privileges, and this freedom allows his ingenuity to flourish with schemes for making money on the side to aid his eventual escape (getaway plans, you see, continue to be the first and last thoughts of his days and nights). Throughout the daytime, as he goes seemingly innocently about his duties, he casually gathers excess timber that is lying around the camp, and when an opportunity safely presents itself, he strategically throws the timber over the prison wall. His plan—by now typical in its recklessness—is to sneak out of camp one night to sell his timber, which happens to be in great demand as firewood in the nearby village.

One evening during his third year of internment, as he marches into the yard from an exhausting day's work, he notices the arrival of a small army truck. As the rear doors open, six frail men almost fall out. Even from a distance, he recognises his friend Radu from his first work camp, but is startled by the dramatic change in his appearance. Radu's once-thick dark hair is now matted and colourless, and his olive complexion has sallowed.

'Radu! Hey, Radu!'

Radu turns and looks at him but his empty eyes show no sign of recognition. Suddenly he collapses to his knees. Istvan runs over to help him up.

'Radu—it's me, Istvan. Remember?' But he receives no reply as Radu sinks slowly to the ground once more.

'Take him to the hospital,' a soldier orders. 'We should never have brought this one. He will be of no use; he won't live.'

Istvan and three other prisoners carry Radu to the hospital, but as visitors are forbidden, Istvan never lays eyes on his friend again.

The thick Russian snow of 1948 begins to melt and drip from the corrugated rooftops in the camp and the needles of the surrounding pine trees reluctantly let their white blanket slip in sporadic thumps onto the ground. Istvan walks about the yard and looks down at the patches of russet mud that begin appearing underfoot. *There are some things that remain constant*, he reflects. *How many more dreaded winters will I see here instead of home? But I will not be like Radu—I choose to be a survivor. Soon I will try once more to get away.*

Some days later, providence turns its hand upon Istvan, allowing his restless mind some respite from its unrelenting thoughts of escape. During a compulsory medical examination—whereby annually some fortunate detainees are classified unwell and economically inefficient—an elderly doctor strikes up a conversation with him.

'What are you doing here, son?' he asks in genuine concern. 'You are so young ...'

Istvan draws a deep breath and tells him his story.

Days pass without event. Then one evening, as he lies resting on his bed of thinning straw, yet another impassive soldier enters his dormitory and begins calling names from a list.

'Istvan König.'

Istvan stands up and joins two other men, whose eyes stare absently over the ridges of their sharp cheekbones. Impossible, he thinks. He can't be transferred again, he has done nothing wrong. Besides, there can't possibly be anywhere stricter than here. He stands behind the soldier with the list and peers over his shoulder. Now he's even more puzzled as he reads the heading 'SICK' above the list of names.

But I'm not sick ...

Within a few hours, he realises that the ink of the letters of his carefully printed name symbolised the most powerful word of all: *hope*. After more than three years in a gulag[25], nineteen-year-old Istvan again finds himself on a crowded train, only this time heading home, or so he thinks.

---

[25] Functioning from the 1920s to the 1950s, the gulag was a harsh penal system of labour camps located mainly in remote regions of Siberia and the far north of the USSR which many did not survive. Housing criminals, rich or resistant peasants arrested during collectivisation, purged Communist Party members and dissident military officers, German and other Axis prisoners of war or innocent citizens accused of disloyalty, they made a significant contribution to the Soviet economy in the Stalin period as a source of free labour for large economic projects. At its height the gulag imprisoned millions of people.

24

Istvan

1948

The temperature is sub-zero. Deemed unfit for manual labour, a hundred or so prisoners are released from a gulag somewhere near Kiev. Under minimal supervision, they are walking on a snow-covered road towards a railway station. They are of mixed nationality, but mainly Hungarian and German 'enemies of the Soviet state'. They are mostly aged, but not all—one is just nineteen. They have no hats, no coats, no gloves, only the flimsy striped pyjama-like clothes given when interned. Their bodies are numb from pain and cold, unable to feel the snow that creeps inside loose-fitting boots or seeps through worn soles. The feeble procession stumbles along, each of them grasping a section of long rope so they don't get blown away by gusts of snow. For some, however, this makeshift lifeline is not enough and the gruelling five-kilometre trek will be their last.

Once on board the train, Istvan looks around at the weathered and twisted passengers who appear as if they may turn to dust if touched. Their shoulders droop from the grime layered through their clothing. He knows they are freezing to death. He needs to take control or these people will not make the long journey, he thinks. With no guards in his carriage to stop him, Istvan huddles the passengers together to maintain their body heat and begins breaking up wooden planks of seating for a small fire he lights in a rusty, old cast-iron stove in the centre of the carriage. The passengers gather around it. They exchange no words but their eyes, saucers in their withered faces, thank him, as a meagre warmth starts to radiate into the carriage.

Each carriage is given cans of American food and a bag of raw potatoes. 'Spam,'[26] Istvan reads on the tin as he tastes it. Promptly deciding it's the best food he's had in years, he washes it down with water melted from the snow.

As the endless days and mercilessly severe nights rattle on, Istvan begins to count the stripped bodies that are being casually thrown off the train like pieces of unwanted baggage, their number steadily increasing by the day. And when the excess wood from the carriage is all but used up, he knows he needs to do more to help his people stay warm. So each time the train stops, he jumps off to gather twigs and branches from any gaps in the snow that reveal the stray woody treasures. He then dries them off as best he can with his tattered clothing, breaks them up and restocks the stove.

With the train paused once more, Istvan is busy filling his arms with firewood. Suddenly, he registers the grind of metal on metal and the groan of the engine. He runs back to the train as fast as he can, his arms laden with his fresh stockpile, which he

---

[26] Invented in 1937 by a US food company Hormel Foods Corporation, Spam is canned pre-cooked pork shoulder meat with added ham, salt, water, sugar and potato starch to bind and sodium nitrate as a preservative. It became popular in many countries as a convenient and storable protein source, especially during World War Two.

refuses to drop despite the sinking of his feet into the soft, thick snow. When he is close enough to the open door of his carriage, he tosses his prized collection on board the slow-moving train. But the train begins to pick up speed and Istvan runs frantically, trying to keep up.

'Istvan, *grab hold of my hand!*' yells one of the stronger passengers leaning out of the train and dangling his arm out to Istvan's extended fingertips. With only seconds to spare their palms interlock and they grip each other's wrists. With the help of another, he is hoisted back up onto the train.

'If we get through this journey, it will be because of you, Istvan,' says Erik, a middle-aged passenger.

'Yes, we owe you our lives …' From tragic eyes and gaunt face in the corner of the carriage comes a weak female voice.

At one point the train is purposely derailed in Poland, where the detainees are made to wait several days, anxiously watching other trains pass them by. This morning, as the night's cold wind quietens, Istvan sits mute with not knowing, as he has done for the past six days, staring out through the grimy window.

The mild winter warmth of the sun, which fractures the early fog like a shard of glass, feels soothing against his skin but does little to compensate for the suffocating pungency that hangs within the carriage. He doesn't blame his fellow passengers who would leave the train for toilet necessities if Istvan let them. But they are beholden to his authority, grateful for his direction, as if their lives hang from his words. Which they do since all but him are too weak to survive the piercing arctic temperature outside the carriage, even for a few minutes.

He sighs, as if a long sigh will ease his tension and suppress his writhing anger at the delay. Through the lifting fog, clusters of silver birch trees make an early morning appearance, rigid and ghost-like, not unlike the living cadavers inside the carriage. Soon Erik breaks into his thoughts, informing him that the trains they have made way for are returning from Germany to Russia.

'Have a good look inside as they pass, Istvan. You will see they are laden with confiscated treasures of all kind. With the war now over, it looks as if the Soviet Union is claiming her spoils of victory.'

Istvan thinks his train is heading back to Romania, but after three weeks of travelling he is surprised to find himself in the East German city of Leipzig.

'How will I get home to my mother?' he asks Erik.

'Listen, you might not be aware, but we are much more fortunate to have ended up here in East Germany, *not* Romania. If you have plans to escape the bloody communist regime, there will be less chance of getting out from Romania's strict borders. Before I was sent away, I heard of many who died trying.'

Once they disembark in Leipzig, Istvan and his travel companions become the property of the Germans. They are taken to yet another camp-like building. Istvan is put in a room and told to remove the vestiges of his shirt and pants—the same he has worn for three years—and ordered to shower. This is his first shower in that time too, and when he looks down at his naked body he is embarrassed to see it covered in lice and sores.

There are seven other men in the showers with him who are also covered with scratch marks, red sores and whose bones protrude through their thin veneer of amethyst flesh. All too quickly the soothing water is turned off and they are told—by a man wearing a mask and protective clothing—to stand with arms raised and legs apart. Each person is then sprayed with de-contaminate.

When Istvan comes out from the shower and into a room on the opposite side, he is given fresh underclothes, long pants, a shirt, a jacket and a pair of boots. He is then asked in what trade is he qualified, and realising that food is still a scarcity, he quickly answers.

'Farmer. I'm a farmer.'

25
Frici

1948

American troops enter Salzburg in May 1945. By the time Frici and Gyuri arrive, Salzburg is the centre of the American-occupied area in Austria. As the brothers make their way through the small streets of Altstadt, or the 'old town' of Salzburg, whose beautiful baroque towers and churches are tragically battle-scarred, they find a comfortable and moderately priced guesthouse named the Railway Hotel. For unlike most refugees who have no alternative but to take up accommodation in displaced persons' hostels and camps, Frici and Gyuri are, of course, used to living in style.

'The rooms are nothing fancy, but good enough.'

'I agree,' Frici replies, throwing their suitcase onto his single bed. 'I'll go and check out the bathroom down the hall.' A few minutes later he returns to their room. 'There's no light bulb in the bathroom so I went down to Reception and asked for one. The woman said that for one schilling extra you can purchase your own light bulb to take with you when you use the bathroom. Can you believe it?'

'Yes, I believe it. Anything is possible these days. I just hope they have some decent food. Did you see all the people queued at that building across the road? It must be for rations.'

During the following months of idleness, Frici, who is by nature neither patient nor idle, has taken to observing with great interest the movements of seemingly ordinary people wheeling and dealing in various goods. The brothers are now without their father's deep pockets, and are beginning to realise they will need to generate their own income. Regrettably, Frici sells his precious stamp collection for far less than its market value and the disappointment sits with him for weeks.

'Listen here, Gyuri. I didn't sell my stamps for you to waste on afternoon tea and dances at the Grande Café Winkler.'

'Oh yes? And what would you waste it on instead?' Gyuri retorts. 'Anyway, you should never have packed that stupid thing to start with.'

'You're complaining? I'm the one who carried our suitcase across Europe! And lucky I did pack it—how else could you afford your high-society girlfriend!'

Before long, Frici comes to understand that Salzburg is home to a lively black market and, after some careful asking around, finds out that American cigarettes are difficult to obtain. More importantly, large sums of money can be made from selling them across the border in Germany. His questions lead him towards a point of contact: a Polish man who is residing in one of the nearby Displaced Persons' camp. There are several such camps in and around Salzburg: Riedenburg, Camp Herzl, Camp Mülln, Bet Bialik, Bet Trumpeldor and New Palestine. Frici's enquiries lead him to the latter. As he walks through the large camp, he is surprised to hear his name.

'Frici! Hey, Frici!'

He turns to see the familiar plump outline of his friend and neighbour.

'Viktor, how did you get here?'

'Probably the same way you did,' he laughs. 'And you know who else is here? Alex Gerrard.'

'You're joking! I've travelled thousands of kilometres and find one face from next door and another from around the corner. How is our debonair friend? Smooth-talking all the girls, no doubt.'

'He's here with his mother Olga. She doesn't let him get too popular—if you know what I mean.'

'Well, it's good to see you, Viktor. Gyuri and I are staying at the Railway Hotel.'

'Hah! That doesn't surprise me. This place wouldn't be good enough for the likes of you two. What are you doing here, then?'

'I'm looking for a Mr Meyer.'

'Oh, I see. He's not a very reputable character, Frici. You'd better be careful with him.'

'Don't worry about me, I can take care of myself. Just show me where to find him.'

Mr Meyer is a pale, skeletal man whose bulging eyes and close-cropped hair suggest to Frici that he may be one of the fortunate few who escaped death in one of the notorious concentration camps, the horrifying details of which he is learning more about with each passing week. Meyer is guarded at first when Frici approaches him, but after a lengthy discussion, Frici wins his trust. Frici also convinces the old man that he is realistic enough to understand the associated risks, assuring him that it will only be a temporary assignment—merely a matter of topping up his and Gyuri's lifestyle.

Within days, under detailed instruction from Mr Meyer, Frici begins a daring escapade smuggling cigarettes across the patrolled German borders into Munich and escaping back out again.

Seduced by a temptress named chance, and not knowing that it will be a lifetime affair, Frici looks forward to—is in fact impatient for—his weekly affair, and is making good money. Along with his new friends, whom Frici meets in an isolated mountain chalet close to the German border, each time he prepares by cladding himself in a white doctor's coat, which is worn over a rucksack stuffed with as many packets of cigarettes as possible strapped onto his back. On his first expedition, he had enquired from Mr Meyer as to the why the doctor's coat.

'It's good camouflage in the snow if the border guards are around.'

Meyer didn't go on to say that these coats were the easiest white clothes to get hold of because they could be readily 'acquired' by his fellow refugees employed in the US military medical stores.

'Oh, I see,' Frici replied, having not actually pictured himself in this dangerous scenario.

Now, however, after a dozen or more expeditions without incident, as he is trying to cross an icy, shallow river by leaping from snowy rock to snowy rock, he is shocked when sudden shots ring out and begin ricocheting off the rocks around him. Stopping quickly without losing his balance takes some dexterity. His natural agility and laborious hours of football training prove invaluable. Frici drops down into the freezing water and tries to blend in with the snow-covered rocks, promptly gaining full appreciation of the purpose of the white coat. When he looks up in the direction he thinks the shots are coming from, he can make out a soldier about two hundred metres from him, rifle in hand, taking aim.

26

Istvan

1948

Some days pass in a holding camp in Leipzig when a large, barrel-chested German with heavy fists arrives and takes Istvan away to work on his sprawling dairy farm. He is given a room over a barn and, although it is scant in furnishings compared with what Istvan has endured these last three years, it is plentiful. The hearty home-cooked meals served to him three times a day slowly nourish his emaciated body and start to replenish his spirit.

'Right, Istvan, it's been two weeks. You look healthy enough now to help me with the cows,' says Herr Bauer in his clipped speech.

'Thank you, Herr Bauer. I'm keen to work and earn my keep. I'm feeling much stronger now, thanks to the good food provided by Frau Bauer.'

'Good. Tomorrow after breakfast we begin. I'll show you how to milk the cows, then take them out from the barns and across into the pasture for grazing. Then there is much to do around here until sundown, when we will round the cows up again for milking and return them to the barns for the night.'

'I know how to milk cows, Herr Bauer.'

Knowing no other life, Istvan works diligently seven days a week. He is very appreciative of the food and lodgings which he is provided with, but more so the small payment of deutschmarks he receives whenever Herr Bauer has enough to spare. Most of the couple's money comes from their busy weekend work when long queues of people travel from the city to their farm to buy milk and vegetables. In post-war German towns and cities ravaged by war, like those all over Europe, many have no money and instead bring wares to trade in exchange.

'I have more watches and my wife has more jewellery than we know what to do with,' the farmer says over dinner one weekend. 'But these people walk for many kilometres and queue up for hours with such desperate expressions. I can't say no, even though I don't want their valuables. I can only hope that when things are better, I'll be able to sell them.'

For the first time in four years, Istvan finally feels safe, warm and well fed—as if the long monochrome of winter is over and he can begin the slow mental journey from the horrors he experienced in the gulag.

'You must stop thanking me, Istvan.' Frau Bauer tucks her silvery bob behind her ears before reaching across the table to pass a second helping of potato pancakes. 'I am pleased to see you putting on weight. You were so thin when you arrived. And you're a great help to Herr Bauer too.'

After dinner, in the quiet of his small room above the barn, Istvan decides it is time to write home. He had seen others write home from the gulags, but did not wanted to burden his mother with what he had endured there, and also believed that a letter home from remote USSR would probably never find its way. He keeps his letter brief, not yet knowing if his father has returned.

Some weeks later when he walks into the homely farmhouse for dinner, Frau Bauer is smiling as she waits to greet him with an envelope in her hand.

'It looks as if you've got a letter from home.'

He reaches out to take it. Recognising the cursive script of his mother, his heart begins thumping with anticipation. He closes his eyes to gather himself, but instead sees that rainy day awash with grief when he farewelled his mother and sister. Their eyes are red and swollen. He can feel the touch of his mother's tear-soaked glove against his skin when he reaches for the basket of food … Hear the heartbreak in her voice as she calls his name through blasts of smoke as the train edges away.

Now, fingers trembling and face flushed with a rush of emotion, he tries to open the envelope without tearing its contents.

'Here, let me,' Frau Bauer offers, gently prizing the envelope open.

He takes the open letter from her and starts to read.

'It's good news! My father has been home for over three years. In fact, he only missed seeing me by a few days …' His voice trails off and his brow knits. 'What I would have given to see him. Still, I am *so* relieved to know he has been there for Mama. And she mentions where my brothers are now. Joszi and Jani are home, Ferenc is in Germany and my dear brother, Nick, is in Austria.'

Although she says nothing, the deep smile lines around Frau Bauer's luminous eyes show her happiness for her boarder.

Istvan spends the next few months working solidly for the farmer, but with the arrival of his mother's letter he has set his sights on visiting his brother Ferenc, who is nearest to him, in the southern German city of Munich. When he manages to save enough money for the train ticket, he informs his hosts that he will soon be off.

'It is time for me to leave, but I will always be indebted to you both for the kindness you showed me. I can't thank you enough.'

Clouds scud across the sky on the morning of his departure. He breathes the clear air into his lungs, savouring the fresh fragrance of damp grass, muddy farmyard and the warm breath of the milking cows. He has already packed a bag of few belongings, containing a toothbrush, spare underclothing, an extra shirt, one pair of trousers, plus a hand-knitted cardigan from Frau Bauer. Throwing the small bag over his shoulder, he says a fond farewell to her, then heads off down the drive in search of Herr Bauer who is repairing a gatepost. The farmer puts down his hammer down and shakes Istvan's hand heartily.

'Are you sure you don't need a ride?'

'No, thanks, Herr Bauer. I can walk to Leipzig station. Two kilometres is no problem for me.'

'Well, young man, good luck and have a good life. Knowing you for just a short time, I have no doubt that you will succeed in whatever you choose to do.'

Once in Munich, it doesn't take him long to find Ferenc, who, as his mother's letter informed him, is working as a cook for the US Army.

'Istvan?' Is it really you?' Ferenc shouts over the noisy clatter of kitchen pans, 'I hardly recognise you after all these years!' He wipes his hands down his white uniform and fondly embraces his brother.

'My God, Istvan, how did you find me?'

'Mama's letter ... and some asking around for a short, fat Hungarian cook. It wasn't hard. Everyone seems to know you. You're a popular fellow, Ferenc.'

'Wait around until my shift finishes and I'll take you home. It's nothing much, but these days nobody has anything fancy. You won't mind sleeping on the floor, will you?'

'Not after where I've slept since we last saw each other!'

After many years of living away from home, Ferenc is keen to return to Timişoara, talking of nothing else each evening over dinner. In the next few weeks they spend together, having made up his mind, he tries to persuade Istvan to go with him.

'No way! People are risking their lives to flee from Romania and Hungary now that they're under the communists and *you* want to return? It's craziness, I tell you.'

'Well, I'm going back. That's where our home is. What will you do?'

'I don't know where I'm going, but I do know where I've been and I'm not going back.'

Istvan cannot dissuade his brother from his decision and so, with much regret and sadness on both sides, it is soon time for Istvan to move on once more. Before separating, however, Ferenc engages the services of a local man to smuggle Istvan across the Austrian border. For the golden price of a kilogram of butter, the people-smuggler gets him securely into Salzburg, leaving him at a railway station. From there, Istvan quickly boards a train to Villach where he knows his brother Nick is living.

On board, it is cold and a rain-laden wind whips the windows. A middle-aged woman in neat but well-worn clothing is seated next to him.

'You're young,' she whispers, 'perhaps not from these parts? I only ask to see if you understand that the occupying countries have enacted new treaties across Europe and there are now fresh borders. If you are heading to Villach, you must have the relevant paperwork to cross into new territories. There are guards everywhere.'

Before he can answer, the train comes to a sudden stop, sending Istvan and the other surprised passengers lurching forward in their seats. Menacing footsteps echo down the aisle. Istvan keeps his head down but is horrified to find the footsteps have come to a standstill in front of him. He slowly raises his eyes from the polished black boots, up and over the grey jacket and leather gun holster, and into the surly face looming over him.

'Papers!' It barks. 'Where are your papers?'

27
Frici

1948

The border guard is edging closer. Frici stays down on his hands and knees in the freezing shallow river, all the while trying to keep the cigarettes dry. Never has he been so cold, the river of ice making his arms and legs ache heavily. Realising the soldier will soon be upon him and that his legs are rapidly becoming numb, he springs up with the sudden agility of a mountain cat and runs for his life. He leaps over the bullets as they reverberate off the rocks around his feet and spray across the water. He makes it to the bank and, no longer caring about his precious bounty, disentangles his arms from the straps of the backpack. He continues running frantically for several more minutes, ducking and weaving between the snow-covered pine trees as speeding missiles whiz past his head, until he realises he is safe.

Despite his brush with death, a few days later Frici decides he will make one final run, this time financing the whole deal himself so that he can make more money than the cut Mr Meyer is giving him. He can't sway Gyuri to join him, but instead persuades his friends, Viktor and Alex.

They arrive at the mountain chalet not far from the German border where Frici usually meets up with Mr Meyer and his collaborators. Just as the three young men are filling their rucksacks with the American cigarettes, and laughing as Viktor stuffs extra packets down the front of his baggy trousers, Mr Meyer enters the small room and asks them to join him for a beer in the bar.

'I wasn't expecting to see you today, Mr Meyer,' Frici says. 'I don't think we'll have time for a beer—we have to get going. Anyway, it's not the usual routine.'

'Ah, but you're the one breaking with usual routine, Frici,' he smiles. 'Just have a quick beer. It's my treat. One for the road.'

The bar is noisy and filled with smoke. Frici is somewhat apprehensive at the sight of a large number of border guards leaning on the bar, drinking raucously.

'Take it easy, Frici,' Mr Meyer says, 'this is your last foray, enjoy it.'

'Everybody here seems to know you, Mr Meyer.'

'Yes, they are ... my friends.' His bright eyes as alert as a fox's.

After they finish their beers, they head back to their small room and begin preparing again. Frici can see that Viktor and Alex are nervous.

'Just follow my lead and we won't have any problems,' he reassures them.

All goes according to plan. They make it across the border into Munich, sell their cigarettes to their contacts and return to the Salzburg chalet without incident. Then, just as they are leaving the chalet, the group are jumped from behind by a gang of border guards. Frici knows, without doubt, these guards had earlier acknowledged Mr Meyer in the bar. He struggles to break free from their strong grasp, but to no avail.

'We don't want to hurt you. Just hand over all your money and we'll let you go,' a burly one says.

'You are a stupid idiot, Frici!' Gyuri yells when they return. 'Lucky for you I've kept some money aside. I knew you couldn't be trusted. And your friends won't be staying here any longer. I haven't got enough to put them up now that you've blown almost all we own.'

After ten months of boarding at the Railway Hotel, their money all but gone, the brothers are instructed by coded letter from their father not to wait for their arrival, but to continue with the plans to leave Europe and find refuge elsewhere. Crestfallen at the thought of leaving without their parents, at the same time they realise they have reached the point of no return. So with mixed emotions they register as displaced persons with the International Refugee Organisation.[27]

They are told they can choose between the United States of America, Canada or Australia. Frici has read that Australia is bidding for the 1956 Olympic Games and, being the sports fanatic he is, argues for emigrating to that unknown land. Gyuri, surprisingly, has no preference.

Photographs are duly taken and they are instructed to return in two weeks to collect their official IRO papers and passports. They will be given train tickets to the Italian coastal city of Naples where they will await a ship that will take them away from everything and everyone they have ever known. Once back in their hotel room, Gyuri immediately writes to his parents telling them of their plans.

---

[27] International Refugee Organization (IRO) was founded in 1946 to deal with the massive refugee problem created by World War Two. In 1952 it was replaced by the Office of the United Nations High Commissioner for Refugees (UNHCR).

On arrival in Naples, the brothers are transported to a refugee camp where they find hundreds of others from all parts of war-torn Europe. Some families, Frici is told by his new friend Mario, have been in camp for up to eighteen months.

'I am here one year—*capisci?*—understand?'

Mario's animated sign language naturally aids Frici's comprehension.

'*Si*. Now I speak to you in English. Tell me if you *capisci*. My brother Gyuri, he say my English not so good. I know Mussolini second most hated man by Allies. *Numero uno*—Hitler.'

'*Si*—good.'

'But I not want to talk about war. Tell me, where can I go for the fun tonight? Somewhere with the music and the dancing and the girls—*si?*'

'I can tell you, but you will have trouble getting pass-out. What you should do, Frici, is practise your English. In Australia they speak English, you know. Here—listen to my short-wave radio. I pick up BBC from England.'

'Ah, plenty time for English on ship.'

Suddenly the BBC announcer has their full attention:

We interrupt this morning's program to bring you news of a tragic plane crash in Turin, Italy. Yesterday, Wednesday 4 May 1949, shortly after five p.m. an Italian Airlines aeroplane carrying thirty-one people, among them eighteen players from the Torino Football Club, along with officials and journalists travelling with the team, crashed into the 2,200 foot-high peak Superga on the outskirts of Turin. The Grande Torino, as they were known, had won the previous three Serie A titles and were on their way to clinching a fourth when their aircraft encountered poor visibility due to low cloud from a thunderstorm and crashed into the side of a basilica near the top of the mountain.

'You hear, Mario? This terrible, terrible news. Football team—all die.'

'More than just football team,' Mario's face is drained of colour. 'Il Grande Torino was pride of our country. Three European cups. This team was like … like … symbol of *la redenzione* for our country.'

'What mean this word *redenzione*?'

'Redemption, Frici. Learn English. That will be *your* redemption.'

Finally, after four months in the camp, where days stretch endlessly to the horizon, followed by interminably long nights fuelled by testosterone-filled, hard-spitting, card-playing men, Frici and Gyuri are relieved to receive boarding documents. They are instructed to be ready for passage to Australia on 22 May 1949.

'The *Anna Salen*, Gyuri. There it is,' Frici exclaims as he lugs their crammed suitcase towards the busy dock. He has heard that it is an old Scandinavian cargo ship turned into a temporary passenger liner. From a distance, she looks in tiptop shape, but as they get up close, pimples of rust break through the fresh layer of white paint, making futile any effort to disguise her haggard appearance.

As Frici makes his way up the gangplank, the salty air mingles with the stench of oil stinging his nostrils. Queuing, waiting to be given instructions by the crew, he lets his gaze wander, quietly observing the spectacle of hundreds of people clambering aboard in orderly chaos, all looking very alike in their well-worn attire and their faces of trepidation. The dock workers whistle as they move luggage around, while on board a crew member shouts orders to uncertain passengers. This portrait of uncertainty and desperation encircles Frici, intensified by the sound of distressed children crying as they cling to their parents' hands.

After dumping their solitary suitcase in the stifling cabin in the hull of the vessel—with no portholes for fresh air and one communal bathroom—the brothers make their way back up on deck for departure. As the old ship groans and pulls away from bustling seaport, Frici casts his eyes back for a final glimpse of the continent of his birth. He feels his parents, their absence. Silently, he asks the fading shoreline if he will ever see them again.

The clean fresh air up on deck is where the brothers spend almost the entire four-week journey, usually in conversation or playing cards with other young men of similar background, those who speak Hungarian, Romanian, German and even some English. The ship is carrying close to two thousand passengers, of whom approximately one-quarter are children. Most have come from displaced persons' camps. Some discuss their remarkable tales of escape from concentration camps or from the gulags of the Soviet Union. Others share nothing from their past.

Sometimes, in the depths of the unrelenting monotony, conversations turn acrimonious as tension builds between those who supported the fascist governments and those who had suffered or witnessed their unimaginable brutality. At such times, Frici is often keen to voice his own strongly felt political opinions—after all, he is now eighteen. But Gyuri usually ensures his confrontational younger brother stays in control, with a sharp dig of his elbow into his brother's side. Often, the tedium is simply passed staring vacantly into a choppy cobalt sea that seems to have no prospect of an end, as the ship rolls and slides towards the horizon.

The bunks are jammed so tightly into each cabin that Frici can't even sit on his bed without hitting his head on the bunk above. Most nights, he sleeps up on deck, preferring the discomfort of sitting up all night under a black sky speckled with a multitude of distant stars and the chill of the night air to the clammy overcrowded conditions below. So it is that in an uncomfortable loose canvas deck chair under the glow of a splendourous moon, he spends many a night feeling surprisingly free, while observing shipboard romances either blossom or stall.

Leaning out over the ship's railing three weeks into their journey, Frici deeply inhales the salty smell of the ocean and watches the watery undulations below gathering in intensity. Out on the horizon, clouds are slowly assembling—dark clouds that remind him of angry fists—and he knows the sea is preparing for her dance in the rain. He wanders back inside to where is brother is playing cards.

'Oh God, Gyuri. This voyage is never-ending.' He drags out a chair and slumps down next to his brother. 'Each day it seems we are no closer to that faraway line where the ocean meets the sky. Will we ever reach Australia?'

'Patience, Frici. You must have patience. We'll get there when we get there.'

'Ah! If I had money, I would buy you a dress—you sound just like Anyu!'

As it is not the smoothest of passages, there is much seasickness as well as other illnesses. Soon the brothers hear of an outbreak of measles on board. Rumours that hundreds are very ill and that five children have already died spread among the disgruntled passengers. The captain appoints twelve burly young Yugoslavs to act as police and help the crew maintain order.

The multilingual bickering over missing possessions or food allocations at times resembles a feast of frenzied animals.

'You would think that after six years of war, people would have had enough of fighting,' Gyuri comments to his brother amid the chaos.

'Even though we're all from different parts of Europe—how quickly they forget it is from one Europe that we're all leaving for the very same reason.'

'Ah Frici, it's not like you to sound so philosophical. This trip is giving you way too much time to think. By the way, do you have any cigarettes? The men want to play cards so we're betting cigarettes instead of money.'

'Very funny, you big clumsy idiot. You know I haven't touched them since they nearly cost me my life.'

Tonight, the sky is vast and black and every few minutes lightning slices through the darkness. Frici likes peering out into the cosmos. It gives him some perspective on how insignificant people—even their precious lives, their stories—might be. He is far too excited to sleep because tomorrow they are due to arrive.

On 22 June 1949, after exactly one month at sea, the *Anna Salen* finally sails between the heads and into the calm teal waters of Sydney harbour. Exhausted passengers make their way to the bow of the ship. There is only a sprinkling of children on deck, most wrapped in woollen clothes or blankets to protect them against the fresh breeze as the vessel glides towards its much-anticipated destination.

The ship sways and groans to a final stop as she docks at Circular Quay. Frici looks about the deck, hoping to finally see smiles on the faces he has come to know over the long journey, but the only other spirited people he can see are the young—those like him, in their teens or early twenties. The older passengers look on flatly, showing neither hope nor pessimism, but clearly apprehensive. Families soon begin gathering and preparing to disembark. A scattering of passengers is waving to expectant friends. But there is no such welcome for the brothers. Aged eighteen and twenty-one, and although arriving with hundreds of other nameless weary faces, they are all alone—with Frici carrying their solitary suitcase of possessions down the gangway.

'Stay together and in line,' orders a uniformed man in nasal tones of English the likes of which Frici has never heard. 'You must have your documents ready. After processing, follow an official to the waiting green and yellow buses.'

28
Istvan
1949

Being unable to produce any suitable paperwork that will allow him to cross a newly designated border in Austria, Istvan is removed from the train by an Austrian gendarmerie and taken to a nearby police station.

'Please, I have been interned for three years in a Russian work camp. They released me with no paperwork. What am I supposed to do?'

'How am I expected to know that you are who you say you are?' The tone in the policeman's voice is confusingly pleasant, catching Istvan by surprise. 'Look, son, we're all facing a new world now. The truth is hard to find and there are some whose values have been compromised, some who would act in an unscrupulous manner for payment.'

'I don't understand.'

'Let's just say that you look like a genuine refugee, but there are those who are not. Those who may be war criminals willing to do anything to escape punishment. So I need you to prove your identity in some way. Can you do that?'

'Yes, I can if you let me write a letter to my brother, Nikolaus König. He lives here in Villach. He'll be able to identify me.'

Before locking him in a large square cell with long benches and barred windows—a space that breeds the familiar odour of confined, anxious occupants—the kindly officer lets him write a letter to Nick.

Within a few days Nick verifies Istvan's identification and states that it is his brother's intention to live with him and seek work in Villach. With that, he is released into the arms of an overjoyed Nick and given temporary Austrian identification papers.

They go straight to the comfortable rooms his brother is renting from an elderly lady. As they relax and enjoy a simple meal of bread and salami, Nick expresses his delight at Istvan's arrival, and then, not keen to discuss his involvement in the war (now, nor at any time in the future), instead fills Istvan in on life in Villach.

'It is just so good to see you again! I've barely been able to sleep since your letter arrived. Though honestly, Istvan, I hardly recognise you. Your skin … the pock marks. Your weight loss. I think tomorrow I'll take you to see a doctor.'

'Ah, no doctor for me! You should've seen me before. Now I'm good. Now everything is good!'

'All right, Istvan. But I need to tell you, not everything is as good as you think. Soon you'll see that the people of Austria are struggling to find food or work or even shelter.' In comparison to most, Nick tells him, he is lucky because he has a job as a cabinetmaker in a furniture factory owned by the US Army, where he is gradually picking up English.

He arranges to leave work early the next day so that he can take Istvan to register at the local government facility that will enable him to receive food-ration coupons.

'Then I'll buy you a suit so you can look for work. It won't be easy, as I said, because so many people are struggling to find any work they can at the moment.'

It doesn't take long, however, before the enterprising Istvan finds work in a company that is building a hydro-electricity dam in the mountains, about one hour from Villach. He begins as a labourer, working all day with a jackhammer holstered to his shoulder, digging through large boulders that will eventually form a tunnel through the mountainside. Being a quick learner and a hard worker (as well as good with numbers), Istvan is soon promoted to assisting the surveyor.

A year passes by without major problems, both brothers' lives revolving around work. Oh, that's not to say there aren't occasional Saturday night dates, but Istvan has more pressing interests. Football. He's joined a local club and now Sundays can't come fast enough. Letters from home arrive every few months, but apart from writing an initial letter to say he has been with Ferenc and is now living with Nick, twenty-year-old Istvan is tardy in corresponding, preferring to leave that to his elder brother. However, despite both young men working hard and managing well, with the depressed environment and the haunted, hungry faces that confront them at every street corner, there is little to tempt them to remain permanently in a country stripped bare of its lustre and opportunities into the foreseeable future. It's Nick who first broaches the subject of leaving Europe and emigrating to America.

'Tomorrow, Istvan, we should go to the US embassy and ask how to get passage to this land that promises "liberty and hope". What do you say?'

'Sure. Why not.'

'Sorry fellas,' the uninterested US official drawls. 'Can't process your paperwork. We've reached our full quota of immigrants for the year. Go across the street and try the Canadian embassy.'

But when they try to register for migration to Canada they are met with the same response. This time, however, they are told they should try the Australian embassy.

A few weeks after registering with the immigration department for refugee status in Australia, they receive a letter with relevant documentation and tickets, informing them to board a train for the Italian coastal city of Naples, where without delay they will board a waiting ship that will take them halfway around the world to their new country of residence.

The brothers feel both a tremendous surge of excitement but at the same time apprehension, not knowing what the future will hold in this unknown country, so far from everything and everyone they have ever known. As they leave Austria for Naples, it hits them with profound sadness that they may never see their parents again and cannot even see them or talk to them before their departure.

One evening, as their ship makes its six-week passage to Sydney, the brothers sit quietly assessing and picking at their dinner when the hush is broken by the yelling of a German woman who carries her little daughter hitched high on her hip. She is demanding to see the captain.

'Why are your officers all drinking hot chocolate, when my little Renata goes without milk?' she shouts at the captain as he approaches.

'Quiet, please, madam. No need to shout and upset your fellow passengers. Come with me, we shall get her some milk,' he replies, as he ushers her away from the busy cafeteria.

'He's doing his best to placate the enraged woman before the rest of us joins in,' Nick whispers to his brother.

'Yes, he doesn't want a mutiny,' Istvan chuckles.

The route takes them via the narrow hundred-mile stretch of Suez Canal and the ship docks for a day at Cairo for supplies. However, the passengers are not permitted to disembark. Istvan is intrigued by the sights of this arid, sandy landscape. Never before has he seen such exotic colours: men and women clad in hues of sultry sunsets, their loose-fitting clothes flowing softly in the dusty wind, tall baskets balanced precariously on their heads. The aromas, too, intrigue him—so far removed from the familiar culture of his boyhood.

Hanging over the ship's rail, he watches with a wry smile as beggars run alongside the ship, crying out for alms from the already deprived passengers. At one point he laughs out loud when he observes a hawker persuade an elderly German to buy his wife a pair of shoes.

'Send money down pegged to this pulley-rope and I send you up shoe,' yells the hawker.

The old man obliges but when he opens the bag that was sent back up to him via the rope system it contains only one shoe.

'The second shoe!' he calls down to the hawker. 'Send up the second shoe!'

'You want more shoe, you must send more money!' yells the turban-clad vendor.

Feeling sympathetic, Istvan strolls over to calm down the agitated man.

'Those fellows can't be trusted. Forget about it now—there's nothing you can do. My name is Istvan,' he says, offering his hand.

'Yep, he stung me all right,' the man replies, pounding his fist on the ship's rail. Then turning towards Istvan, his frown fades. 'But you're right, no point worrying now. I've noticed you around, Istvan. My name is Mr Schulz.'

They begin talking and, before long, are sharing their histories and aspirations.

'Why do you and your wife want to make such a long trip to Australia?' Istvan asks.

'Why indeed? Perhaps you think we are too old to want a new life?'

'No. That's not what I meant.'

'Well, maybe not, but regardless … these eyes have seen too much, Istvan. For too long men have been killing each other in Europe. And although I lived in the countryside, where the fields look green … they are bloodstained. So I go because Australia has none of my history, and I like that.' Leaning over the rail, he makes a broad gesture with his hands. 'It's spacious, and I believe it to be civilised. At this time in my life, I want for nothing more.'

With the sun searing down upon them hour after hour, Istvan decides he's had enough of the relentless heat and, ignoring his older brother's disapproval, climbs over the rail and dives into the tempting waters. Within minutes he is ordered to get back on board the ship and is severely reprimanded by the captain. He takes it all in his stride—even the ire of the captain cannot dampen the reignited glint of his youth. Now, for the first time since he was sixteen, he feels free and excited about where his travels are taking him. He knows he has to live by instinct and feels inferior to no one.

'Nick, I am just so happy to be heading to a new life. It's hard to describe but … it feels as if I've finally come out of a long dark tunnel. Do you know what I mean?' He wipes himself dry with his shirt. 'Right now, as I dry myself, I feel as if I'm shedding my skin and all my scars … They're all gone.'

'Yes, yes. How you survived … I can't begin to imagine. But let's not talk about the past. Let's look only forward. And Istvan, we have time on this long voyage for you to learn some English. The sooner you learn the basics, like me, the better it will be when we get to Australia.'

As the *SS General Muir* sails into Sydney harbour on 16 March 1950, the glimmer of the early morning sun lights a corridor that seems to guide the vessel across the harbour waters towards its destination. Istvan leans over the railing and lets the breeze kiss his skin and the warmth of this new land welcome him. The brothers, weary from the long voyage, are anxious to disembark. As the ship draws closer to Circular Quay, hundreds of passengers make their way to the bow where conversations gradually cease as a current of anticipation travels through the crowded deck. The ship sails by small coves with sandy beaches, past large tracts of parklands with sprawling green lawns that meet the water's edge and around a tiny island with an old brick fort, before weaving its way through slow-moving craft with green hulls ferrying groups of passengers. Nick whispers in awe into his brother's ear but receives no reply. Istvan is mesmerised by the sight of a magnificent steel arch bridge that spans the full width of the harbour.

SYDNEY, AUSTRALIA

1
Frici

1949

As Frici queues with the rest of the immigrants who have come ashore from the *Anna Salen,* the line is endless, but his self-discipline is not. He shuffles from foot to foot, peers over heads and around shoulders, counts how many in front, curses under his breath. Finally, as he nears the counter a young female officer takes to a loudspeaker.

'Welcome to Sydney, Australia. Thank you for your patience.' Is it his imagination or do her eyes fall directly upon him?

'Please have your documents ready. Once you have been processed, you will be escorted to waiting buses. You will then be transported three miles to Central Railway Station, after which you will be placed on a train that will take you to a migrant hostel in the western New South Wales town of Bathurst. The train trip will take approximately six hours. Australia's immigration rules and regulations will be outlined to you once you arrive in Bathurst.'

The rickety train trip is a long one. Staring out through the smudged and dusty window, Frici's throat becomes increasingly parched. His only distraction is the immense landscape with scattered dwellings and tall grey tree trunks with metallic green foliage unlike any he has seen before. Because he wants to take it all in without distractions, he becomes irritated by the fingerprints that now interrupt his view and frustrated that the sticky panes refuse to give way to his efforts to slide them open. As the hours linger inside the cramped carriage, he grows desperate for the light breeze that occasionally filters through the carriage doors which don't quite meet, or comes in through the concertina of small windowpanes in the rows in front.

On arrival at the migrant hostel, Frici and Gyuri agree that the camp resembles military barracks fashioned from old corrugated iron sheds. The camp director, a rugged, loud ex-military man, introduces himself and the senior staff who are responsible for the administration of the camp. Frici is tired from the long journey and his mind starts to wander. How amusing, he thinks: the catering officer looks plump, the hygiene officers look dirty, the watchman sleepy, the butcher beefy and the plumber is dripping with sweat. At least the medical staff look efficient. Controlling himself just before he laughs out loud, he turns his attention back to the camp director.

'Everyone will be given a list of the camp rules and a camp pass. However, you are not allowed to permanently leave camp until you can prove you have sponsorship for employment. Please take the time to familiarise yourselves with the rest of the rules. We all need to abide by the rules if we are to live together and maintain order. For those who require assistance with translation, an interpreter will be provided. In the coming days, English classes will be set up. Please line up now to receive your provisions. After you have unpacked, please make your way to the canteen, where a meal will be served. Thank you for your attention.'

Again Frici has to wait as each new resident is allocated a

stretcher bed, a thin mattress, two blankets, two sheets, one pillow and two pillowslips, one towel, two plates, one mug and a wash tub. Unmarried men and women are then separated into single-sex barracks, while married couples and their children are accommodated in long dormitories, separated by the thinnest of partitions. Bathrooms, laundries and dining rooms, they are informed, will be shared.

Having spent just as many hours studying English as Frici has devoted to football, Gyuri can speak and read it fluently. As they sit down to their first meal in the busy canteen, he begins to read out the camp rules: 'You must attend all meals promptly. You must clean your lodgings for daily inspection. You must take care of all camp equipment and report any damage.'

'Is there a rule saying that we must eat this stuff they call food?' Frici interrupts his brother as he attempts to saw through a tough and unfamiliar piece of meat.

A canteen orderly is clearing trays near the end of the trestle table at which the brothers sit.

'You've gotta speak English here, wogs, or you won't get on.'

The colour rises in Frici's cheeks—even with his limited knowledge of English he can grasp that 'wogs' is not a compliment. He pushes his chair back abruptly and stands. Gyuri stands too. Then he abruptly grabs his brother by the arm, and leads him out of the canteen.

As the days progress, the brothers begin making plans to leave without permission from the camp authorities. They have the name and address of a friend of Sigismund's who he studied with in Crasna and who now lives in Sydney. Before they left Salzburg, Sigismund had written to them with the contact details and informed them that he had also written to his friend,

Dr Green. They are not entirely sure if the letter ever made it past the Romanian authorities, but knowing their father, they are sure he would have been very selective in his use of language.

'I think we should go and find this Dr Green,' Gyuri says.

'Yes, we must try. But how do we get back to Sydney without money?'

'We'll hitchhike.'

As the wind sweeps the ochre dust between the joins in the identical walls of corrugated iron and into the suitcase Frici is packing, his annoyance rises to the surface.

'Look, orange everywhere,' he says, shaking out another pair of trousers.

'Keep your voice down. We don't want anyone to know we are packing.'

Picking up the unwieldy suitcase that he has lugged across Europe for over a year, its weathered handle breaks free from the bag's grasp.

'Gyuri, how do you say a bad word in English?'

'Damn.'

'You sure? I thought I heard an 'f–something'. But all right, damn! The suitcase is broken. Now I must carry it … like so,' he says hurling it up on his shoulder.

'Great, now you really look conspicuous. Come on, follow me. And don't speak to anyone.'

Gyuri leads the way between the rows of barracks and towards the camp exit. As he approaches the watchman's shed, he peers inside then turns back to Frici smiling. He closes his eyes and tilts his head on his hands to simulate sleeping. When Frici catches up, he looks inside the small shed.

'I knew it—a sleepy watchman,' he laughs.

When they arrive at Dr Green's consulting rooms and give their names to the receptionist, the doctor comes out to greet them immediately.

'Come in, come in, boys.'

Underneath his unbuttoned white coat, the doctor's crisp white shirt and blue tie—held neatly in place by a silver tie pin—are immaculate. His age and dapper appearance remind Frici of his father. He pats Frici warmly on the back as he ushers them into his office.

'I've been expecting you. Didn't know when I'd see you, but I knew it was only a matter of time. Sit down and tell me everything. How and where are your dear parents?'

Gyuri recounts their escape from Timişoara and their fourteen-month wait for their parents in Europe before setting sail for Australia.

'Oh dear. I only wish you had all left when my family did … before this ungodly nightmare.'

When the Nazis take power in Germany in 1933, the next few years see Dr Green's family paying close attention to the creature of fascism and the spread, like tentacles, of anti-Semitism. They already have family living in Australia, so when they discover that the Australian government is permitting entry to Jews who want to immigrate as 'victims of oppression', they quickly take advantage of the visas before the outbreak of war.

It wasn't all plain sailing, though, as Dr Green's Hungarian medical qualifications were not recognised by Australian authorities. He, therefore, had no alternative but to go back to university and do a six-year medical degree all over again. After studying long hours each day, he worked late-night shifts and weekends as a hospital orderly, to support his family.

'Now, tell me how I can help you boys?' the kind doctor asks. Gyuri replies that they have nothing and know no one. If he were able to assist them find somewhere to live and some form of employment, as well as a small loan to tide them over, they would be most grateful.

The doctor makes some phone calls right there and then. In due course, he replaces the heavy, black telephone receiver and instructs them to go and see a Mr Brown, who has rooms to let in Birrell Street, Bondi.

'You boys will like the beachside suburbs around Bondi. They've become a hub for many Hungarians, Romanians and Polish immigrants since the war.'

As directed, they catch a tram from the city to Bondi Road. The terrace-style boarding house appears rambling and old in comparison with some of the more modern buildings they have seen, but once inside they are surprised to see how well it is maintained.

After Mr Brown has shown them around and introduced them to the other boarders, the brothers retreat to their own one-bedroom flat which includes a tiny kitchenette.

'Even though we have to share the bathroom, this place is like a palace compared with where we've been, Gyuri,' Frici says.

He notices that inlaid on the front of the cupboard door is a bevelled oval mirror. It has been a while since he's had a decent-sized mirror from which to glimpse his eighteen-year-old image. He looks a little ragged around the edges, but for the first time since leaving home, he feels a certain stability. Yes, a new life in a new country ... what many would give to be so lucky!

'We mustn't waste a precious day, Gyuri. Live life to the full, that's what I intend to do.'

'What? Give it a rest, Hercules.'

With their surname already officially changed to 'Loew', the brothers hope to blend in even further by adopting 'Fred' and 'George' as their first names. It takes some getting used to for Frici, who finds it strange to call his brother something entirely new—except, of course, in jest or mockery.

Dr Green has arranged for them to begin work in a steel foundry not far from their new residence, starting immediately. But after only one week grinding away in the heat and noise, George decides that the work is too physically demanding.

'I'm going to ask the landlord if I can drive his taxi like some of the other residents,' he informs Fred. 'You're too young to get a taxi licence, but I overheard the men talking about a store in the city that makes confectionary and sells nuts. It's owned by a Jewish man—he's looking for a young trainee.'

'All right,' Fred relents. 'I'll go. It's not the hard work that concerns me—but then we both know who the stronger of us is. I know I'll only end up in a fight without you at the foundry. The way the Australians make fun of my accent and my rye bread and salami really makes me furious.'

Located in the Strand Arcade in the city, the Nut Shop is only a short bus trip for him from Bondi. The owner, Mr Mendels, is a small, balding man with owl-like spectacles that match his round head. Over the next few weeks, Fred is taught how to make various toffees, boiled candies and sugar-coated nuts, as well as how to serve customers. Mr Mendel's son Paul is a year older than Fred, and the pair soon discover they share a passion for soccer—as the Australians call football—and cars.

Fred works for several years at the Nut Shop, but as soon as he turns twenty-one and is old enough to get a taxi licence, he commences driving one of Mr Brown's cabs on the weekends. He works hard, and being young, single and without parental supervision, plays just as hard. Most of his wages are spent on expensive suits and Italian-made shoes, as shortly after his coming-of-age in April 1952, he is already enjoying a Saturday night ritual of dressing up to go out to upmarket nightclubs.

'After all,' he says to George one night as he slides his bow tie into place and slips on his dress jacket, brushing flecks of lint off its shiny black lapels, 'I have to look the part if I'm to pick up any girls.'

He finishes dressing and hurries out the door so that he can catch a lift from the replacement driver to the city, as he does every week.

Standing in the foyer of Chequers Night Club, Fred looks down into the cabaret room, the encased mirrored walls amplifying the swollen crowd of animated people. He experiences his usual rush of excitement and anticipation. The conductor picks up his baton and the brass band dressed in their red sateen dinner jackets begins belting out a tune. He skips down the staircase to the trumpet's ritzy beat of 'Fly Me to the Moon', each step bringing him closer to his anticipation of an evening that will take him into the small hours of the next morning. Leaning against a mirrored wall, he acknowledges the proprietors and regulars, who he is now on a first-name basis with, as he observes the couples swaying to the bluesy tune.

His eyes are drawn to the stage as a heavy-set saxophone player steps forward and begins a solo rendition of 'Somewhere over the Rainbow'. To and fro his body arches as his cheeks puff and flood with colour. The instrument gleams under the spotlight, producing a texture of bright notes and mellow tones that demand everyone's attention and culminate in jubilant applause. The clink of glasses and peals of laughter from women seated in a lounge booth near Fred attract his attention. Each of the three women is clad in an elegant cocktail dress: golden-rose flocked taffeta, beige lace with sweetheart neckline, hot pink strapless chiffon. Mmm … each one is worthy of inspection, he thinks, as the subtle wafting of their cigarette smoke lingers in the air.

Before long, his Saturday night ritual evolves as he finds himself spilling out onto Goulburn Street, following the seamy crowd further along the road to the nearby illegal gambling casino: the Goulburn Club. He would never have stumbled upon its inconspicuous metal-grille door on his own but he is propelled by the click of high heels and musk-scented dress suits.

One night, Fred is recognised and is immediately allowed in with his loud friends, all glad to escape the cold of the small hours. The girls must be freezing in their lace and fineness, he thinks, as he catches the group's reflection in the mirror that panels the corner of the L-shaped stairway. The landing opens out onto a grand room. As he enters, Fred's heels sink into the velvet of the lime-green carpet. Waiters carrying trays of drinks and tempting morsels of food move around a swarm of people dressed very stylishly, but whose brazen behaviour betrays their lack of class, as elbows prod, push and shove to get closer to the action. The waiters seem to glide through the crowd, only pausing each time a hand reaches forward to lighten their consignment. Copious food and drink are, of course, supplied *gratis* to entice patrons through the door.

In one corner is an enormous roulette table, surrounded by a circle of focused individuals, some of whom sit on stools while others stand—all with varying stacks of red and green gaming chips kept in close check. Fred is mesmerised by the scene.

'No more bets,' the croupier announces with a spread of his upturned hands.

A woman cheers. She holds a single daisy between her fingers, which she places in her lap as she leans forward and smiles with entitlement at the croupier. Her chiffon-covered arms encircle three high stacks of chips and she draws them towards her chest the way a cat would her young. Forcing himself to look away, Fred takes in the many other dice and card tables, each lined with inscrutable faces, wads of cash in front of them.

With time, he discovers other illicit gambling rooms, the Celebrity Club in York Street and the Carlisle Club in Kellett Street becoming two of his favourites. He finds himself drawn not only by the lure of his old temptress, chance, but also by the thrill of prohibition. Front doors to clubs such as these are usually indistinguishable from their neighbours, apart from square little casements covered with metal grating that face the street. After knocking, the small insert is cautiously opened, allowing men with extremely unpleasant faces to scrutinise punters before granting admission. A dimly lit staircase then leads to a hive of clandestine activity. Soon the clubs all look the same to Fred, as do their inhabitants. However, there seems to be a current of adrenalin that flows throughout these establishments—a magnetic attraction that lures him, arousing feelings of excitement and euphoria … but later it will bring drama, conflict and entrapment.

One day at work in the Nut Shop, the owner's son Paul introduces Fred to a talent scout for Hakoah, the first grade soccer team in eastern Sydney. Without hesitation, Fred signs up.

At the same time as his football career is regaining traction, he and George have become a part of the Sydney horseracing scene. It doesn't take long for Fred to work out that by becoming a starting price (SP) bookmaker, he can use his contacts from his gambling world to build a clientele base. It's just a matter of setting up a phone line in their boarding rooms, he assures George. Some of his friends from the boarding house and soccer team are eager to be part of the action, so he decides to take them on as agents and give them a ten per cent cut.

Arriving for work one morning, he heads straight for the small caged lift, behind the ornate wooden staircase of the arcade, where his friend Ray works. He finds him seated on his stool in the corner. Usually, as he passes by the lift on his way to or from work, they enjoy sharing a joke or brief chat.

'G'day Fred. Want to go for a ride?'

Knowing Ray is a chancer—like himself—he hops inside the lift.

'I've got a proposition for you, mate.'

In the time it takes for the barred enclosure to go up to the third floor and back down, Fred explains his scheme, all the while watching Ray's expression change as the moving cables cast weird shadows across his face.

'Well, what do you say? Do you want in?' he asks, as the lift jolts to a stop.

'You bet I do—I've got nothing to lose, have I!' Ray replies, using both arms to hoist his body higher up on his stool.

Pleased with the outcome, Fred races off to work. Along the way, he thinks back to the day Ray volunteered what had caused the loss of his right leg and right eye. He only ever spoke about it once, proudly telling Fred that he had enlisted as soon as war was declared.

'I trained as a pilot in the RAAF and was sent to England. Flew in the RAF under Fighter Command 11 Group, I did. Battle of Britain. That was until a damned Jerry got me.'

'Jerry?'

'Ha! Jerry was our nickname for the Germans. Well, a Jerry from the Luftwaffe sent me crashing to earth over south-east England. Lucky to be alive, really.'

'Incredible! I feel honoured to know you, Ray.'

'Ah! Nothing honourable about me, Freddie. We've all had it rough. What about your lot, eh?'

On a balmy Saturday afternoon, as Fred is playing centre-back, his concentration drifts with thoughts of what George is doing on the betting phone line. When the opposing side is awarded a corner kick, however, Fred's attention returns as he must mark a nimble striker. In the air, Fred has got a full head and shoulders on his opponent and easily heads the ball well away from the goal, but on the way back down the striker gives him a sharp elbow directly on the bridge of his nose. He falls to his knees, tasting blood and jerking him back to his after-school fights in Timişoara. The pain is intense, but he ignores it and gets to his feet, furious. Grabbing the striker by the collar he gives him a sound beating, after which he is called over by the referee and unceremoniously sent off. Once inside the dressing sheds, he cleans himself up and dresses. Checking his reflection in the change-room mirror, his nose is huge and his eyes are beginning to puff up. But, on hearing the half-time whistle, he forgets his pain and dashes to the nearest phone to contact George.

'You have to be careful running off like that every week, Fred,' a teammate says on his return. 'The coach is getting annoyed when you're not around for the team talk.'

'I have to contact George and give him instructions.'

'Can't he handle it himself? What instructions do you need to give him?'

'It's to do with the larger bets,' his voice sounding more nasal with each syllable. 'It's about knowing the odds—seizing your chances—and I'm better at gauging these things, you see.'

2
Istvan

1950

Not only imperturbable but patient too, Istvan fills the tedium of the lengthy disembarkation process joking with Nick and their new friends made at sea. Although the brothers share the same spirited character and enthusiasm for work, they couldn't be less alike in appearance. Istvan, now twenty-one, is pleased to have regained his former muscular build. Never one too fussed with his appearance, he does take time each morning, however, to tame his thick tresses into a fashionable 'pompadour' wave, but after that everything is done without bother: shave, splash on the masculine scent of Old Spice and dress without too much fuss. The haughty head tilt and wry half-smile—not to mention confident swagger—all come effortlessly.

Nick is smaller in stature, with a more subtle profile than the typically Slavic facial breadth of Istvan and the other brothers. Living with Nick is an eye-opener for Istvan. Observing him painstakingly tending to his toiletry—combing every strand of his fine dark hair back from his forehead, followed by an efficient rubbing of hands with Brylcreem, which he then meticulously slicks onto his sculpted mane—almost drives Istvan crazy. Oh, yes, they are different in appearance and taste, Istvan thinks, as they stand in line at Circular Quay and the lavender-citrus scent of Tabac floats in Nick's wake.

Along with several hundred other immigrants from the *SS General Muir*, they are transferred by bus to Sydney's Central Station, where they are informed they will be boarding a train that will take them to a migrant camp in a town called Bathurst. As they wait under the covered archway, the concourse swarms with other travellers, most of whom are well dressed: men in grey flannel suits and matching fedora hats carrying folded newspapers underarm; women in cashmere twin-sets over pencil-pleat skirts with pillbox hats, white gloves, court shoes all finished off with mandatory strings of pearls. Istvan admires the scene before him for several minutes, until a rattling red train groans to a halt and his group is ordered to board.

Although still in yet another restrictive holding camp, Istvan is determined not to let it blemish his optimism for life in this adopted country. Unlike those around him who complain incessantly about the conditions in the camp, he finds an energy that manifests itself in his every stride as he swaggers about the buildings. So it's not the environment that he has difficulty with, but rather the enforced idleness. It takes just a few short weeks before the enterprising brothers make plans to leave the sparseness and inertia of the countryside.

Despite knowing it is against immigration policy to permanently leave camp without providing proof of sponsorship or employment, under a heavy autumn rain as the wind jangles the corrugated tin around him, Istvan pulls the collar of his jacket up around his neck and prepares to leave. Each brother with their one small suitcase in hand exit the camp without notice and walk the short distance to the station, where they make their way back to Sydney paying their fares with the little money remaining from their hard work in Villach.

On board the train, as the town of Bathurst becomes a speck on the horizon, Istvan turns to his brother and asks, 'When we get to Sydney, Nick, what will we do then?'

'When we arrived at Circular Quay, I overheard some people talking about a migrant centre at a place called Lindfield. It's somewhere in Sydney. I'm sure we'll have more chance of finding work in the city. Let's find out how to get there.'

It is late afternoon by the time the train arrives at Central Station. They join the bustling peak-hour commuter crowd until they come to a bright-red neon sign that flashes 'KIOSK', and ask the man behind the counter how to get to Lindfield. He shows them where to change platforms and take the line to Sydney's northern suburbs. The setting sun sends a burnt orange haze across the horizon as the train rattles across the Harbour Bridge. There is just enough light left in the day for Istvan to see through the grey metal lines of this engineering wonder and below to the tiny white sails and hulls of slow-moving boats.

Once at Lindfield, after asking directions again, they find their way to the centre on foot. From the way in which the exasperated immigration officer stamps their papers, issuing them temporary residence in what appears to be disused army barracks, it's obvious the man is not at all pleased with their foray. Within a few days, they are summoned back to his office.

'Pack your belongings, lads. After breakfast you'll be boarding a bus. The Metropolitan Water and Sewerage Drainage Board have commissioned several hundred single male immigrants to dig trenches for a new sewerage project in Wollongong.'

'Where is this place, Wollongong?' Nick asks.

'Sunny coastal town a couple of hours south of here. Actually, too nice an area for reffos like youse.'

Istvan is ecstatic to receive his first week's wage.

'Nick?' he calls as he runs in search of his brother between the hundreds of tents where he and a further two hundred refugees are accommodated.

'Three pounds. Is this good money here in Australia?'

'Not exactly good, but it's a start. Only way we can go from here is up. And Istvan, here your name is Steven. Nick is the same in English, but from now we should call you Steven.'

In the mess tent that evening, Steven overhears two men at the end of their trestle table speaking Hungarian. He approaches them and introduces himself, inviting them to join him and Nick.

'Nick, this is George Nagy, and his friend Major. They're cabinetmakers like you.'

With much in common, all four bond immediately and before long are working alongside each other in the same trench. Nick, George and Major find the labouring heavy-going, but not so Steven who often works up such a sweat, he strips down to his shorts, soaks a handkerchief in water and ties each corner in knots before placing it over his head.

A couple of weeks go by, then one day the manager of the Water Board project approaches the trench where the brothers are digging. He introduces them to the director of Berryman Furniture, who says he has heard on the grapevine about these cabinetmakers who are digging trenches. He offers them jobs and asks them to return to Sydney with him that same day.

'Yes, yes. But I won't go anywhere without my brother,' Nick insists.

The director takes a hard look in Steven's direction—clearly noting a strong, hardworking young man with lots of potential. Wasting no time, he beckons him out of the trench.

Later that day, after showing them around the factory, the director takes them to a nearby block of land full of caravans and simple shed homes.

'We employ the men who are living there temporarily—some with their families—until they get themselves established,' he says, before taking them over to a pile of building material. 'Here's some timber. Build yourselves a house.'

In time, it comes to Steven's attention that one of the on-site caravans houses a large family of German origin. The father is also employed as a cabinetmaker. Steven is keen to meet him because one of his daughters has caught his eye. So, one afternoon, Steven hurries to clock off, intent on catching up to the dark-haired lanky man as he makes his way to his makeshift home.

'Hello, my name is Steven,' he says, putting out his hand to shake.

'William Heidrichas,' comes the wary reply. 'Where you come from, Steven?'

'Romania. You?'

'Born Germany, but most my life I was living Lithuania. My wife—she is born in Lithuania.' As they approach his caravan, he stops and adds, 'I am not staying much longer here. I have bought a small brick home in Hillsdale. You must come to dinner—meet my family before we go.'

'Thank you. I would love to,' Steven replies eagerly.

A few days later, Steven receives an invitation from his co-worker to come to dinner that evening. Arriving punctually at the family caravan, he is welcomed in and introduced to the whole family.

'Steven, this is my wife, Stefania. My eldest daughter Aldonna and her husband Bob. They are living in Malabar. And this is my daughter—also Stefania—but we call her Steffie. And my three sons: Albert, Louis and Paul.'

'Very nice to meet you,' Steven says offering a bunch of flowers to Stefania, who accepts them with a nod. Without making eye contact, she turns her stout frame away and disappears with the flowers. As the evening progresses, he is led through to two additional rooms that William has built onto the side of the caravan in order to house his large family. Seated tightly around a laminated table, Steven makes pleasant conversation in German with William's sons, whose slim builds and dark hair resemble their father's. However, other than let his gaze momentarily meet hers or purposely brush hands as she passes the platter of schnitzel, he cannot engage the vivacious Steffie. William's wife does not sit with them to eat, only appearing at the table to bring food or clear plates. She has few words to say all evening and Steven is surprised by her curt manner. After a filling meal completed with the flakiest, most buttery apple strudel he has ever tasted, Steven gravitates towards Steffie, whose quick-witted conversation with her brothers only intensifies his interest.

'Why don't we go outside where it's cool?'

She shyly agrees and shows him outside, letting the wire screen door close behind her with a slap.

'Your mother—she doesn't like me so much.'

'Mutti? Oh, that's nothing,' she gestures with a wave of her hand. Then brushing her dark curls from her hazel eyes, she adds, 'She is the same with everyone. She's had a very hard life—you know—during the war.'

'I understand.'

'You speak German good. I will explain in German. My English is not so good.'

'Ja. Sprich doch Deutsch mit mir, Steffie.'

'Well,' she begins more naturally in her native tongue, 'trying to raise all of us children on her own during the war, it was very difficult—you would understand how poor the living conditions were then and especially afterwards. Food rations and all. And Mutti—actually all of us—lived knowing that we didn't dare say what we thought, especially to strangers. We never knew who we could trust. I think in trying to shelter us and herself, she has become a bit reclusive.

'What made your family come to Australia?'

'Just like you and your friends, I suppose,' she replies with a shrug of her shoulders. She pauses, as if reflecting for the first time on the reasons, or weighing up whether to trust this man she has only just met.

'We came in the hope of a better life.' She pauses. 'This is not something I generally talk about, but I feel I can trust you,' she smiles, suddenly warming to his attention.

He is taken by her charming dimples as she smiles up at him.

She continues with her story, telling him that even though her family lived in Lithuania, her father was German by birth, which meant he was forced to join the German army after Lithuania was invaded. The rest of her family was then taken to Germany and made to live in a camp with other foreign German families whose husbands or fathers were forced to enlist.

'Ausländer, that's what they called us—we came from nowhere, we were foreigners. Some of the women in the camp

convinced their children that war was necessary, that Hitler and his men should be revered.'

Not an uncommon theme throughout Germany, of course, but her father was a pacifist, with no choice but to comply.

'Powerless to the Nazi wartime machine, was how Papa described it,' she concludes.

'That's how I felt after the war when I was forced to leave my mother and sister behind. I was sent to a Russian labour camp for three years,' Steven replies with his gaze fixed firmly on the middle distance.

'Not many survived the gulags, I'm told,' Steffie replies, her voice subdued but sympathetic.

'I was lucky—that's all.' Then, after pausing for thought, he adds, 'Although, I remember thinking to myself that I *must* survive. You see, I just couldn't bear the thought of my mother receiving bad news.'

'Did you see your family before you came here with your brother?'

'No. Once I was free, I had to make another choice. And when I learnt that my father and brothers had returned home, I knew my mother would be all right. So I chose not to return to my family in Romania. With the Russians in control, I knew I would be punished—maybe gaoled or even sent back to a gulag—so really I just couldn't go back.'

'I can see that you really didn't have a choice, but it must have been so difficult to leave your family behind.'

'It was and yet it wasn't, if that makes sense! The way I justify my decision is that I believe it's what my parents—especially my father—would have wanted for me. To be free. As you said earlier: to make a new life … and a better life.'

'Do you think that one day your parents might come here so you can all be together?'

'Who knows? I hope I can work hard and save enough money to get them safely out of there. I really miss them. All of them, even my crazy brothers,' he laughs, trying to disguise his emotion. 'Anyway, enough about me. Keep going with your story.'

There is something about her soulful eyes and disarming smile that makes him feel at ease inside, as he watches her continue.

'When Hitler's war began to fail and Germany was under fierce attack—bombs falling from the sky every day—Mutti thought we would all be killed, for sure. So she decided to flee to Poland to live with my aunt. For many years we did not know if Papa was alive or dead. But when the Russians took control of Poland,[28] Mutti decided to flee again. She and my aunt fled into Lebenstedt, which had become a safe city in Germany—you know, in the British zone. It took Papa two years of searching after the war ended, but incredibly he traced us. And once we were all finally reunited, Papa desperately wanted to begin afresh and take his family to a country that was as far from the horrors he'd experienced during the war as possible. And a country that wouldn't hold grudges against him as a German, too.'

Wanting to save up to secure a future in his new country and being the son of a father who believes a man rolls up his sleeves and works hard, Steven is on the lookout for after-hours work in addition to his fulltime job. So on weekends he begins touring the Hungarian communities of Sydney to ask if he can help with renovations or new buildings. Very quickly, through word of mouth, he has jobs covering almost every weekend, yet still

---

28 Near the end of World War Two, the advancing Soviet Red Army pushed out the Nazi German forces from occupied Poland.

somehow maintains his vitality and enthusiasm for his week-day job at Berryman Furniture.

Very soon he is happy to be earning the princely sum of six pounds a week at Berryman. In addition, whenever he completes his assorted weekend jobs, he has extra cash—most of which he prides himself on his ability to carefully save. However, now that he is dating Steffie, for the first time he is conscious about his appearance and wonders if perhaps he smartens his style, maybe he can even make headway with the implacable Mutti. So early one Saturday morning he catches a tram into the city to the large department store, Mark Foys.

After trying on several suits, Steven settles on two: a grey flannel one with wide lapels and the standard cuffed pants, and a basic black one with a double-breasted vest.

'The gold buttons really set off the contrasting colour of the tan vest,' the salesman assures him. 'Now you just need to add a black-and-white spotted tie, like this one ... And with the grey suit, may I suggest a bolder new fashion maroon silk?'

'Yes. Good. I'll take both.'

'And in the pocket, sir, a plain white handkerchief is worn like so ... There. Perfect.'

Finally, he slides on a pair of black-and-white wingtip shoes and asks the salesman to bring him some gold cufflinks for his white shirts. Turning from side to side, even he has to admire the suave reflection he cuts in the long mirror. Apart from the brown suit Nick bought him in Austria, these are the first good clothes he has ever owned—all his life, he has only ever known hand-me-downs. With that, he makes a conscious decision that from now on he will present himself in a style that says not only who he is but also who he wants to become. So with parcels in hand, he makes his way up Elizabeth Street and finds a small jewellery shop. Two weeks later, he makes the same trip into town to pick up his order.

'Look at you with your gold chain and fancy ring,' Steffie teases, as she picks up the golden soccer ball that hangs around his neck and then slides off his new black onyx ring. She slips it on her slim fingers.

'Oh dear, much too big. What a shame.'

'How about we see a movie and go dancing tonight?' he suggests.

'Yes, I'd like that.'

'Good. Then you should have something new to wear,' he smiles, producing two packages from behind his back, one larger than the other.

'Oh, my goodness, Steven,' she laughs nervously, as she tears open the larger of the two brown paper parcels. She stands up holding an apple-green dress against her, its taffeta rustling as she twirls around.

'Oh, I love it! It will fit me perfectly, too. Thank you *very* much. You're spoiling me!' she exclaims.

'Now open this one.' He passes her the smaller parcel. She holds her breath while carefully untying the tissue paper.

'Pearls! What have you done? Really Steven, they must have cost a fortune.'

He stands behind her and fastens the clasp.

'There's a Doris Day movie showing at the Regent—*Lullaby of Broadway*—would you like to see it?'

'Sounds great.'

'Why don't you wear that dress and afterwards we can go dancing at the Trocadero. Nick wants us to meet his new girlfriend so we can meet them there. It's not far from the theatre.'

Later that evening, as they enter the Trocadero, the melody of Cole Porter's 'I've Got You under My Skin' drifts into the foyer. Steven notices Nick and a young woman with a profile of fine features framed by a tumble of blonde curls waiting on the large circular seat in the foyer's centre. Behind them, vases massed with scarlet and cream flowers blend perfectly with the decor.

'Steven, Steffie! I'd like you to meet Edna,' Nick says, as he stands and helps the slim, poised young woman to her feet.

'Lovely to meet you both. I've heard so much about you, Steven,' Edna smiles. Her eye shadow matches her eyes as well as her chiffon frock of soft blue, which hangs gracefully from a georgette neckline. 'I love your dress, Steffie,' she leans in to say. 'You have the perfect figure for a pencil skirt. But have you seen the new poodle skirts? They're the *latest* thing.'

'Ah, no. I have not heard of such—'

'Oh? They're a very full, flowing skirt. Ideal for dancing. Some even have poodles embroidered on them—that's where they get their name.'

The two couples enter the large, resplendent auditorium and are immediately shown to a table on the edge of the parquetry dance floor. The glass-coloured lights present a constantly changing mural against the shell-shaped glass bandstand.

'Have you been here before, Steffie?' Edna asks over the orchestra.

'No. First time.'

'Do you get out very much?'

'Not really.'

'Uh huh … Have you been in Australia long?'

'I, um …'

'You are *very* young. But if you mingled a bit more, maybe your English would be better.'

Steven knows from conversations with Steffie that despite her youthful seventeen years, she takes a worldly view on matters and doesn't respond well when faced with prejudice. So, noticing a glint of defiance light in her green eyes, he quickly slides his chair back.

'Please excuse us, Edna. Let's dance, Steffie.'

They waltz cheek-to-cheek, and as he feels her shoulders begin to relax, he draws her to his chest, close enough to feel her heart beating against his own, despite the competing rhythm of the band.

In late 1951, after a courtship of less than a year, Steven proposes.

'Your father is very happy, Steffie,' he says, 'but Mutti ... not so much.'

The wedding takes place at Maroubra Catholic Church and, as William has recently moved his family into their three-bedroom brick home in nearby Matraville, he insists the reception be held there.

The sound of loud and cheerful German, Polish, Hungarian and Australian accents fills every room of the small home, while the aroma of succulent pork knuckles with sauerkraut, *piroshki*[29] and Steven's favourite chicken *paprikás*[30] tantalises the guests. As Steven squeezes through the living room jammed tight with an assortment of people on borrowed chairs, he stops to admire his bride laughing freely with her brothers. He feels her belonging, her simple and radiant joy. Yes, she is fortunate to have her family around her, he thinks.

---

29 Boiled, baked or fried stuffed dumplings/buns made from yeast dough, commonly contain meat (typically beef or pork) or a vegetable filling (mashed potatoes, mushrooms, onions and egg, or cabbage).
30 Classic chicken-based creamy paprika stew/goulash.

Of course he wrote to his parents, told them of his impending wedding, but unfortunately they were unable to get permission to come—at least that's what his father replied. If only he could persuade them that this land with its broad horizons offers a freedom that is unfettered. Steven is joyous, yes, but not without cost.

3
Anna

1953

The arctic winds blow in from the north and Anna shivers as tree branches scrape against the bedroom window of her small apartment. She stands in front of her open suitcases willing herself to move, but feels caught between the known and the unknown, trying to decide which way to turn. What remains of her good sets of cutlery and fine china, as well as the few small pieces of antique furniture she managed to salvage after the government took over her grand townhouse for use as police headquarters, is already packed. But now it comes down to the final packing of their clothes, and suddenly it all becomes very real. She says nothing to Sigismund as she prepares for their momentous journey, but beneath her feet the sands are shifting.

'I have the passports and documents,' he says patting the breast pocket of his coat. 'Are you ready?'

'Yes and no.' She looks up at him with a half-frightened, half-determined look as Sigismund holds open the front door.

'Don't be anxious, Anna. All will be fine. Our packing cases have been sent ahead and should already be at the docks by now.

Come along. Janos is waiting in the car with our luggage. And Anna …'

'Yes, dear?'

'I have decided to give Janos my car. After all, he was my most loyal employee and trusted friend. The boys would never have escaped without his assistance.'

Three and a half hours after leaving Bucharest, after a potholed bus ride towards the east coast of Romania, they arrive in the old city centre of Constanta. Anna stands by the suitcases while Sigismund hails a taxi to take them to their hotel.

'Have a look around,' he says as the taxi drives through the city streets. 'We are only here one day, but perhaps we can visit a museum after lunch. Would that make you smile?'

'Oh, yes. That would be very nice,' she replies absent-mindedly.

Holding hands in the rear of the taxi, they continue to take in the sights during the short drive to their hotel. The taxi pulls to a stop in front of a large whitewashed concrete building.

'Here you are: the Casino of Constanta.'

'Thank you, driver.'

Anna picks up her black-and-gold-tapestry toiletry bag and climbs the hotel steps. From beneath a large archway, she turns and takes in the view of the sea, its rich indigo gently lapping the white sands of the shore. As they enter the foyer, her eye is drawn to the art nouveau decor. Beautiful, impressive, she thinks. And with that she admits to herself that her interest in anything other than her family feels like a lifetime ago … when innocence still prevailed, before the world cracked, before the sky was torn open with hatred.

In the cool autumn light of the next morning, Anna finds herself standing on deck of an outsized ship, awaiting their exodus.

She feels peculiar. She desperately longs to see her sons again. Not a day passes that she hasn't thought about them, wondered what they are doing, how they look, in the morning, at night, a special date, a place, a smell—each thought causing her heart to yearn for them. But over the years, she has languished, almost succumbed to her ignorance. Now to be leaving all that is familiar fills her with fresh insecurity, even dread. A man standing beside Sigismund strikes up a conversation.

'Good morning,' he says, tipping his felt hat to reveal a mop of silvery hair. 'Let me introduce myself. I am Sol Gutmann, and this is my wife.'

'I am Sigismund Löw. How do you do?' he offers his hand, 'And my wife.'

'Are you bound for Israel?'

'No. We're staying on the ship and travelling to Australia.'

'Australia? Such a long way to travel. Do you have family living there?'

'Yes. Our two sons have been there for nearly four years.'

'I see. We're disembarking in Israel.'

'Do you have family there?' Anna asks.

'No. We have no family left ...' Mrs Gutmann replies, reaching for her husband's arm. The small woman's head is covered in a scarf and Anna notices her hands are pale and delicate with knuckles that speak of arthritis.

'I am very, very sorry ...' Anna feels the colour stain her cheeks as a pause fills the air.

'Yes, well, that's the trouble with being a Jew, *nu?* I take it you also are Jewish, Mr and Mrs Löw?' Sol asks.

'Yes we are.'

'Then, as I was saying, Mr Löw, the trouble with being a Jew is not only have we lost our families but many of us now have no home. And although this is also true for many other Europeans, if you consider history, there has never been a place where we have lived and felt safe. There's no country that has not turned against us. We exist everywhere, but under sufferance.'

'But we have done nothing to warrant it. It is a gentile problem and therefore only the gentiles can resolve it,' Sigismund replies.

'True, Mr Löw,' Mrs Gutmann's frail voice breaks in, 'and now it is up to the good people of this world to open their hearts as well as their minds.'

'*Nu* ... so,' Sol looks at his wife with gentle brown eyes. 'We now live in a time which is in dire need of harmony and unity. No longer can the world wince from life's hard truths.' Then, turning toward Sigismund, he adds, 'How else can we avoid further tension and conflict like that which has stained the first half of this century?'

'You dream, I would say, Mr Gutmann,' Sigismund replies with an edge of cynicism in his voice.

'Ah, but without dreams, hopes, aspirations—a man is nothing. But ... *Oy vey!* Enough talk of such things. We are all setting off for a new life. We shall see what happens in Israel—and you in Australia. It has been our good fortune to meet you and I look forward to continuing our discussions at another time. Perhaps over dinner?'

'Certainly.'

'Peace be upon you, *shalom aleichem*, friends,' he says, tipping his hat again, as he leads his wife to an empty deck chair.

Anna stands quietly again. Her apprehension at the thought of such a long sea voyage has returned. Two stretched and deafening hoots send black smoke billowing from the ship's funnels and blast away her contrived calm as she looks down to the dock and the scurrying of the crew as they unravel the last of the thick twine that ties her to her homeland. Slowly the vessel begins to edge away from port. Suddenly, Sigismund lets go of her hand and dashes towards the gangplank as it is being hastily drawn back into the open mouth of the ship.

'Stop! Wait! Our furniture … our belongings … They are still on the dock!'

What remaining good spirits they previously had fade quickly when they make the unpleasant discovery that not only have their tea chests been left behind but all of their suitcases have been removed from the ship prior to departure by the dock workers, who are renowned for topping up their meagre wages with theft of passengers' belongings—even though so many are survivors of appalling losses, of family members, of their homes and even of their nation.

'Too late,' replies a disinterested officer. 'If you want your precious belongings, you can swim back to shore and stay with them.'

4
Fred

1953

As his parents' vessel docks at Circular Quay, Fred recognises the outline of his mother and father, standing tense and huddled as one, gripping the railing, their faces searching the line of beckoning people below.

'Anyu! Apu!' His voice is lost amid the noise.

His mother's eyes have found him. Her gloved hand rushes up to her face. Pushing people aside in her haste, she rushes down the gangplank with Sigismund close behind.

'Frici, Gyuri … Gyuri, Frici, my darling boys!' She weeps, as she hugs them fiercely in turn. Fred is transported to that day when her arms had squeezed him so hard he thought he would break. Yes, even though he is now all of twenty-two, he has to admit it feels good to succumb to his mother's embrace.

'My sons, my sons! How my arms ache to hold you!' Anna wipes the tears that spill down her cheeks. 'Your letters were not enough! Now, stand back. Let me look at you. You are taller, but skinny. Now show me your teeth. First upstairs, now downstairs.'

'Anyu, *nem*. Not here,' Fred says, gently brushing her hand away from his face.

'*Jó*, good,' she continues. 'Cleanliness is good. But good food you don't have—I must be cooking for you. You see my English, how good she is? Your father—*nem*—not so good.'

'*Tinédzserként mentetek el és felnött férfiként tértetek vissza,*' Sigismund whispers against Fred's ear as they embrace.

'What did he say?' yells George over the noisy crowd.

'He said, "You left home as mere teenagers and now you are grown men",' Fred yells back.

Fortunately, his parents do not have to go to a migrant camp because they have the necessary paperwork with proof of residence. After they pass through immigration, they walk along Circular Quay with the sea breeze at their backs, his father animatedly recounting in Hungarian their voyage and the unfortunate loss of their belongings. Fred leads them up the small incline of Argyle Street, into George Street and towards his parked car. Sydney is a very young city, only 180 years old, he tells them.

'Mmm … I see,' Anna says softly, trying not to let the emotional undertow of the journey pull her away from the moment.

'Here's our car,' Frici declares proudly. 'I'll put the roof down and we'll go for a drive through the city and out to the beaches.'

'Car nice, Frici. Is new?'

'Yes, it's a Hillman Minx. Your English isn't bad, Apu. You have to keep using it.'

'How about I tell Apu how much you paid for your shiny blue toy?' George whispers, sliding across the front leather seat.

'You do and you'll be sorry, you big-footed oaf,' he replies through gritted teeth as he puts the car into gear.

'What are you saying?' Anna asks from the back seat. As they take off, she removes her silk scarf from around her neck and ties it over her ebony bob, revealing her gold-rope chain which has been around her neck since they left Timișoara.

'Not important, Anyu. *Nem fontos*,' Fred replies over his shoulder.

After a brief look around the city and the eastern Sydney beaches of Bondi, Tamarama, Bronte and Clovelly, Fred pulls to a stop on the incline in front of the pale blue boarding house in Birrell Street.

'That will do for today. I'll show you around some more tomorrow, after you've had a good night's rest.'

'No garden,' Anna says, looking at the squares of concrete that fill the front yard, 'but the tree is beautiful. Sweet perfume. What is its name, Frici?'

'Frangipani. Here—I'll pick you some.'

They walk down the curved path and enter through the undercover archway on the side of the building. 'Follow me up.' Fred leads them past the front doors of the downstairs flats and up a flight of L-shaped stairs.

Mr Brown is waiting for them on the first-floor landing.

'Welcome to Australia, Mr and Mrs Loew. I have a two-room bedsitter ready for you on the second floor next door to your sons. That way, you'll be able to keep an eye on their comings and goings,' the lanky landlord winks at Fred.

'What does he mean, Frici?' Anna enquires from her son in Hungarian as they make their way down the hallway.

'Nothing, Anyu, nothing.' He opens the door to their rooms. 'Anyway, here we are. It's a shame about your clothes and things, but we'll go out shopping when you're ready tomorrow. I'll buy you whatever it is you need, all right?'

'Good, thank you, *drágám* [darling].'

Fred watches as his mother stands in the doorway and assesses her new home. She smiles as she enters, but he can tell it is forced.

'The sideboard is nice,' she says as she removes her white gloves, runs her hand along the dark stain of the oak and inspects her fingertips. 'Matching round table—enough for four—good. But why are the sofa, bed and armoire all in one room?'

'Well, because there are only two rooms, Anyu. Although … come, step over this small step. See, this open balcony is undercover like an extra little room, and you have a view of the whole street—even water glimpses if you lean out over the windowsill,' he says, demonstrating. 'It's only small but it gives you the fresh air you're so fond of. And from here … we go into the kitchen. Sit down at the table and I'll brew you some coffee.'

Her mouth twitches as she forces a smile again.

'And the bathroom?'

Fred looks to his brother, who jumps in.

'It's just down the hallway, Anyu.'

'We must share?'

'Yes, unfortunately. But before you know it, you'll be used to it.'

He digs his hand into his pocket and brings out a pile of coins.

'Here are some pennies. You, um … have to put them into the gas meter to run the hot water. Don't worry, I'll show you how later.'

'Anyu, you won't have to go far to feel like you're back home—Bondi Road delicatessens are all run by Europeans, the fruit shops are run by Italian families and the cake shops are mainly run by Hungarians. You'll find all the ingredients you need to cook for us: paprika, chillies and capsicums of every colour and variety … I even spotted some Belgian cocoa powder just like you use for your chocolate *dobos*.'

'Yes? Good then.' Avoiding eye contact, Anna turns to take in the view from the kitchen window.

'No matter how far she has travelled, she is still tied to the past,' Fred says to George, a few days later, after retreating to their room following dinner. 'And Father won't even try to learn more English. I'm more worried about him, to tell you the truth.'

'What do you mean?'

'Haven't you noticed how he now walks around with his chin tucked firmly on his chest? He's not the same confident man I remember.'

True, Sigismund now views the world differently. Living through the loss of his home, business and the extermination of most of his family and friends is taking its toll. Some weeks after their arrival, when Fred senses his father is in a conversational mood, he makes a casual enquiry.

'Apu, can you explain to me what happened to all the money you sent to that Swiss bank account?'

Sigismund explains that his first cousin went to England prior to the war to study law. When war broke out, he couldn't continue with his studies, nor could he get home. This Swiss bank account was one that Sigismund and other members of his family had been contributing to prior to and during the early part of the war. However, after the war ended, it was discovered that there were no funds left in the account and, as the English cousin was the only family member who was able to travel to Switzerland, he was asked to explain. His explanation was that he had sent someone close to him to withdraw the money because he had nothing to live on, and this 'someone' was robbed and shot dead on the way back. Naturally, his family denied any suggestion that he or they had stolen the funds and even went so far as accusing Sigismund of embezzling the family money.

'If they could see how we ended up living in communist Romania and now here in Australia, with nothing to claim as our own, except our dignity …' he finishes.

The deeply hurtful accusation that Sigismund has embezzled his own family's money is a wound that gnaws away inside him leaving him increasingly sad and withdrawn. A few weeks later, Fred returns home from work to find his mother crying.

'Oh Frici, your father is very sick. The doctor sent him to the hospital. You must take me to him.'

'Let's go, then. What did the doctor say was wrong?'

'Heart,' she replies with hand on her chest and fear in her eyes.

5
Steven

1952–55

Steven and Stephanie have purchased their first home—a quaint little cottage on busy Botany Road in Botany. Perhaps 'quaint' is going too far. It is so old it rattles at the passing of a truck. Regardless, as they settle in on this humid Sydney afternoon, there is a knock at the door. Steven opens the door to a dark-haired stranger about his own height and age, with brown eyes that shine with intelligence.

'My name is Alex Pongrass. I hear you're a builder. I would like you to build me a factory in Botany,' he says directly, with an accent Steven immediately recognises as Hungarian.

He invites Alex into their small living room and they sit down opposite each other. Steven is drawn into piercing eyes that look out at him from an angular face, as he listens to Alex describe his vision.

'My brother George is an amazing engineer. I am not just saying this because he is my brother, but he has an incredible knowledge, an immense feel for manufacturing of any sort. He has designed and made a universal clamping machine to be used in carpentry for assembling dovetail joins. We have already been using it with great success, but we need a larger factory, we want to mass-produce it. I can pay you well for your time.'

Steven quits his job at Berryman Furniture and begins working for Pongrass Brothers. Before long, the factory takes shape. After almost a year, the project is complete and, having only agreed to build the factory, it should be time for Steven to move on. But Alex has other plans.

'Listen, Steven. I like what I've seen of your leadership skills,' he says. 'My brother has invented a pneumatic tube-bending machine and we want to start manufacturing furniture. Stay with me and be my factory manager—I'll offer you even more in the way of remuneration.'

Characteristic of his father before him, Steven knows his own mind, especially in business, so without any discussion with Stephanie he accepts the offer immediately. And it's a good decision—for the Pongrass brothers (Alex, the entrepreneur, and George, the innovator) have vast and varied visions. They will be trailblazers, whose belief in the grand opportunities of their new country inspire them to take risks. And yes, they will turn their visions into reality; they will go on to use their wonder-machine to not only make an array of tubular steel furniture but indeed modernise the automobile, construction, whitegoods and even boating industries throughout Australia. No mean feat for two Hungarian immigrants from exceedingly poor origins. And no mean feat either for their 'right-hand-man', Steven, who for the next forty years will work as if the business is his own.

In February 1952, Stephanie leaves her job as a process worker in a cigarette factory to give birth to a daughter whom they name Rosemary. When Steven holds her for the first time, he is overcome with emotion.

'You know, with her brown hair, broad nose and chubby cheeks, she reminds me of my mother. How I wish she could be here to see this beautiful little one.'

'We'll send her photos, darling. Who knows, another letter might convince them to come.'

'I doubt it. Nick and I have pleaded with them to join us, but they are too set in their ways, too frightened to travel so far.'

Three and a half years later, their second child, Robert, is born.

'A son, Steffie—now I have a son. I can't wait to teach this handsome little one how to play football,' Steven says, as he cradles him in his arms.

'Soccer! When are you going to learn to call it soccer?' she laughs.

'Have you ever seen such a shock of black hair on a baby?'

'He takes after my dad, don't you think?'

'Yes, he's very much a Heidrichas.'

In his limited time off, Steven somehow wangles time to take up the sport he played as a boy in Timişoara. He hears on the grapevine that a few Hungarian fanatics have established the Budapest Soccer Club and are looking for players. Relaxing in his favourite armchair after dinner one evening, with the sound of the children giggling in the background, he turns the pages of his newspaper as he draws back on a pungent Peter Stuyvesant cigarette.

'Steffie,' he calls, 'listen to this news from the *Soccer Weekly* about a young Romanian guy: he just signed with Hakoah Soccer Club. They're giving him rave reviews in just the few games he has played. How about we go and watch him play this weekend?'

'I think you should go alone. It's getting too cold in the afternoons now for the children.'

The following Sunday evening, Steven arrives home and removes his corduroy jacket, tossing it casually over the teak arm of the Parker lounge suite. The aroma of chicken soup and fried schnitzel greets him. He's been expecting it. Stephanie cooks the same meal for him each Sunday. Her welcoming voice sounds from the kitchen.

'How was the game?'

'Good game. Hakoah won. Their new player is very good—agile, good ball skills. Defender, like me, although he plays much more roughly than me. And I notice he's very argumentative with the referee. He needs to control his temper.'

6
Fred

1955

Late autumn, and the bare branches of the summer-scented frangipani have stretched across the front path at the Birrell Street boarding house. Fred ducks his head to pass, as he carries a small suitcase to his car. He has decided to treat himself to a weekend away in the Blue Mountains, about two hours' drive west of Sydney.

Late that afternoon, as he sits gazing out the oversized windows from the lounge of the exclusive Hydro Majestic Hotel—captivated by the golden sunset as it lingers longer than it should over the mist that rolls in to blanket the gum trees—the reflection of a slender woman's silhouette catches his eye. He turns in his chair, suddenly uninterested in the poetic backdrop of the Megalong Valley below. What a stunner, he thinks. As she passes, he silently admires her graceful carriage and proud tilt of her head. He can't believe his luck when she sits down alone at a nearby table. He picks up his beer—perhaps a bit too quickly—and makes his way over.

'May I join you?'

She smiles and nods, her auburn hair falling in points about her face like the leaves of a maple. With long, delicate fingers, she brushes it aside and looks at him almost as if she is mocking his awkwardness. Pulling out the lounge chair opposite, Fred asks her name.

'Joan.'

'I'm Fred. Can I buy you a drink?'

'Yes, thank you. A cocktail would be lovely.'

Fred signals for the waiter and orders two martinis.

'I like your accent. Where are you from?'

'Romania. But I live in Bondi.'

'How long have you been in Australia?'

'Six years now. Where do you live, Joan?'

'Well, it's a long story, but I'm living in Oatley. Actually—and I probably shouldn't even be telling you this over our first drink—I'm here trying to get over a recent divorce.' She continues as she sips her drink. 'I've probably scared you off now …'

'It doesn't worry me, Joan, Not at all.'

Chatting casually for the next few minutes, Fred does well to conceal his admiration of her beauty.

'I'm playing golf tomorrow,' she says. 'Would you like to join me? I suppose I should first ask if you can play.'

'What? Oh, golf—of course I can play. I even have my own set of clubs,' he lies.

First thing the next morning, Fred skips breakfast, hops in his car and drives like a bullet back down the winding mountain road and into Sydney. He heads straight to a large golf shop on Parramatta Road and buys himself a decent set of clubs. *This game looks easy enough*, he thinks in his eagerness to get back up the mountain.

After only playing a few holes, Fred is feeling very sheepish.

'You surprise me with your skill. Are there any other sports you're good at?'

'I don't know about "good at", but I certainly enjoy watching most sports.'

Without lifting her head, she adjusts her feet into a stance in line with her shoulders, and keeping her back straight with knees slightly bent, she arches both arms back over her right shoulder. Then in one fluid movement she swings downward, generating a *swish* with the club head as she whips the ball from its tee.

'Great shot,' he says, as the white dot disappears against the pale sky, wondering if she'll ever agree to see him after he's made such an idiot of himself. He perseveres. 'I play football, or soccer, I should say. Would you like to come and watch me play next weekend?'

'I'd love to.'

'Great! But I don't think I can wait a whole week to see you again. How about dinner tonight? Then tomorrow, before we each head home, let's take a walk—a bush walk—if you'd like to, that is?'

'Yes to both. I should tell you I love getting out into the bush. The beauty, the sounds, the smells—especially early mornings or after it rains—there's nothing quite like it.'

He has no idea what sounds or smells she is talking about but, not wanting to appear ignorant of such things, agrees with her. Joan, he will soon discover, is enamoured of the natural environment, besotted by the fecund freshness of the earth when it opens up and releases its invigorating spell. And very quickly he will also discover that he will fall for Joan's grace and simplicity—which, like the sweet-scented frangipani, flowers easily with little maintenance.

The next morning they head off along one of the many bush trails that lead from the expansive manicured grounds of the hotel. As the path becomes steep and uneven with tree roots and loose stones, Fred takes Joan's hand. They venture deeper into the shadows of the canopy and, though he longs to speak to her, Fred remains silent and tries to immerse himself in the surroundings. He notices how the splintered sunlight delicately silhouettes the tall dark trunks and creates hues of olives and greys on the undergrowth. Farther on, he sees how this shimmering light animates the droplets of morning dew, draping the foliage in natural fairy lights. Without really listening, he hears an orchestra of birdsong and the rustle of bushes as something slithers nearby. Amazing, he thinks, filling his lungs with the clean air. Leaves crunch underfoot and quite unexpectedly a flock of sulphur-crested cockatoos flies from the tree tops screeching hoarsely in a cacophony of protest at their intrusion.

The pair trek on for another half hour before stopping to rest against a large boulder speckled with lichen. Leaning back against the cool mossy rock, Fred thinks to himself how different this landscape is from the forests he holidayed in as a boy. The Romanian mountains where he skied most winters were filled with soaring pines, and their grandeur and distinctive scent produced an entirely different sensation. Not that he misses it—he loves his new home. But being in these mountains evokes memories of fond times with his family—of trekking through forest or skiing with his many cousins … almost every one of whom has perished.

Just as he is about to share his thoughts, Joan whispers, 'Shh, Fred, don't speak or move.' She points to a squat furry animal rubbing itself on the bark of a nearby tree. 'Wombat,' she whispers to the question in his eyes. She leans close to again speak softly in his ear, but instead he gently cups her chin, guiding her lips to meet his own.

When Fred tells his mother he has fallen in love with a woman who isn't Jewish and is going to marry her, she does not withhold her opinion.

'But Frici, she is not *like* us!' Her look is dejected as she sets the table. 'In halakhah, Jew must marry Jew.'

'Don't be ridiculous, Anyu. You know I have never cared for all that fuss over religion.'

'Yes?' And when the children they are born … what will become of them?'

'It's not important, Anyu. They will be who they will be.'

'No, Frici, the children take the mother's religion.'

'I don't care, I'm telling you!'

'Don't get angry with me. Can't I say that you should not be marrying a *shiksa*?'

'Anyu!'

'Stop yelling, please. She is a very beautiful lady. I like her. But for marriage? No. Believe me, I know how these things work—she will not allow you to live in the way we raised you.'

'Anyu—that's it. I don't want to discuss this with you. I don't understand how you can even *think* such things.'

'Will she cook the food we eat? Will she clean, sew, do everything I do for you?'

'One minute it's about being Jewish, the next it's about living up to your standards. You should hear yourself. Anyway, when were you ever so orthodox? Ah, don't answer that. Just leave me alone.'

7
Anna, Fred

1956

'We have a long way to go today, Sigismund. Are you well enough?'

'Yes. All good.' He ties a flawless Windsor knot and slides it into place under the collar of his white shirt.

Anna has done the homework that Sigismund assigned her. She has looked up 'Miley' in the telephone book and written down the address on Canterbury Road in Canterbury. Then she has walked down to Bondi Road and made enquiries from a tram conductor about the best route.

'I'm only asking because this one is a long trip and there will be some walking.'

'I'm fine. Let's go.'

Two hours later Anna knocks on the timber door of a semi-detached brick dwelling. It is opened by a diminutive woman whose short auburn hair falls in composed waves away from her face. She seems pleasant, neatly dressed in cream slacks and lacy cream cardigan, even though Anna herself would never wear anything but a dress or skirt.

'Hello, can I help you?' Her teeth are white against the smile of her bright poppy lipstick.

Anna can detect the surprise in her tone, as they haven't met before. But this surprise visit was the only way to appease Sigismund. Too late to turn back now, she thinks, as she enquires, 'You are Mrs Miley?'

'Yes …' her pencilled eyebrows arch in a question, as her blue eyes look from Anna's face into Sigismund's.

'We are Frici's parents. Anna and Sigismund Loew.' Anna smiles, trying not to reveal her nervousness.

'Oh … oh, please come inside. This is a nice surprise. Come through, just down the hallway is the living room. John? John, are you there, love?' There is a simplicity in her manner.

'Yes dear.'

'We have visitors. Fred's parents. Anna and …'

'Sigismund,' he says a little too severely.

'Of course. Sigismund.' Lorna blushes through her thick dusting of face powder and rouge as she continues to move down the hall.

They walk into a combined lounge and dining room. Despite the faint odour of cigarette smoke emanating from the furnishings, the home is spotlessly clean—a fact that doesn't escape Anna.

'Hello, I'm John. How do you do?' says a well-groomed middle-aged man with a thatch of wiry black hair and matching moustache, in a voice that falls soothingly upon the ear. With introductions complete, John indicates they should sit on the three-seater settee, which has two matching chairs all carved from mahogany and filled with plump, rich tapestry cushions—antique and expensive, another fact not lost on Anna's discerning eye.

'Would you like a cup of tea?' Lorna asks politely.

'Not tea, but coffee would be very nice, thank you.'

Sigismund sits quietly throughout the pleasant enough conversation, with Anna casting him anxious glances every so often. But when he clears his throat, she almost spills her coffee in her lap.

'John, Frici wants marry Joan.'

'Yes, we know. At first we were surprised, I'll admit, but we like Fred—Frici—very much.'

Anna knows what's coming, and she can't stop the roses on her Royal Albert cup from rattling in their saucer.

'What you provide as dowry?' Sigismund says.

'I beg your pardon?'

'Dowry. Is custom bride for family provide dowry.'

The colour rises in John's cheeks as he shifts in his seat.

'Well, it might be the custom in *your* culture, but it's certainly not our custom.'

'But once Frici marrying, how are we to live? He looking after us. We have nothing here in Australia.'

'Look, Sigismund, you need to talk with your son. This has nothing to do with us. I am sorry, but it's just not our problem.'

Now it is Sigismund whose cheeks turn crimson, and Anna is immediately worried about his blood pressure.

'You not understand. Your daughter taking our meal-provider? How can you say not your problem?'

'I don't wish to argue with you—and I can see this is very upsetting for Anna and Lorna.' Rising from his chair, John continues, 'I think it would be best for all concerned if you would leave now. I'll show you out.'

'I am very sorry for upset, Lorna. Anna stumbles, trying to repair the moment. 'Please try to understand, I don't want to lose my son. We together have been only a short time.'

'Yes, Anna, I understand,' Lorna replies, squeezing her arm

gently on the way down the long hallway. 'I felt the same way with Joan. But there comes a time as a mother when you just have to let go.'

'I have already let go once. It is too much to let him go again.'

'Apu!' Fred shouts, bounding through the front door.

'Why you are screaming, Frici?'

'What the hell have you done? How could you go over to the Mileys' house and do such a bloody stupid thing?'

'Not stupid. What I say true!'

'What bloody nonsense. Have you lost your mind?'

'You don't talk to me like this! I am your father!'

'I have never fought with you my whole life, Apu, but now … now I am so angry. I don't know if I can ever forgive you!'

'Go then. Go! Leave us!'

'Frici, wait!' he hears his mother call, as he slams the front door behind him.

A light rain begins to fall as he drives the one hour to Joan's house. The windscreen wipers thump back and forth against the thick damp air that alternates between drizzle and mist. The wipers help clear his view, but not his mind. *How could they do that? I'm already having trouble getting them to like me … Now what will they think? My stupid father asking for a dowry! Doesn't he understand that people have struggled here too, from the Depression and the war? Damn! It'll be so embarrassing to go to dinner there this week.*

The roads are glassy, reflecting the changing colours of the traffic lights. Suddenly, on an innocuous curve in the familiar road, he has no control over the steering of his new Zephyr. The car swings out sideways and continues skidding, as if on glass. It slams into a telegraph pole, then rolls back and flips over onto its roof. With his head bent awkwardly, Fred hangs upside down for several minutes in shock and disbelief. Patting himself down, he realises he has no broken bones or serious injuries, so proceeds to pull himself out through the window. The sound of squealing tyres and metal crushing has drawn people from nearby shops.

'Do you need help?' asks a man who must be a butcher, as his white coat is splattered in more blood than Fred has on his shirt.

'No, I'm fine. Really. Just a bleeding nose and cut hand,' he replies, wiping his nose with his handkerchief. 'But can I borrow your phone to call a tow truck?'

As the flashy Zephyr disappears from sight, he hails a cab and arrives at Joan's just as she is finishing dinner.

'I suspected there was something wrong with its damn steering!' He tries to control his temper but he is still livid. 'That will be a £1500 write-off.'

'Oh, darling it's so lucky you weren't hurt!'

'Yes, lucky,' he says, 'but it certainly doesn't feel like it.'

Fred marries Joan in late 1956 in an unprepossessing ceremony at the registry office at Circular Quay. He would marry her anywhere—including the Catholic church at Dulwich Hill, which Lorna and John attend—but she tells him that because she's divorced it's against the doctrine of the church to take her vows twice. With that, he thinks his parents will be satisfied—after all, they don't have to sit through a church wedding—so he's deeply hurt and disappointed when they and his brother fail to turn up on his wedding day, emphasising their disapproval of him marrying out. Nevertheless, he is pleased to have Lorna and John's support.

'Don't let it worry you, darling. I'll win them over yet,' Joan says, linking her arm through his as they walk out of the building and down the steps.

When it comes to determining their honeymoon destination, Fred states his case emphatically for attending Melbourne and the Olympic Games, telling Joan that it was one of the main reasons he decided to come to Australia.

'Well, lucky for me you love sport or we'd never have met.' She laughs happily.

With the honeymoon over, Fred moves into Joan's house and with it inherits a hefty mortgage from Joan's parents. The Mileys have been covering the mortgage since Joan's divorce. Despite working as a dance instructor for Arthur Murray Dance Studio, Joan's income is very low.

Not one to hold grudges, Fred soon forgives his parents and visits often, leaving them a few pounds whenever he can spare them. At twenty-eight years old, George continues to live next door but, having tired of working irregular hours in the taxi industry, drifts in and out of employment as a salesman. He will continue to live next door for the next ten years until he meets and marries Margaret. A talented florist with an upper-class pedigree and elite private school education, Anna will approve of the match despite her second daughter-in-law not being Jewish.

Some weeks later, on a stifling summer's day, Fred has had enough of the traffic snarling on the city's hot, black streets. Enough of people, too. The ill-assorted lot that fill his rear-vision mirror are usually world-weary. Some chat pleasantly, but others make him feel foreign. As he drives from the city towards Mascot airport, which usually proves his best source for a good fare, he is flagged down by a scruffy young man on Botany Road in Redfern.

'Where to?' he asks, as the youth closes the rear door with an unnecessary force that always grates on Fred's nerves.

'St Mary's.'

'Long way out west … Over twenty-five miles. You can cover it?' Fred catches the liquid eyes in his mirror. There is a long interval when neither lowers his gaze.

'No worries, mate.'

Suspicion produces silence, as Fred heads towards the outer western suburb of St Mary's. A good hour later, as they approach the suburb, his passenger begins giving directions. The streets are wide, treeless and intermittently scattered with standard fibro houses which all seem to match each other, even down to the uniform height of the fences. Just as Fred is slowing to stop at a T-intersection, and waiting for the obligatory 'left' or 'right' instruction, the young man opens the cab door and takes off through a deserted paddock. Fred brings the cab screeching to a stop on a sixpence and leaps out after him. He tears through long grass and flies over mounds of clay and tangled weeds as if he is competing in the 110-yard Olympic hurdle event.

The evader has a good start, but Fred is a naturally fast runner and, being twenty-five, he has never felt fitter. After a furious dash, he has almost caught up. *Now I've got you … you little lout … Just a few steps more …* He reaches out to grab the guy's flapping flannelette shirt and suddenly he steps blindly into a small depression. His knee buckles and he stumbles and falls.

'Bloody hell!' he yells, as he rolls onto his back.

He stands up, wipes the sweat from his brow and swears some more before limping back to his cab, which stands abandoned in the middle of the road with both driver and rear passenger doors wide open. Awkwardly, he slides himself onto the vinyl seat and sits behind the wheel, his hand resting on the key in the ignition, the breaths coming hard and fast. Whilst he is hurting, the pain isn't really physical. Fred is not used to losing and doesn't like the emotion it stirs. He consoles himself by thinking of all the others whose fortune has not escaped his fist on their face. Not just the many brawls or scrapes he finds himself in recently—sometimes over unpaid fares like this one, or when things get too heated inside the gambling joints. Some have tasted his fury over blatant prejudice, like those who persist in calling him a wog. It's at these times he is reminded of being a naive Jewish boy growing up in times of fickle friendship, times when friends were just a nod or a finger-point away from becoming your enemy. It was then that he learnt that his fists served as his valour; as if bearing witness to humans at their worst has informed his nature.

Deficient in verbal conciliation skills, Fred will continue to use his physicality to right his perception of injustice well into the future. And although his vehemence will mellow with time, when aged sixty-two, Fred's final fight will be his most violent; one which will see him draw from his reservoir of survival instincts one day when he suddenly finds himself looking down the barrel of a sawn-off shotgun. And it will be his childhood mantra of taking his opponent off guard that will save him when he uses it to distract an armed robber half his age. He will wrestle him to the ground, overpower him, remove his weapon, and be proclaimed a 'town hero' for his audacity.

The Ford engine rumbles as he turns the key and begins the long drive home.

Annoyed and sore, he arrives home just as the sun is setting. Limping towards the front veranda, even the birds seem to sense his mood as they argue in the tops of the eucalypts that line the drive.

'Joan?'

Hearing no answer from the kitchen at the end of the narrow entrance hall, he walks through the glass doors that open onto the living room—his footsteps resonant on the floorboards—and opens one of the French doors which lead directly onto the back patio. He stands leaning against the architrave unnoticed for several seconds, watching as she sits on her slatted-timber chair, immersed in the pages of a novel, while in the background the cicadas deliver their electric song. The fading sunlight glistens through the leaves of the many trees she has planted—mulberry, banana, lemon, magnolia, poinsettia, bottle-brush—he can't remember all their names.

Joan looks up, startled at first, then greets him with a smile.

'Darling, I didn't hear you come in. How was work?'

'Don't ask,' he mutters as he hobbles towards her.

'You're limping! What happened?'

'I'd rather not talk about it just yet. I'll tell you over dinner. How was your day?'

'Well …' her eyes suddenly sparkle. 'I've got some news.' She pauses, for effect, and also because she knows this is going to add to their financial strains.

'What? Tell me.'

'Darling …' A breathless silence fills the air and he is drawn deeper into her emerald eyes. Then, 'I'm pregnant!'

'Sweetheart!' He draws her close, his arms encircling her waist. 'I couldn't be happier.'

Extracting herself from his embrace, she walks into the house.

'Mum and Pop will be so happy as Bert always blamed me for not giving him any children in the four years we were married.'

'Yes. I'm sure my parents will be happy, too, especially Anyu,' he replies, as he follows her inside, both his pain and anger having dissipated.

'I hope so, Fred. I hope this bridges the gap between us.'

Nine months later, a static-filled voice delivers a message over the taxi radio.

'Make your way to St Margaret's Hospital. Your wife is in labour.'

'Roger that! Over.'

For the next forty-eight hours, Fred paces the sterile corridors of the hospital—his footsteps echoing over the polished linoleum—only going home late each night to sleep with a promise from the nursing staff to summon him at any hour. Anxious looks are shared between himself, Lorna and John, and his own parents, who all come and go in a haze of visits. Finally, a timid young nurse appears.

'Mr Loew?'

'Yes?'

'You are the proud father of a healthy baby boy,' she says in a well-rehearsed tone. 'You can go in and see your wife and son now, but doctor's orders are not to stay too long as your wife has had a very tough time of it.'

Tentatively, Fred follows her into the room and peeks around the blue-and-pink striped curtains.

'I'm fine, darling. Come in.' She sits propped up with several pillows, smiling as she gazes at the tightly swaddled bundle in her arms from which tiny black curls protrude. She sounds exhausted. 'He looks just like you, Fred.'

'Does he? Can I see?' He inches closer, taking care not to touch the stainless-steel pole that stands beside the bed snaking thick scarlet fluid into her veins. Despite her attempt at colour with lipstick and rouge, the contrast makes her appear even paler.

'Here, Fred. Come closer. Now take him in your arms … support his little head. That's right … Do you still want to call him Stephen?'

'What? Yes, darling. That's what we decided. Stephen. It already suits him.'

'Fred? Is that you? Where have you been? I've been up all night with Stephen and worried like hell …'

'I, uh, did a double-shift for Bob. The other driver called in sick.'

'Why didn't you let me know? There are phone boxes on every street corner. We need food, baby formula, the Walton's man was knocking on the door for their payment and I had to pretend I wasn't home. Did you get paid?'

'Ah, no—you see, Bob's a bit short this week …'

'Again? You don't have to stand for that! Did you tell him?'

'I did. He said he'd fix me up tomorrow. We've got to cut the poor guy some slack.'

'Well, that sounds odd coming from you of all people …' She casts him a suspicious look as she rocks the crying baby.

The hour is just as late the next night when he arrives home. Silence, complete and still, greets him as he opens the front door and steps into the darkened hallway. Creeping up the staircase, a creaking floorboard suddenly betrays him as he turns at the narrow bend.

'Fred?'

Damn, she's awake, he realises, beginning to craft his alibi.

'There's one thing I'm not, Fred, and that's a fool. So don't treat me like one. I can smell stale smoke from here,' she chides, as he enters the bedroom.

'Here you are, Joan. Here's £500.' He tosses a pile of notes onto the bedside table. Silence. 'Are you still angry with me?'

Thank goodness it's dark, Fred thinks, as he slips into bed beside her. Lucky, too, that Mr Quigley paid dividends tonight. He'll have to devise a story by tomorrow when Joan sees his split lip. But it wasn't *his* fault.

'Freddie, the wog,' the fellow called him. 'Been eating that salami crap again?'

Well, he got what was coming to him. Shame about the whack across his mouth. Broke his own rule and let his guard down. And now the guard has to stay up, even against his precious Joan. Why? Because Quigley's is an illegal two-up joint—a charming little tin shed structure with just a tarp on the ground and wooden benches around all four walls hidden in the back streets of Paddington.

Two years hurry past, with Fred falling victim to his gambling habit again. Of course *he* doesn't see it that way. He can't understand that he is in a relationship where nothing exists between giver and recipient. Or that the one relationship that matters most is suffering from neglect.

'I'm pregnant,' Joan says, as he climbs into bed exhausted after another long night.

'Again? Mandy is only three months old ...'

'I know that. I'm the one looking after a toddler and a baby. It's Stephen's birthday next week. Do we have any money to buy him that spaceship he wants?'

'Do you want me to find it now, when I've just got into bed?'

'Well, you'll be gone before I wake up and if you've got any money on you, I've got to get it now.'

'For goodness sake, don't start on me! You could tell your parents to buy him that expensive spaceship. They spoil him too much as it is.'

'Don't be ridiculous, Fred. We have to have something for him.'

'All right, all right. Just let me go to sleep right now so that I can get up and do it all over again tomorrow.'

'No problem.' Her tone is sarcastic as she rolls over, turning her back towards him. 'Just make sure it's work you're talking about.'

Just as Joan says, she's no fool.

8
Steven

1962

A few weeks after putting a deposit down on a modern three-bedroom red-brick home in the middle-class suburb of Beverly Hills, Steven receives a letter from Timişoara. When Stephanie arrives home from shopping, he sits her down to explain what has happened and what he's decided to do.

'Steffie, my father is not well. Cancer—' he chokes on the word, pauses, then slowly brings his hand up and strokes his strong jaw, grimacing as if in pain. 'My mother says the doctors don't hold out much hope that he's going to recover. I really need to go home. It's just so awful that the first time I see them after all these years will be at a time like this …'

Two weeks later, after obtaining the appropriate travel documents, he leaves not knowing whether he will arrive in time to see his father one last time.

Arriving at Budapest airport, Steven sees his two brothers before they see him. They are easy to recognise—they are older versions of him, eagerly scanning the line of emerging passengers. Then their eyes meet his. All three move urgently towards each other, Steven dropping his hand luggage to embrace both brothers at once. They hug each other fiercely, let go and hug again. As they stand back and look at each other, Steven sees his own tears reflected in their eyes. Seconds pass without words.

'No crying, right? This is a happy occasion!' Joszi finally says.

'Yes, for goodness sake, we are all grown men. What would people think to see three men crying?' Steven laughs.

'Hey, little Istvan, we can't call you "little" anymore—you're stronger and taller than us both.' Ferenc pats him on the back as they walk through the airport.

'Joszi, what happened to all your hair?' he teases. 'You had a full head of thick brown hair last time I saw you.'

'Well, that was almost twenty-three years ago. Don't worry, little brother, I'm just showing you what you'll look like in another ten or fifteen years.'

'Where are your families? Here or in Ózd?'

'They're home in Ózd. As it's so late, we'll stay here overnight and tomorrow we thought you might like to see the sights of both Buda and Pest,' Joszi says. 'A lot has changed since you were here as a boy. We can start with a visit to Szent István-bazilika (St Stephen's Church), which is fitting for someone who is named after that particular saint, don't you think,' he laughs. 'And in the afternoon we have a special treat for you. We remember how much you enjoyed your tortes, so we're going to take you to the best cafe in the city—the Gerbeaud Café on Vorosmarty Square.'

The following day after their fill of sweet delicacies, the three brothers set off on the long drive to Ózd. As they reach the outskirts of the town, Steven is struck by how similar all the streets look, lined with similar-looking small houses, giving the impression of a flat and depressing landscape, despite the town being surrounded by green hills.

'Where are you working now, Ferenc? You gave up cooking, I hear,' Istvan enquires.

'Yes, yes. It's taken me some years, but I've worked my way up to be a leading-hand at Ózd Steelworks.'

'Very good. And you, Joszi? What happened to the bakery you used to own?'

'It still exists. I'll show you tomorrow when we have some time. But, as you know, I no longer own it—not for many years—since the communists took it from me. Now I'm just an employee, like everyone else.'

'He's not really like everyone else, Istvan,' Ferenc intercedes. 'He's a stubborn one. He fought the government for so long, created such a stink for them when they took his bakery—which, by the way, was the largest bakery in all of Hungary—that they punished him by rostering him on night shifts. Only night shifts. And he's still only given night shifts, even after all these years.'

'Well, here we are. Ferenc's house is that one and mine is next door, see?' Joszi says pointing to two identical small brick homes. As he pulls into the drive, both front doors fly open and two middle-aged women and several teenagers gather around the car excitedly. Steven is once again struck by how similar—and somehow grey—not only the houses look but also their inhabitants.

'So good to meet you!' he exclaims, leaping out of the car and fondly embracing each of his relatives.

'Come inside, come inside. We have a special meal cooked for you,' Ferenc's wife Eszti says.

'Thank you. I hope you didn't go to too much trouble, though.' He follows them inside and the smell of cooking fat almost overwhelms him. 'Before we eat, let me open my bag. Steffie has sent some gifts for the children.'

After four days in Ózd, the highlight being a visit to the warm mineral baths situated by a lake at the foot of the mountains, Steven farewells his brothers and their families and takes the train to Timişoara.

9
Homecoming

1962

'I am shaking with excitement,' Katarina's voice echoes in the otherwise empty station, bouncing off the concrete as she, Nikolaus, Jani and Hermina wait eagerly for the eleven p.m. train from Budapest. She stares down the darkened track waiting for the first glimpse of train lights. When he doesn't reply, she turns toward her husband. Flickering shadows from the lone fluorescent light emit strange patterns across his face. 'Nikolaus? Are you feeling all right? It's late, perhaps you should have waited at home.'

'Eighteen years is a long, long time …' he says quietly.

'Here, come and sit down on this seat,' she says, guiding him towards the empty bench. 'Jani, come and sit with your father.'

She paces back and forth along the platform, plucking at the gathered waistline of her dress, then adjusting her good coat, making sure the fox-fur collar sits correctly. When Katarina received word that he would be coming home, each passing day seemed like a month. For so long, she has visualised this very moment in her quiet times. She wonders how, if at all, the years have changed him. In her mind, she still sees him as the sixteen-year-old boy leaning out of the train window to say he will be back very soon. *Yes, eighteen years is a long, long time but if feels like a lifetime …*

Now, just as a train has taken him away from her, another will bring him back, on the very same platform. She hears it before she sees it, a faint click-clack of distant wheels against joints, which grows to a squeal of steel wheel against steel rail. She turns and looks into the blackness and sees two round lights gradually growing bigger. Her heart swells and tightens with the crescendo of approaching noise. *He's here … he's here.* 'He's here!' she calls out to the others, who stand to welcome the train as it draws alongside the platform.

'There he is,' Jani calls out as he scampers towards Steven, who has stepped down off the train, suitcase in hand. He drops the bag and runs his fingers through his ruffled hair, brushing it back from his forehead—a mannerism Katarina well remembers—then he zips up his grey leather jacket against the cold. Even from a distance, she can see his familiar swagger and bold grin as he picks up his bag and begins walking in their direction. The stout frame of Hermina trundles towards Steven, her short, mousy perm motionless in the breeze as she gently leads Nikolaus by the hand.

Katarina wants to follow, but her feet feel glued to the spot. She drops her eyes to her tightly clasped hands and wills them to relax, then pinches herself hard to shake off the dream state she has entered. As she watches him hug and kiss his brother and sister, she feels her eyes well with tears. But when he embraces his ailing father, her fist flies to her mouth to smother the sobs.

Then he turns. And it feels as if all the years have disappeared between the cracks of the old platform. He looks to where she stands frozen in time. He walks towards her with outstretched arms, his palms upturned as if to say, 'I am sorry it has taken me this long.' His voice, when it comes, is thick with tears.

'*Mama.*'

'*Istvan.*'

As the car moves up the long dirt drive of the Chişoda farmhouse, Hermina's husband stands on the front step awaiting their arrival. A letter from his mother, years earlier, had informed Steven that nothing was ever heard from Hermina's first husband Hans, and that Hermina was going to remarry.

'Istvan, this is my husband Ludwig and my daughter Evelyn. She's a couple of years younger than your Robert and should really be in bed at this late hour.' Hermina places her hands proudly on her small daughter's shoulders. Steven can see that Ludwig is a pleasant man with a gentle manner. Little Evelyn takes to Steven immediately, as most small children seem to, wrapping her arms around his legs and looking up inquisitively into his face, her black fringe falls back to reveal round dark eyes.

'Oh, no!' Steven says as he picks up the little girl.

'What is it?' asks Hermina with concern.

'I forgot the koala. Stupid me!' he strikes his palm against his brow. 'Steffie sent a big fluffy koala for Evelyn and I carried it so carefully for the whole 24-hour plane trip. I had it sitting next to me on the train trip here but was so excited to arrive, I've left it behind on the train!'

'Don't worry, Istvan, we have you. That's all we need,' his mother's voice tender as she holds his arm with both hands. She hasn't let go since they first embraced.

'It's late,' Nikolaus says. 'Istvan is tired, as am I. Let's all go to bed and catch up with the news in the morning.'

'Papa, have you news on the cancer? Are there specialists here for prostate?'

'Certainly. Good doctors. Don't worry—I'm doing fine. I'm just tired. Good night, Istvan. It's wonderful to have you home again,' Nikolaus says before moving off down the hallway to the bedroom.

Katarina motions to Steven to follow her into the kitchen.

'Before you go to bed, Istvan, I have cooked your favourite— nut *beigli*. Would you like a piece now with a hot milk coffee?'

'Wonderful, Mama. Thank you.' The small kitchen, still just as he remembered it from childhood, smells slightly smoky with a hint of paprika lingering in the closed air.

'Tell me more about Steffie. Your letters don't say enough and it is hard to get to know a person from a photograph. She looks very nice.'

He fills her in on what a wonderful wife and mother Stephanie is—how she would have come too, but didn't want to leave behind the children, who are now eleven and seven. And, of course, what fine children he has.

'Ah Mama, you should see Robert play football. He's the best player—he can outplay an entire team. What? Don't smile, it's true. He scores two or three goals every week. I tell you … he will be something when he grows up!'

Sleep takes forever to come to Steven that night. Thoughts of how his parents have aged, especially his father, play on his mind. Apart from that, everyone and everything look and smell the same. He is also concerned about his brother. From the letters he has received from his father, Steven knows that Jani has never fully recovered from the war. He hasn't worked a day since, an unimaginable choice in his family. And upon seeing him again, especially the next morning in the light of day, Steven can tell from his unkempt appearance and agitated manner that Jani's life has indeed spun out of control.

'Hey, Jani. Let's go for a walk outside—I want to look around.'

Making idle chat, the two brothers walk down the drive and out into the open field opposite the farm. The wind leans on the long grass and wild daisies, making their path an easy one.

'So, how is Papa faring? He looks better than I thought he would.'

'Yes, he says he's feeling much better now that he's home from hospital. But I don't think he wants to admit he's sick.'

'No, he wouldn't,' Steven says, as he takes in his brother's profile. His greasy black hair and thin black moustache only add fuel to the rumours of his gangster-like lifestyle. 'Listen, Jani, why don't you get a haircut, clean yourself up. Maybe then you could get a job. You must be bored doing nothing all day.'

'Did Mama tell you to say that? Is Papa worried about the company I keep? Well, I'm happy with my life. I don't need your interference—'

'No, Jani, don't take it like that. I just want to help you, that's all.'

'Yes, of course, help … Anyway, talk about worrying Mama and Papa! You know that we thought you were dead, Istvan?'

'What? What are you talking about?'

'Mama and Papa both thought you were dead when you didn't write home from the labour camp you were sent to. For years they thought you were dead. Tibor saw your body on a stretcher.'

'I have no idea what you're talking about. I don't remember being on a stretcher. It's so long ago, for God's sake. Anyway, I wrote home as soon as I could when I got to Germany.'

'Yes, yes, as soon as you could, you say. But you should have seen how worried Mama and Papa were. Of course Papa pretended not to be, but he was harsh with Mama—I would hear him shout and pound his fist on the kitchen table. That was his way of telling her not to worry. And I saw her crying on and off for years. Until your letter came from Germany. Only then did she stop.'

'Look, Jani, I had no idea. But truthfully, I didn't know who was home and who wasn't during that time. Whether you, the others, even Papa, had survived. I wasn't going to write home and burden Mama. Don't you understand that?'

'Don't look so worried, Istvan. You wrote. Mama stopped crying. All is good. And now here you are …' Without warning, Jani suddenly changes topic again. 'You know Papa is revered here by the government because of his engineering knowledge. But no matter what your status, under communism you can only own the house you live in—nothing more. Papa bought the old wooden house on the next property for me to live in, but when the government found out they wanted to take it from him. So you know what he did?'

Steven shakes his head and looks questioningly.

'He took an axe and smashed the house to pieces. There was nothing left for them to take,' he laughs.

'Do you remember how I used to follow you and Nick around out here all the time with my football—begging you boys to play with me?'

'Not so much. I don't remember much before the war.'

'Really?'

'I'll tell you something I do remember,' he pauses and rubs his head. 'No, that happened during the war …'

'Maybe don't go there, Jani.'

'I remember being in a field, by the banks of a river. I am not sure where. And I remember a German soldier shouting at us, warning us what would happen if we panicked and didn't follow orders. I can see it so plainly now—'

'Jani—'

'I can see him turning and scooping up a baby duck—the last in a row of baby ducks that were swimming behind their mother. And while he was still yelling at us, he simply put the duckling under his boot and squashed it.'

'Jesus. That's horrible!' Steven exclaims. Then, trying his best to bring Jani back to the present, he points towards the oak tree near the house. 'That tree has grown so much—it must be twice the size of what it was when I last saw it. And I can see a nest of starlings in its branches. Can you see it? Jani—are you listening to me?'

'He screamed at us, "This will be your fate if you should choose to be weak. The weak shall not survive!"'

'Jani, Jani—we all have bad memories. It does no good to think of them.'

'You, Istvan? What bad memories could you possibly have? Nothing bad happened to you.'

'Plenty happened to me. But it's a lifetime ago. And now I *choose* not to let the past haunt me. We all have to move forward. We have to live life now.'

'Yes, all right. So, tell me about your life in that far away country. How does it compare? I bet you wish you still lived here, eh?'

Despite being overcome with emotion at seeing his family after almost twenty years, it doesn't take long for Steven to realise he made the right decision not to return with Ferenc all those years ago. As the weeks linger, he finds each day painfully uneventful.

To watch the people he loves so disengaged from life—meandering from one day to the next without ambition—frustrates him with disappointment. For not only has time stood still in terms of economic growth but the sophisticated city centre he remembers from his childhood is now dreary and lifeless. It has lost its grandeur. And the bleakness infuses not only the buildings but also its occupants. How are people managing to survive in this repressive regime? From his discussions with family and those he meets, there is so much frustration with, even rebellion, against the authoritarian government. Yet many, including his own family, are unwilling to seek out another way of life. It puzzles Steven, who also harbours a fear of again being held against his will, this time behind bars that can't be seen.

Finally, the day he has been both dreading and willing for, arrives. As he slowly packs his bag, his mother stands in his bedroom doorway. He can't look at her—he knows she is crying. Closing his suitcase, he stands back, taking one last look around his room. *His* room ... where vestiges of a contented childhood dwell. He takes a deep breath and leaves, closing the door behind him. For several seconds his hand rests on the worn handle—the punishment of his conscience, his guilt about leaving, weighs heavily through his grip. At last, he forces himself to let go.

In the hallway, his family is gathered by the front door, lined up like a chorus about to perform their final act. Approaching little Evelyn, he squats and hugs the child, and feels her small hand patting his back. He stands. Wordlessly he hugs Hermina. Her short arms barely circle him but her grasp is tight, and it takes Ludwig's strong hands to peel her arms away so that he, too, can hug his brother-in-law.

'Take care of everyone, Ludwig, will you?'

'Of course.'

Steven then turns to his elder brother.

'Jani, what can I say?'

'Why is it we've talked for hours without really saying much, and now we linger at the door and no words will come, eh?' Jani replies.

He moves down the line till he draws level with the hazel eyes that are a mirror of his own. His father looks even greyer today.

'Papa …'

'Istvan, it hurts, I know. I feel it too. It's because we feel this must not happen again. And yet it must.'

'Papa, this is the hardest day of my life.' Their embrace is intense. Nikolaus lets go and rubs his son's head in the same playful manner of days long past. Steven takes a bulky envelope from his pocket and, after kissing his father on both cheeks, passes it to him.

'Don't open it until I've gone because you won't want to take it.' But he knows that no amount of money can lessen the ache in his chest.

Finally, he turns towards his mother, whose sobbing has been getting louder with each goodbye. Looking into her tear-filled eyes, he tries to find the words he needs. A sound is born deep in his throat but by the time it reaches his mouth it has vanished.

'*Istvan, Istvan …*' Katarina whispers raspily as she raises her hand to brush aside the tears that roll down his cheeks. 'Will my eyes ever see you again? Will my arms ever hold you once more?'

'Of course, Mama. I will be back very soon.' As the words leave his lips he knows them not to be true. And so does his mother.

'No, Istvan, my adventurous one. You said those same words to me twenty years ago. Something tells me to hold you close for this one last time—long enough for me to feel your strong embrace for the rest of my years.'

After six long weeks away, he feels such relief to be finally back on Australian soil, but is confused by his wife's greeting.

'Steven! I have been so worried about you. Why didn't you write, as you promised?' she asks in the car on the way home from the airport.

'But I did write—a long letter—about everyone and everything. How tough they are doing it there. How wonderful it was to see everyone, but how depressing it was at the same time. It'll probably turn up in the coming weeks.'

But the weeks roll on and no letter arrives—the Romanian government doesn't want any letters critical about conditions behind the 'Iron Curtain' making it across the borders to the West.

10
Anna

1963

'Hello?'

'Hello, Joan. It's Anna. How are you and the children?'

It took some years but, with the gift of adorable grandchildren, Anna has come to accept and admire her spirited daughter-in-law and has become a source of genuine support in Joan's life.

'Anyu? I can barely hear you—it must be a bad line. It's very hot for you to have walked down to Bondi Road to call, but I'm so glad you did. I need to talk to you about Frici. He's back to his old tricks and I have to do something to stop him.'

'Yes, Joan. I know what you want. I will come over to your place to be with the children. You know I talk to him many times, but he doesn't listen to me. He is very wilful, always, since a little boy.'

'Yes, I know. Would you be able to come tonight?'

'Of course. I'll ask Gyuri to drive me.'

'Thank you, Anyu. You are always such a great help to me. How is Sigismund?'

'So-so.'

It is late when Joan and Fred arrive home. Fred storms into the house, barely acknowledging his mother as she stands in the lounge room, wringing her hands, helplessly.

'Frici, wait. Please help me open the sofa bed. I always have trouble with it.'

'Anyu, I've shown you a hundred times,' he scowls. 'Hold it here—by the top corner—and bring it forward until you hear it click. Then lift it back up and it will open right out.'

'I tried, Frici, but it's too heavy for me,' she replies, looking up to see Joan standing in the hallway. They exchange knowing looks, before Joan follows Fred upstairs to their bedroom.

As she lies on her improvised bed listening to the yelling, Anna is embarrassed, even ashamed. Thank goodness Joan's parents have no inkling of her son's gambling, she thinks, for she's certain an upstanding man like John Miley would never tolerate such behaviour.

'I was going so well tonight, until *you* bloody well showed up!'

'We've been through this in the car coming home, Fred. It can't go on. *I* can't go on. It's too much. Now keep your voice down or you'll wake the children.'

'You're the one who makes it hard on yourself, traipsing down dark alleyways late at night to find me.'

'Do you even care what it's like for me? I worry about you night after night. Too frightened to answer the door in case it's people looking for money. Tell me the new location for Thommo's two-up joint. I'm going to go and get a bar put on you from that place, too.'

'No, Joan, you can't! You know what happened last time: "mad-dog-Milton" threatened to kill you if you showed up again. He blames you for their big raid.'

'I couldn't care less about him, or Thommo's other cockatoos. You think they scare me?

'If you just left me alone, I could make ends meet.'

'If you think I'm going to leave you to your own devices, think again!'

A tense silence fills the air before Anna hears Joan sob, 'Oh Fred! What's happening to us? We used to be so happy … but now all we do is fight.'

'I don't want to fight with you, Joanie. I'm no saint, I know. But believe me when I tell you that I love you, and the kids, and … I'm just trying to provide for you all as best as I know how.'

When she hears their bedroom door shut, Anyu gets up to make sure the children are still sleeping. She finds Cheryl sobbing under her covers.

'Don't cry, Cherie-ke—everything is all right,' she says, gently stroking the girl's head 'Shh, little one'.

'I hate it when Mummy and Daddy fight. Why do they do it?'

'You know, your mummy named you Cheryl so she could call you Cherie, which means darling in French?'

'Yes, Anyu, but—'

'And your middle name, Jane, I chose for you.'

'Yes, Anyu, I know.'

'Go to sleep now. I will be here in the morning when you wake up. I will make you breakfast.'

'But Anyu, why does Mummy have to yell at Daddy like that? Why does she pick on him?'

'Listen to me, darling. Your mummy, she is right to yell at Daddy. She is a good mummy to all you children and a *very* good wife for Daddy—just what he needs. She is strong and determined and when somebody, they do something wrong, your mummy will fix. This Anyu knows for sure. Now, sleep little one, sleep.'

In the mid-1960s, Joan gives birth to two more girls—Melinda in 1964 and Susan in 1966. Fred continues to work around the clock and Joan finds herself ever more lonely in the leafy suburbs on the outskirts of Sydney. With five children under ten, she is unable to work, and must scrimp and scrape money together to buy food and pay bills.

In Fred's mind, Joan deserves the world on a plate, and that's exactly what he's trying to do—get hold of this illusive creature called 'money' to provide Joan with the kind of life he experienced in Timișoara: a life of *quality*. What he can't comprehend—how could he?—is that his undeveloped young mind was then influenced by a paradigm that now affects his thinking: an innocent child who bore witness to the manipulation currency wielded as the lifeblood of wartime Europe. How was he to know it was a corrupting one?

Fortunately, Joan is resolute in her love for him—but more than that, there's an energy that flares between these two independent spirits, an imperceptible force that transcends transgression. In the intimacy of their relationship, Joan not only forgives but also accepts Fred along with his failings, making allowances in light of his background. She has no way of knowing, however, that as imperfect as he is now, before long he will transform himself into the most reliable, devoted and selfless life partner she could have wished for.

11
Fred

In the late 1960s Joan is pulled by an undercurrent of feminism that bursts into the public consciousness with the publication of ground-breaking popular books such as Germaine Greer's *The Female Eunuch* and the rise of political groups campaigning for equal rights for women in all areas of society.

For some years she quietly rides that wave within the confines of her small world. Each time Helen Reddy's song comes on the radio, she dances flirtatiously through the house twirling her tea towel in one hand as she sings, '*I am woman, hear me roar, in numbers too big to ignore ...*' and oh, how Fred roars with laughter! Only she can make him laugh like that.

Privately, however, Fred wishes he could do more to give his progressive-thinking wife, whose habitual defiance against conformity and whose fearlessness mirror his own (albeit her passion lies in *righting* societal wrongs) the fulfilment she lacks within the domestic sphere.

Without knowing what else to do, but aware how jazz music and dancing lift her spirits, as often as he can afford he suggests they go out to nightclubs such as Chequers or Whisky-A-Go-Go.

Having connections to many underworld figures, he can sometimes score tickets to see big name attractions.

'Joanie, I'm taking you to see Shirley Bassey tomorrow night. Get your hair done and I'll organise Anyu to come over to babysit.'

Anyu welcomes every opportunity to be with her grandchildren and Fred takes great pleasure in seeing her busying herself in his own kitchen. And during these times, Anyu starts to induct Cheryl into the secrets of some of her delicious Hungarian dishes.

Rising late one morning after a night out in the city, Fred stands quietly in the doorway observing the intimate bond between his mother and ten-year-old daughter.

'Cherie-ke, are you watching? *Egy, kettö, három, négy, öt, hat,*' Anyu says as she counts out six tablespoons of sugar, then flour, then cocoa, for their favourite rolled *dobos* chocolate cake. Fred looks lovingly at his ageing Anyu—a name that her grandchildren, including George's two girls, Rebecca and Annabel—have adopted. He notices that nature has begun to deftly streak her hair with silver and create soft folds in her once flawless skin as it inevitably takes its course.

'Yes, Anyu, I see.'

'*Nem, Cherie-ke, beszéljen hozzám Magyarul.* No, Cherie-ke, talk to me in Hungarian.' Turning to her son, she continues, 'Frici, why don't you teach the children to speak Hungarian? Are you listening?'

'*Igen, Anyu,*' son and granddaughter say in unison.

'*Hogy vagy, Cherie-ke*? How are you, Cherie?'

'*Köszönöm jól.* I am always good when I am with you Anyu!'

'*Szeretlek, Cherie-ke.*'

'I love you too, Anyu!'

It's 21 September 1969. Anyu's sixty-ninth birthday. Dawn spills through the broken slats on the metal venetian blind, filling the alcove of the east-facing dormer window of Joan and Fred's bedroom, warming the leaf-green paint of the walls. The sudden ringing of the telephone summons Fred from his tender thoughts as he watches Joan sleep. He leaps from bed and runs down the stairs to answer the phone before the entire household is awake. *Who the hell would ring this early?*

'Hello?'

'*Frici, Frici!*'

'Anyu? What's wrong?'

'*Your father … he's gone,*' she sobs.

'What? Gone to the hospital?'

'No. Too late for hospital. *He's gone … dead.* I found him in the bathroom this morning. He was as cold as the tiles on the floor where he lay. *He's dead, Frici, he's dead …*'

'I'm coming Anyu. I'm coming right now.'

The passing weeks barely lessen the heaviness inside Fred's chest. Without Sigismund's presence, Anna's world has tipped on its axis. Fred spends as much time as he can at Bondi. With George now married, Anna is mostly alone but she refuses to come and stay with him.

Over the ensuing months, Fred watches with rising concern as Anna tries hard to piece together her brokenness. She is, of course, comforted by both sons' attentiveness, but her conversation always turns back in time to the pastel imagery of her early years of marriage prior to the austerity of war.

It's now that she begins to pass on to the grandchildren, but particularly Cheryl, her most valuable possession: her life story, her legend. And even as a young girl, Cheryl sees that her grandmother's rose-coloured recollections are the world to which she retreats, the crutch she chooses to hold onto in place of her husband's strong hand.

12
Steven

1970

Not one to rest on his laurels, 'Steven the builder' has been scouring the new southern suburbs of Sydney for a block of land to build his dream home. Eventually, he comes across a beautiful block tiered with tall trees and leafy shrubs, and emerald views of the Georges River. He buys it on the spot, without even consulting Stephanie. When he takes her out to see it the next day, her initial reaction is not enthusiastic.

'Steven ... you didn't say it was on a cliff face. How on earth will you build a house on this? Surely we'll slide down into the river!'

'No problem. You worry far too much. You know me—the bigger the challenge, the more I enjoy it,' he laughs.

He immediately sets about designing a magnificent three-storey home, including a fifteen-metre swimming pool which, he assures Stephanie, will not crash to the ground below, as he has engineered its weight to be held up by enormous concrete pylons. He brings the draft plans home to show her. 'On the top floor there will be four bedrooms and two bathrooms. The middle floor will be a huge open-plan living area, and the bottom floor will be a games room—you know, big enough for a pool table and table tennis table.'

As he spreads himself between work, the running of the Budapest Soccer Club and the building of his home, he also receives two letters from Timişoara separated by less than twelve months. The first, informing him that Nikolaus has died from prostate cancer, he has been expecting, and takes comfort from the fact that he managed to spend those few weeks visiting his ageing father. However, the second completely devastates him.

'What's wrong, Steven? You're as white as a ghost.'

'Here,' he says, handing his wife the letter. 'My mother has passed away suddenly from appendicitis complications. They have already buried her. My poor Mama … She was so good to everyone, always so good.' With that, his feigned composure almost abandons him as he begins to tremble. Stephanie rushes to embrace him.

'I'm so sorry, darling,' she says, cradling his head on her shoulder. When no tears appear, she gently coaxes, 'Just let it out, my darling. No matter how old you are, losing a parent, especially so suddenly and unexpectedly like this, is … is shocking!'

She reminds him how devastated she was when her father died suddenly from a heart attack aged only fifty. And recalls how fortunate she was to be surrounded by her family to share the grief. And yes, without Steven's unwavering physical and financial assistance, Mutti would still be struggling.

'Your mother was a good woman who raised a good man!'

'You would've loved her, Steffie. If only …' his legs feel shaky so he sits down on the kitchen stool.

'Of course. It's my loss not to have met her. But for you to be so far away at a time like this … I can't even begin to imagine.'

In bed that night, Steven lies on his back staring into the

blackness. At first it's his anger that keeps him awake—why didn't Hermina let him know earlier? But soon that feeling dissipates, replaced by a profound nostalgia, mingled with sadness. He is thinking about both the magic and mayhem of his earlier life: the magic of his mother's nurturing, the mayhem of that train trip that took him away from her. From that first goodbye, he somehow knew it was an inexorable one-way journey from the warm comfort of her arms that held such a sacred bond. Now the time he has subconsciously feared for so long has arrived. Finally, with hurting heart too much to bear, he turns and weeps into his pillow. Over the coming weeks and months, to lessen his torturous remorse, Steven does what he knows best: increasingly burying himself in work.

After completing their new home in 1971, Steven throws himself into an even greater building challenge. He is put in charge of the mammoth construction of a state-of-the-art football stadium for the flourishing St George Budapest Soccer Club.

'Steffie, listen to this,' he calls out as he returns home after a committee meeting. He is carrying a booklet published by the club.

> *Koenig was king of the project—just what his name means in German—and it took him some three years to see it completed. Hardly a day passed without him visiting the site two or three times a day. Talk to anybody within the club about the stadium and all questions produce the same echo: this is Steve Koenig's baby. For it was this craggy-faced factory manager and old club stalwart who pushed a loose idea into a stunning reality.*[31]

---

31 *Silver Jubilee of St George Budapest (1957–1982)*, page 29: 'Old Dream Come True' by Andrew Dettre.

With his professional life continuing to go from strength to strength, few of Steven's colleagues are aware of the personal tragedy that is gnawing away at him. In addition to recently losing his parents, Rosemary, his gregarious fourteen-year-old daughter with bouncy brown hair, insightful blue eyes and a smile that always lifts him after a hard day's work, is gradually losing balance and co-ordination. Until recently, he has watched her spend her days like most young girls—riding her bike after school, playing tennis on weekends, even becoming a cheerleader for his beloved soccer club. But now, as she dances to the song of adolescent dreams with popular music from her favourite bands—The Beatles, The Easybeats and The Monkees, emanating through her bedroom walls—something sinister is brewing.

As each month passes, Rosemary's condition worsens, with no doctor, not even the best specialists in Sydney, being able to diagnose it. Soon she is unable to keep up with her studies and eventually, at the school's recommendation, leaves—not yet fifteen years old. For a man whose strength over all these years has been to embrace hope and find a solution to even the most intransigent of obstacles, this is the one time, and the most significant in his life, where he is lost for options.

Not knowing what else to do, Steven immerses himself in the management of three hundred employees at Pongrass Industries and begins spending evenings, and most weekends, throwing himself into his duties as vice president of the rapidly expanding Budapest Soccer Club. And for the first time in his married life, subtle cracks appear; for the first time, he and Stephanie feel disconnected. Although living with the same depth of grief, both struggle to give voice to their feelings—as if doing so will somehow turn the unthinkable into reality.

The passage of time does little to bring them closer, as Steven watches his wife bear the weight of traversing unfamiliar territory with a progressively disabled daughter. Stephanie is persistent, relentlessly pushing for answers, taking Rosemary to specialist after specialist. But each time she comes home frustrated and deflated when no one can tell her what's happening. Steven, of course, can't believe that he is presented with a situation where he feels so powerless once again. It is a cold thought that creeps like a worm through his brain during the still of night. And as time marches on, he becomes worried that finding a foothold in this new world, with its adversity and inequity, is becoming increasingly more challenging for Stephanie, who tells him she is often regarded as just another ignorant and emotional mother by patronising medicos and intolerant strangers.

Months slowly turn to years and still Rosemary's deterioration continues unabated. Like sand between his fingers, Steven feels her slipping away. *What good is everything that I've worked for, our beautiful house, our comfortable life, if it can't give me back my daughter?* In due course, she begins to lose the ability to structure sentences and, although she can still walk, her step is unsteady. Then one day Stephanie comes home with the news that she has found a neurologist who suggests they perform a nerve biopsy.

'He wants to take it from her ankle, of all places ... in hospital, under general anaesthetic. And Steven,' she continues, 'please say you will come with me.'

'Yes, of course. All you have to do is tell me ahead of time, so I can organise work.'

Two weeks after the biopsy, as they wait patiently on one side of a large desk cluttered with papers. Steven holds Stephanie's hand. He feels it shaking. The neurologist leans back in his high-back leather chair, his silver beard and thin nose buried behind a ream of white paper. Minutes pass, with no sound except the ticking of the wall-mounted clock. The doctor continues to shuffle through the paperwork as he runs his open hand down the length of the fine strands of silver hair that fall to the top of his collar. Then, leaning forward, he places his elbows on his desk and looks up over his glasses.

'Mr and Mrs Koenig, I have good news and bad news. The good news is that I am able to give Rosemary's condition a name …'

'And the bad news—' Steven blurts out.

'The bad news is the type of disease she has: metachromatic leukodystrophy, or MLD. This is a very rare and complex disease, one of a group of genetic disorders in the leukodystrophy family that impairs the growth or development of the myelin sheath, which is the fatty covering that acts as an insulator around nerve fibres. MLD is caused by a deficiency of a crucial enzyme, one of several lipid storage diseases which results in the toxic build-up of fatty materials in cells in the nervous system, liver and kidneys. Symptoms include muscle wasting and weakness, muscle rigidity, developmental delays, progressive loss of vision leading to blindness, convulsions, impaired swallowing, paralysis and dementia. There are three forms of MLD: infantile, juvenile and adult onset. Rosemary has juvenile onset. There is no cure for this most debilitating neurological disease. It is extremely rare—Rosemary is only one of five in Australia. Unfortunately, she will progressively deteriorate. I don't think we can expect her to live past thirty,' the doctor concludes.

Mesmerised by the metronome of the wall-mounted clock ticking in synchrony with the thunderous beating of his heart, for several minutes Steven can't move. He looks at Stephanie, whose head hangs in despair. Slowly, the doctor's words register, shattering any last vestige of hope. Knowing he must move, Steven stands and guides a fragile Stephanie to her feet, supporting her wilting body as they walk unsteadily from the consulting room to the car. Through the tears that he can no longer hold back, Steven voices their determination.

'While she can still see and eat and get around, we will make sure that she never misses out on anything.'

Each Saturday night that follows, the family of four go out to dinner. And on Sundays, no matter in which part of New South Wales the Saints are playing, they follow. For the first time in Steven's life, work becomes a secondary concern.

13
Fred

1973

After nearly three decades of laborious days which often stretch into hostile nights as he drives for an assorted but pushy breed of cab owners—never once calling in sick and rarely, if ever, taking time off for holidays—Fred is elated to be awarded his own taxi plates by the New South Wales Department of Transport: 'For exemplary record and contribution to the industry'.

'These plates are worth more than fifty thousand dollars, Joan.'

'Maybe now you can ease up a bit.'

'Yes, I'm going to buy a new Ford Falcon and set up my own business.'

Without a doubt, from this time on, there's a distinct relaxation in Fred's manner, as things quickly became more financially secure. *Finally ... no need for me to try and make a quick buck.*

Only six months later, Fred receives a message over his radio.

'Message for Driver 44. Driver 44, urgent message. Do you read me? Over.'

'Roger that, 44 here. Over.'

'Your wife has been in a car accident, 44. Message for you to go straight to St George Hospital. Over.'

'Oh ... right ... ah, roger. Going now. Over.'

'I'm Fred Loew. I'm looking for my wife, Joan.' He has rushed into the busy emergency department and past wheelchairs and trolleys holding restless patients. He is shown to an empty waiting room where he sits down on the corner of the stiff and unforgiving foam sofa staring at the ground and nervously jangles his car keys, as the minutes drag. Finally, the door swings open and a doctor hurries in.

'Mr Loew? I'm Dr Chang, Head of Emergency. Please, have a seat. Right. Your wife has been in a car accident, Mr Loew.'

'Yes, I know. She's all right though, isn't she?' Fred says, sensing that the doctor is going to tell him something he doesn't want to hear.

'Not really. She has a serious injury to her neck.'

'Oh, God!'

'We've taken x-rays that show she has broken a vertebra at the C4 level and, although it's serious, she's also very lucky because it's a compression fracture which doesn't *appear* to involve the spinal cord.'

'I don't understand ... How could this happen?' Fred says, at once confused and shocked.

'It's an unusual thing, actually. I haven't seen it happen like this before. You see, she was in the back of a taxi when it was stopped at a red light and a car ran into it. It was a relatively minor accident, but because she had her head bent forward looking down into her purse for money to pay the fare—well, it's like a diver who hits their head on the bottom of a pool.'

'Is she in a lot of pain?'

'Yes. There's some pain and swelling. She also has some tingling down her arms.' The doctor goes on to inform Fred that Joan won't require surgery at this stage, but as sometimes these things take time to reveal nerve involvement, they will admit her and keep her immobilised for a couple of months. If all goes well, when she leaves hospital she'll still need to be in a brace for a few more months.

'Let's not get ahead of ourselves, though. She's eager to see you. But don't be alarmed to see her lying on a flat board in a brace from her chin down to her waist.'

'Of course. Just give me a moment, will you?'

The door swings closed behind the doctor and Fred leans back on the empty wall and closes his eyes. Never has he felt such anguish. It moves through him like a splinter of ice piercing his heart. He looks down at his hand. A duplicate key could be cut from the impression his car key has left in his clutched fist. He's going to be strong. That's what he tells himself. But as soon as he sees her lying immobilised with a mirror above her head in which she can see his face and he hers, his resolve collapses.

'Darling ... Oh, God! I can't believe this has happened.'

'Fred, don't get upset. I'm okay. It could have been a lot worse,' she whispers weakly, reaching for his hand.

'Yes, I know. I know. But still, you of all people ... If it had to happen to one of us, then it should have been me.'

'Now you're being ridiculous,' she says, wincing in pain. 'Do the children know?'

'Not yet. I'll ring home soon.'

'Good. I want you to tell them. I didn't want them frightened by getting a call from the hospital. I'm sorry to do this to you all. I don't know how you're going to cope for so long at home without me.'

'You mustn't worry about that! The kids are big enough. Mandy and Cherie can look after the other two. Then there's Anyu and your parents for back up. God, I'd better go and ring them now. They'll all want to know straight away.'

'Do it carefully, Fred. Don't panic them.' With that she begins to cry.

'Darling, don't cry. I'll look after everything. There's nothing I wouldn't do for you. You know that, don't you?'

Gently squeezing his hand, she whispers, but with surprising fervour, 'Yes, I know. I've always known.'

14

Steven

1973

Seasons sweep by and time, like a thief, robs Rosemary of all opportunity. Gradually, the ominous prognoses of the neurologist ring true. All except simple communication—'yes', 'no' and her discerningly broad smile—has evaporated. Support is required not solely to ambulate, but in all daily living skills. She needs the fulltime care of a devoted mother which, to her great fortune, she has. And, quite extraordinarily, because of her parent's love and dedication, Rosemary will defy the most important medical expectation: she will live twenty years past her predicted expiry date.

'You've been under enormous strain, Steffie,' Steven says as he watches her plant annuals in her prized rockery, her place of solace. 'I think we should all go back to Europe—visit our relatives in Hungary, Romania and Germany, then take in some other countries you've always wanted to see—maybe France, Italy and Spain. What do you say?'

Removing a soiled gardening glove, she wipes her brow.

'But how? I'm not leaving Rosemary anywhere.'

'Of course not. I've already thought it through. We'll take our time—three, four months—and I'll buy a van where she can lie down as we drive.'

'All right, but just thinking aloud, we could go next year for the World Cup. Needless to say, *you* would like that, but can you imagine how Robert would love it! And the timing would be ideal too, since the doctor said he won't be able to play for a year after having his knee reconstruction.'

'You know what? That's the best idea you've had in ages!'

They travel through France and Spain, marvelling at each country's charm, culture and art treasures. In Barcelona, Steven takes out the map to draw their route across Europe to his home town.

'We'll head back through the French Riviera and into Italy, to Florence, Pisa, Rome and as far south as Pompeii, before heading back up through Venice. We've got a long drive after that through Yugoslavia and then to Romania and Timişoara.'

Providing his family with a holiday of such magnificence—one that will cost the equivalent of a small house—Steven is filled with immense pride: *I wonder, Papa: would you be proud of all my hard work? And Mama: what I would give to see the delight in your tired eyes, just once more …*'

Behind the wheel of the van and waiting patiently for over an hour at the Romanian border control, Steven is finally ushered forward by armed guards.

'Passports?'

'Here, four people, four passports,' he passes them out through the driver's window.

'Australian?'

'Yes, that's correct.'

'Reason for travel?'

'We are here to visit my family.'

'I see. You are Steven?'

'Yes.'

'Why you not speak to me in Romanian?'

'I can't. I've forgotten it. I haven't spoken it for nearly thirty years, but I can speak to you in Hungarian, if you like.'

'Move your car to the side of the road, please,' the guard says, taking their passports back to his booth. After half an hour he returns.

'All of you, get out of the vehicle!'

'Steven, what's happening?'

'Just do what he says, Steffie. Come on, Robert, get out. Here, Rosemary, let me help you. Say nothing,' Steven says, as their bags are emptied of all their contents.

Finally, just before sunset, with their clothes strewn across the side of the road, the same impassive guard approaches them and hands their passports back to Steven.

'You can go,' he says brusquely. Then, as he walks away he turns his head in Steven's direction and adds, over his shoulder, 'You should speak Romanian.'

They continue to drive in the fading light, following what few signs exist. After some hours, Steven reluctantly admits he's lost.

'I've been going from memory, but it's been too long. Let's ask these three old men at the bus stop for directions. Robert, roll down the window: *Tudna adni irányban Chişoda?*'

Nothing. No reply. The three men look at each other and then stare blankly back at him.

'They mustn't speak Hungarian,' he says in exasperation, following up with a loud '*Baszd meg!*' in the direction of the men.

'What did you say then, Dad?'

'I said "damn you",' toning down the profanity, while putting the van into gear as Robert winds the passenger window up. Suddenly there is a *tap, tap, tap* on the closed window.

'Christ!' Robert recoils in shock at the sight of a gnarled walking stick against the darkened windowpane. He quickly winds the window back down.

'Let me in and I'll take you to Chişoda,' a weathered face says in Hungarian from beneath a narrow-brimmed straw hat.

Robert slides across the front bench-seat and the ancient man, dressed in crumpled brown jacket and trousers, slowly climbs into the van and sits down next to him.

'You understood me all along.' Steven leans forward and casts him a wary look.

'Yes, yes, I can speak Hungarian. But you are crazy if you think anyone in these parts will speak it in public. Now, follow my instructions: left up here … now right at the bridge …'

By the time they arrive in Chişoda, it is pitch black and the road ahead is barely visible as torrents of rain pummel the windscreen. They drop the old man off where he asks and inch their way slowly along the dirt road towards the family farmhouse. It is late, past midnight, but Jani, Hermina and her husband Ludwig are waiting up to greet them, with warm hugs and mugs of hot coffee. For the next two weeks, Steven enjoys showing his family around the neighbourhood of his early life.

'Nothing has changed,' he laughs, 'not a thing. Even the roads are still dirt. See here—this is where my mother used to sell her poultry at the markets. I spent a lot of weekends helping her. I never minded … I just loved being with her. You know I can't remember her ever raising a hand to me. Oh, there was this one time when I was very young—nine or ten—and I made her very angry, right here at the markets in fact. Can't even remember what I did, but I remember her reaction. Funny how some things stick out in your memory. That time ... at the market. And the day the planes circled ... Oh, and the day they took my dad away to camp. But ...' his voice trails off as they drive past Chișoda railway station. Steven feels certain that this is no longer his home, that it hasn't been since the day he left at sixteen. And yet, something intangible keeps his soul attached to this place, this cradle of memories.

'Are you all right, darling?'

Clearing his throat, he replies, 'Yes. I was just going to say ... that damn train station ... Brings back some memories, I can tell you.'

15
Fred
1974

After several months in hospital, followed by six months in a head and upper-torso brace, Joan recovers sufficiently well to think about what she wants to do with the next part of her life now that the children are older and their financial position is no longer under constant strain. The seeds of her flirtation with feminism combined with the opportunities that have opened up in Australia recently for mature-age entrance to universities, including the abolition of fees, enable her to realise one of her dreams and enrol in a university course in psychology. A year into her studies, however, after showing an active interest in community affairs and having been persuaded by friends to join the New South Wales Liberal Party, she is asked to run for local government by the sitting federal member for Barton, Jim Bradfield who is impressed by her political nous and judicious charisma.

'What do you think, Fred, should I do it? You're already doing so much for me—what about your work?'

'I think you should do it, Joanie. I can always hire another driver. Just as long as you pace yourself. I know you—you'll want to save the world, but—'

'Yes, I know, I know. I'll take it slowly, I promise,' she says, kissing him gratefully.

From that moment on, Fred goes into election mode and works tirelessly, managing her whole campaign as if Joan is running for the American presidency.

'Money's no object, Joanie, when it comes to publicity.'

He walks kilometre after kilometre, some days through foul weather, door-knocking the electorate and delivering mail-box campaign material, dragging the teenage children along with him. On polling day, he coordinates her many supporters, along with the children, in an effective system of manning all the voting booths. When she is successfully elected to Hurstville Council, his enthusiasm knows no bounds, organising a celebratory party where Seaview champagne flows freely all around.

Nothing is too good for his Joanie.

So Joan begins devoting all her time to enhancing local community services, including a focus on sustainable development, an early success being the preservation of the Lime Kiln Bay mangroves.

In all, she will spend thirteen years on Hurstville Council, including three terms as deputy mayor and one as mayor, and will become patron to over one hundred community groups. One of hers—and the family's—proudest achievements is her successful lobbying of successive state governments to introduce blue lights on the outside of guard compartments of suburban trains so that passengers, especially women and children, will know when there is a guard travelling on board their train. In just a short time, a dramatic improvement in passenger safety results.

In spite of her busy schedule, Joan completes her psychology degree in four years but, with the onset of rheumatoid and osteoarthritis, any further aspirations have to be scaled back. Indeed a time is soon approaching that will see Fred atone for past transgressions by becoming Joan's fulltime carer after she becomes incapacitated when her condition is compounded by osteoporosis so severe that she can barely move without breaking a bone. When Fred loses the love of his life in her early seventies, he becomes half the man he once was. However, before his greatest sadness, something quite serendipitous and wonderful awaits …

'Hey, Dad! Can you drive Yvonne and me down to St George Budapest Soccer Club tonight?' Cheryl asks.

'What? You're too young to get in—you're only fifteen,' he replies, a bit bewildered.

'No, Dad. You don't understand. They've got a family movie night happening.'

Fred drops the girls off outside the club, giving them strict instructions to wait for him inside the foyer afterwards.

Two hours later, he is back outside the soccer club to pick them up.

'How was the movie, Cherie-baby?' he asks on the drive home.

'Oh Dad, I met the nicest boy tonight. Robert, his name is. He's just so handsome. He plays soccer, too. And his father is vice president of the club. And he asked for my phone number. *And*—'

'Did you watch the movie at all?'

'Oh, Dad, don't be so silly.'

The following Friday evening as Fred is relaxing in front of the television, roaring with laughter at the antics of the characters in *The Benny Hill Show* and sharing a long-neck bottle of DA beer with Joan, the front door knocker clangs loudly.

'I'll get it!' Cheryl pounces like a cat off the sofa before anyone can beat her to the door.

A couple of minutes later she returns to the living room followed by a tall, slim young man, with shoulder-length black hair and smiling eyes.

'Mum, Dad, this is Robert,' she says, excitedly.

'Hello, mate,' Fred stands, hitching up his trousers before putting out his hand to shake.

'Hello, Robert,' Joan says warmly, from her gold velvet recliner chair. 'Won't you sit down?'

Noticing he is a few years older than Cheryl, Fred asks, 'Would you like a beer, mate?'

'Yes, he would, Dad. But first listen to this. Robert's dad comes from Romania too. Not only that, but from the same town you said you come from. How do you say it: *Timiswara?*'

'*Tim-i-shara*. Really? Is that right, Rob? Can I call you that?'

'Sure.'

'Well, that's amazing! It's a small world we live in! But Timişoara is quite a large town. Do you know what part he came from?'

'No, Mr Loew. I should, because we went there last year on a holiday, but I can't remember the name of the suburb. It starts with a 'K', I think.'

'Call me Fred, please. Tell me now, how did you find Timişoara? What year did your father come out? Did he notice much change when he went back?'

'Fred, give the poor boy time to answer!'

16
Christmas

1975

'They're here!' The strident motor of the Mercedes Benz signals the arrival of Robert's family. Their car pulls into the curved driveway, the tyres crunching over pebbles before coming to a stop. Butterflies flutter in Cheryl's stomach as she turns sideways to carefully edge past her bed and along the wall where yellowing bits of sticky tape barely hold Rod Stewart's spiky hairdo in place. She bends a metal slat of the venetian blind to peer out from one of three loft windows protruding from the angle of the gable roof and watches the visitors get out of their car and walk towards the front veranda.

I can't wait for them to meet! I hope they like each other ... I mean, why wouldn't they?

With a last glance in the mirror, she quickly brushes her long blonde hair and checks she hasn't applied too much of the powder blue eye shadow that matches her eyes, before hurrying down the stairs, taking care not to catch her platform shoes in the cuff of her pink bell-bottom pants. The loud clanging of the wrought-iron knocker sounds through the house just as she lands on the bottom step.

Fred enters the narrow hallway. Through the diamond-cut facets of the small amber window on the front door, the setting sun gives off just enough light for Cheryl to notice Fred's teasing smile.

'You look lovely, Cherie-baby. What's the special occasion?'

'Shut up, Dad!' she whispers, smiling back at him. 'They'll hear you. And I wish I could say the same about you. Your buttons are undone and your beer belly's showing. Bloody hell, Dad, I want you to make a good first impression.'

Nodding sheepishly, he quickly fixes his shirt and indicates that he will open the door. Joan stands in the kitchen doorway, elegant as always despite her pain, drying her hands on a tea towel.

'Don't embarrass her, Fred, with any of your silly jokes,' she whispers. 'And mind your language, Cheryl, or the good impression you've apparently made will soon disappear.'

When the front door opens wide, Cheryl smiles as Robert enters the house. *He looks so handsome in that green paisley shirt ... It brings out his eyes.* In those eyes, and in his being, Cheryl sees a confidence and pride tempered with an unassuming nature, a smile that tells her all is right with the world. And when he holds her hand, she has a feeling, a certainty, that all she will ever need is right there.

'G'day Fred,' Rob says in his usual cheerful tone as they shake hands. 'I'd like you to meet my fath—'

Suddenly, something isn't right. What has Rob seen in her father's eyes that makes him falter? Standing on the last step, Cheryl can just see Steven framed by the architrave. His broad Hungarian shoulders fill the doorway. He has neatly brushed his brown hair back from his wide forehead. But his eyes have lost their usual boldness as he stands there, feet fixed to the spot. And his expression is odd as he looks past Fred and smiles awkwardly at Cheryl—everything is so unlike his customary confident style. Something is definitely wrong. Rob senses it too, as he looks from one father to the other. Then Fred says something. Strange. He is mumbling. Joan reaches out and takes his arm.

'What is it, Fred? Say something, for goodness sake!'

He turns, slowly. His eyes find Cheryl's. His face is white, as if he has seen a ghost.

17
Fred

1979

On 3 November 1979, dressed in a black tuxedo and seated at the bridal table, Fred stands nervously to make the customary father-of-the-bride speech.

'When Rob first came to me and asked for Cheryl's hand in marriage', he begins, 'my first thought was that she was too young to be engaged at just eighteen. But it only took me a few moments longer to work out that that didn't matter at all. That in fact she could travel the world over and never find a finer young man than Robert …'

The distinctive melodic tones of a Hungarian accent emanate from within the muted light that shines over the guests. It is Alex Pongrass, Robert's employer, who is seated at the end of a table precisely where the parquetry dance floor meets the floral carpet. His voice fills the pause in Fred's speech and stirs the 130 guests to a standing ovation, as with glass in hand he rises from his seat, lifts his glass and shouts, 'Hear! Hear!'

'Well, Anyu, what do you think?' Fred asks his frail mother as they dance slowly together, after the speeches have been made.

'Fabulous wedding, Frici. Cherie-ke looks so beautiful. And

you know I have always thought Robert to be such a handsome young man. They will have nice-looking children.'

'Yes, but give her time, Anyu—she's only nineteen.'

As they continue to dance, Fred looks over at Steven who is busy pouring champagne for his table of Pongrass workmates.

'A lifetime later,' he says, shaking his head in disbelief, 'and Steven is a grown man and part of my family. You know, I could have passed him on the street—and most likely did at the Budapest Soccer Club—but would never have recognised him. All I can see is that brawny kid taking me on in a game of soccer. Of course *he* reckons he saved me from some Brownshirt bashing, but I'll never give him credit for that one,' he laughs.

'Of course, Frici, you would not recognise him because you were not *expecting* to see someone from Chişoda here. Honestly, no one can believe it when I tell them. I still cannot believe myself that you come to such a big country and you end up still living two kilometres from each other!'

They continue their gentle waltz to the three-piece band's slow rendition of 'Moon River', Fred continuing to muse on the conspiracy of the universe that reunited him and Steven. *What are the odds of a child of mine and a child of Steven's actually meeting? Must be in the millions…* Naturally, he thinks of it that way—after all, his whole life has been about knowing the odds and seizing his chances.

And, if he could look into a crystal ball? He would see that Anyu is right. Cheryl and Robert will have fine-looking children—two boys, in fact, who will both take up the sport their grandfathers are so passionate about. Huddled as one, the ageing men will sit through many blustery Saturdays, sharing the joy of watching the younger one, Chris, play at an elite level while debating which one of them their grandson has acquired his talent from. Always conversing in their adopted English language, they never revert to their common native tongue and never really talk of their past experiences—evidence, perhaps, that hope and laughter can erase memories of starvation and degradation.

The band takes a break, and Anna says, 'That's enough dancing for me, darling.' Fred helps his mother into her seat, kisses her on the cheek and turns to leave. Anna catches the sleeve of his tuxedo and draws him down to her.

'Such a nice European family, too. But … Jewish they are not—a shame, *nu?* What can you do?'

18
Anna

1982

'Anyu? It's Cherie. Are you awake?'

'*Igen,* Cherie-ke.'

'How are you feeling?'

'*Jó,* good, darling.' Taking a shallow breath she continues. '*Egy nyelv sosem elég.*'

'I can't understand you, Anyu. *Nem értem.*'

'Cherie-ke, I said, one language is not enough.'

'Yes, I know, Anyu. I wish I had learnt more Hungarian.'

'Here … sit closer to me. Something important I must tell you. Something I just remember the other day.' Her voice is soft, almost a whisper.

'Anyu, I'm here.'

She feels her hand being held. Forcing herself awake, she smiles lovingly at the granddaughter who has given her so much joy.

'Everyone says how much you look like me, darling.'

'Yes, I know. They tell me the same.'

'I must tell you … This week, I was dreaming about my home in Timișoara. You know, I used to have maids to clean for me and beautiful, beautiful furniture.'

'Yes, I know.'

'Well, I remembered Robert's grandmother. She worked at Chişoda markets.'

'What do you mean? Did you meet her?'

'Yes, yes. I bought my chickens and geese from her. She was a lovely lady—*very* good person—I could tell.'

'Are you sure it was his grandmother? How do you know?'

'Her name was Mrs König. She told me one day when I asked her how does she always remember my name. She said, because in German her name means king and mine means lion—not so different really.'

Cheryl sits stunned.

'Wait … I have more to tell you.'

'I'm not going anywhere. I'll sit with you for a while.'

'Your father … now, what was I going to say?'

'Don't push yourself, Anyu. Go to sleep if you're tired. I'll be here when you wake up.'

'No, something important I need to remember. Let me think … It will come to me … Yes, I know. He met Robert's father one day at Chişoda markets—perhaps even more than once. I used to take him with me when he was a little boy so that he would get used to the chickens, alive,' she laughs. 'Your father … how he hated the chickens.'

'How do you know it was Steven?'

'Mrs König had a young boy with her—helping her.'

'Well, I suppose it might have been him … But it could have been someone else. Maybe even one of his brothers.'

'No, darling, I remembered she called him Istvan. That means …'

'Yes, I know what it means in Hungarian, Anyu. Dad and Steven think they met each other when they played soccer in the park after Dad had just started high school. But their story goes back even further? ... You actually knew Robert's grandmother?'

'Yes, yes ... How strange this world is, my darling. Not so big after all.'

'Oh, yes, Anyu—wait till I tell them! You know how many times Dad has told me the chicken story! Never in my wildest dreams could I imagine that it unfolded that way. Anyu, you do look tired. Why don't you have a little rest?'

'Yes, darling—I am a bit. *Szeretlek,* Cherie-ke.'

'I love you too.'

How many days have passed? Anna can't be sure. Voices ... blurry, but she hears them now.

'Look how beautiful she looks, as if all the worry lines have disappeared from her face. I think her mind is finally at peace,' Fred says softly.

'Yes, it looks as if she's let something go. She was never really happy after Apu died.' George removes his black-framed glasses and rubs his eyes.

Frici and Gyuri here? Rarely, they both come ... Strange. I feel strange. And why is it so difficult to breathe? ... Very, very tired ... just need to go to sleep ... Wait.

'Frici? Frici? Where are you my *makacs kisfiú,* my wilful little boy?'

'I'm right here with you, Anyu.'

'Your father is calling me ... but I don't want to leave you ... don't *ever* want to lose you again.'

'It's all right, I will be fine. Go to him, Anyu. He wants to take you home.'

www.ingramcontent.com/pod-product-compliance
Lightning Source LLC
Chambersburg PA
CBHW050625300426
44112CB00012B/1658